JAPAN
AGAINST
THE
WORLD
1941-2041

JAPAN
AGAINST
THE
WORLD
1941-2041
The 100-year War
for Supremacy

Russell Braddon

STEIN AND DAY/*Publishers*/New York

First published in the United States of America in 1983
Copyright© 1983 by Russell Braddon
All rights reserved. Stein and Day. Incorporated
Printed in the United States of America

STEIN AND DAY/ *Publishers*
Scarborough House
Briarcliff Manor, N.Y. 10510

Library of Congress Cataloging in Publication Data

Braddon, Russell.
    Japan against the world, 1941-2041.

    Bibliography: p.
    1. National characteristics, Japanese. 2. World War,
1939-1945 — Japan. I. Title.
DS830.B72 1983   952.04   83-40078
ISBN 0-8128-2941-7

TO
LORD TRANMIRE
IN ADMIRATION

CONTENTS

FOREWORD

The premise upon which this book is based is that the Japanese have brought to post-war industry precisely that spirit of daring and devotion that yielded them such stunning victories in the Pacific in the first five months of 1942, and inspired them to such suicidal feats of valour for three further years of war.

After their defeat, in August 1945, technology, capital and raw materials were less available to them than to any industrial nation in the world. Enduring ten years of harsh poverty, they acquired sufficient of all three once again to become an exporting nation. Since then their once puny industrial machine has become a juggernaut: what has made it a juggernaut, however, is not technology but the unique spirit of those who designed and man it.

Accordingly I have attempted to trace the development of that spirit from 1860 until today. Since the Pacific War exemplified it at its best and worst, it seems to me that there is more to be learnt about the Japanese from a scrutiny of their conduct and achievements throughout that conflict than there could ever be from describing the mechanics of the juggernaut itself.

Ever since 1894, when they attacked Korea, occupied Seoul and sank China's navy, they have suffered an apparently insatiable thirst for international pre-eminence. War failed to slake the thirst. Defeat left them thirstier than ever. As the world's richest industrial nation – which they plan to become within ten years – they will be able to drink their fill. As the world's most influential nation – which they envisage themselves becoming in the twenty-first century – they will be in a position to decide who else must go thirsty.

If their industrial challenge is eventually to be met, we must at the very least, and very belatedly, seek to understand them. To that end, I have quoted their Emperor, statesmen, generals, admirals, philosophers, professors, students, citizens and leading industrialists at length. Those quotations which are derived from interviews are reproduced verbatim from notes. I asked my question in English, phrase by phrase, wached the subject's reaction as each phrase was translated into Japanese, watched his expression and gestures as he replied in Japanese, and wrote down each phrase as it was translated into English. Bear in mind, however, as you read their carefully chosen words, that the Japanese dislike being assertive or forthright, are incapable of being rude, and positively shrink from saying anything that would be displeasing to the listener, especially if he is a foreigner. Rather than say a frank but unwelcome 'no', a Japanese will smile and say 'yes'. It is for this reason that I have quoted from interviews mainly at the end of the book, by which point the reader should understand the Japanese sufficiently well to be able to re-interpret words that have been interpreted already.

The effort involved in such a re-interpretation will not, of course, be small; but shrouded within those courteous, ambiguous and sometimes contradictory words lies Japan's vision of her future and ours, and that vision is one from which we can no longer afford to avert our eyes.

JAPAN
AGAINST
THE
WORLD
1941-2041

CHAPTER ONE

>>>>>>><<<<<<<

The Unknown Enemy

BEFORE THEY ENCIRCLED, attacked and destroyed us, we knew all too little about them, and none of that was true. That they made cheap toys and battleships that capsized, for example. My grandfather told me that; and he was omniscient. Yet it was two of Britain's battleships, not Japan's, that had just plummeted to the bottom off the Malayan Coast, and most of America's Pacific Fleet, not Japan's, that lay ruined in Pearl Harbour.

So what had my grandfather been talking about? And, more to the point, what had our Intelligence Officer been talking about? He who had assured us that the Japanese were unlikely to invade Malaya because they were small, myopic, ill-equipped, frightened of the dark and anyway physically repulsive.

How would he (had he still been with us, which he was not, because one of his unlikely invaders had killed him) have explained the fact that the very first of them with whom we, his subordinates, had come face to face, behind a road-block, was tall, strong, splendidly equipped, conspicuously unbespectacled – and very nearly beautiful?

He was also, of course, dead – or I would never have risked so close an inspection. But death had neither glazed his eyes nor blanched his face, as it did the eyes and faces of our dead. Rather, he lay bare-headed, face upward, as if sunbathing; and had it not been for his too carefully razored eyebrows (like Robert Taylor's) he would have been beautiful.

That would not have suprised his Samurai ancestors, of course, to whom death was so inseparable from beauty that they had ordained that a man should powder his face and paint his lips before committing seppuku (lest those who subsequently beheld him should find his passing ugly).

The countenance we beheld, however, had needed neither powder on coppery skin stretched smooth over high cheek bones, nor

9

paint on lips so deeply red as almost to be purple. He seemed, moreover, to have died serenely.

Perhaps one does if killed by blast instead of shrapnel. Perhaps, even as our profligate shell exploded, in that millisecond between concussion and extinction, he had been able to welcome the deification promised to all who died for their Emperor. Certainly his forebears would have approved his serene beauty no less profoundly than we were oppressed by it.

Curiously, the idiot lie that the Japanese were grotesquely inept and uncomely might have worked had it been peddled not to us but to our enemy. In his book, *Prisoner of the British*, Yuji Aida tells of a British leaflet he read which warned the Burmese about the 'ugly' Japanese.

'It was,' he writes, 'a thoroughly beastly pamphlet.' Beastly, not because he believed the Japanese *not* to be ugly, but because he and most of his compatriots thought that they were, their aesthetic propensity for finding beauty in non-physical things having left them, he claimed, with an inferiority complex about their looks and bodies.

Perhaps, then, had the sweltering divisions of Japanese troops, and the crews of the vessels transporting them to Malaya, been bombarded with leaflets telling them how hideous they were, their convoys would have turned about and the war been won in days rather than years.

It was not just about their looks and equipment that we, who were supposed to defeat them, had been misled, however. The following night a crouched figure flitted warily, almost invisibly, from one rubber tree to the next, toward the long shallow trench that was our only defence. One of ours, or one of theirs – probing? It became my unwelcome task to step out from behind my protective tree and challenge him – but softly, lest I awake my exhausted comrades, or alert the enemy's mortars.

'Who goes there?' I murmured.

At which he stood erect, peered through the gloom until he located me (posturing ridiculously, with my left foot forward and my rifle out-thrust) and then charged, ardent as any lover in a film, and impaled himself upon my bayonet.

He can never have doubted his fate, because I outreached him by a foot, but he hadn't faltered. Doubtless he had expected me to shoot him – had been sent precisely for that purpose – but a rifle flash would have pinpointed our position, so we had only used bayonets that night.

And he, who was supposed to be frightened of the dark, had welcomed it like a nocturnal predator; and, shrouded by it, had skewered himself. As if disappointed that he had failed to provoke a single shot, he sighed and sagged to the ground.

Where dawn revealed a fresh-faced youth with teeth so beautiful it seemed a desecration to have rendered them inanimate. Had I known then that, the instant he died, his soul had sped to Tokyo's Yasukuni Shrine, conceivably taking with it a quite entrancing smile, I might have cared less; but I did not know it, and I cared for so long that one of the first things I did when I visited Tokyo at the end of 1981 was visit the Yasukuni Shrine.

Two massive gates of tawny wood guarded its approaches, each embossed with an enormous symbolic chrysanthemum of gilded bronze. During the day they stood open and welcoming, and a broad path of pebbles led through a grove of trees into the temple's enclosed forecourt.

The temple was single-storeyed, wide, pagoda-roofed and dramatic – an empty stage with a proscenium of carved wood artfully draped, as if by a raised curtain, with a white calico banner on which were inscribed a dozen bold ideographs, each of them a minor work of art. The polished wooden floor below and beyond was bare and uncluttered, wide and deep.

A small crowd of pilgrims waited their turn to stand before the waist-high stage, then walked almost cheerfully forward two or three at a time, bowed a greeting from the footlights (as it were) reflected a moment, clapped twice, bowed a farewell and withdrew contentedly – leaving millions of spirits to enjoy an eternity of divine peace in the empty, glossy depths behind them. It was my turn. I approached, halted, bowed, muttered, 'Sorry little Nippon' – and waited. But he did not answer, perhaps because he was unwilling to absolve me, or unable to hear me. Or maybe because Shinto spirits are forbidden to communicate with lapsed Protestants who kill people about whom they know only what they have been told by their grandfathers and Intelligence Officers. I could not bring myself to clap, but I did reflect and bow before I withdrew, so he should at least know that I cared about killing him.

I have also cared about the faceless cretin who created the ludicrous fictions our Intelligence Officer was required, in the hideous language of the Army, to promulgate.

Before we were asked to bayonet them, a potted version of the truth about the Japanese would not have gone amiss. It might even

11

have put us on our mettle – which the prospect of meeting a foe who was bow legged, buck-toothed, half blind, frightened of the dark and armed with bows and arrows never did. And even *our* Intelligence Officers could have promulgated a potted version of the truth.

Not of Japan's beginnings, of course. What with goddesses and dragons, divinely created islands and emperors, shoguns (who did the Emperor's actual ruling) and the samurai (who did their shogun's dirty work) Japan's beginnings would have addled the brains of any Westerner. Indeed, Kenichi Yoshida (whose father was to become Japan's most famous Prime Minister in the early years of reconstruction after World War II) is very funny on the subject. 'Make believe' is what he calls it.

Commodore Perry, however, was not make believe, because it was he who precipitated the era that was ultimately to produce a generation of warriors like the officer we had killed with a shell and the private I had killed with a bayonet. But first there had been the Emperor Meiji.

His shogun having failed to eject the barbarian Perry, Meiji had dispensed with his services and set about modernizing and motivating a nation that was feudal. From 1890 onwards, therefore, and even after his death, until 1945, every school child in Japan, every school day of his life, dedicated himself to his emperor.

Every morning of every school day every pupil bowed in the direction of the Imperial Palace – 'Worshipping at a distance' – then repeated by heart the long Imperial Rescript on Education, and finally waited breathless for the question, 'What is your dearest ambition?'

To which, in passionate unison, the entire school responded, 'To die for the Emperor.'

Meiji gave them their first opportunity to do so in 1894, when he allowed his Army to be provoked into occupying Seoul. This distressed not only the Emperor of Korea, who took prompt refuge in the Russian Embassy, but also the Emperor of China, who sent his navy to Korea's assistance. When the Japanese sank his navy, however, the Chinese sued for peace, and surrendered not only the island of Taiwan and the Manchurian peninsula of Kwantung but the right to protect Korea as well.

Unfortunately, though, Korea's border touched that of Russia, and Czar Nicholas cared not at all for the idea of Japanese neighbours. With the full support of France and Germany, Nicholas required Japan to forego the fruits of her first foreign conquest.

Explaining to his people that Japan must now 'eat stones and drink gall', indeed 'endure the unendurable', Emperor Meiji accepted the terms of this so called Triple Intervention. Japan could not defy the collective might of three great powers; but that was not to say that later she would be unable to pick them off one by one.

Russia's turn came suprisingly early. In 1904, without declaring war, the Japanese Navy made a daring raid on the Czar's Asiatic Fleet in Port Arthur, sank it and blockaded the Port while the Japanese Army laid seige to the Czar's Army in its formidable fortress.

Thus provoked, Nicholas dispatched his mighty Baltic Fleet three quarters of the way round the globe to raise the siege and punish the Japanese. Britain (with whom Japan had the forethought to sign an alliance in 1902) and America (whose President Theodore Roosevelt had promised his good offices should the Russians win) awaited the outcome, enthralled.

Just in time, Port Arthur's fortress fell. At a cost of 20,000 lives, the Japanese had captured 25,000 Russians (whom they treated with great chivalry) and 500 guns. Better still, they had freed Admiral Togo's fleet from its task of blockading the harbour. Togo at once sailed southwards, deployed his fleet in the Strait that separated Japan from Korea, and lay in wait.

The Czar's great Baltic Fleet steamed into the strait and was classically outmanoeuvred. The Japanese sank twenty capital ships, captured five more and drowned 12,000 Russians for the loss of 116 of their own sailors. Five years later, adding insult to injury, they annexed Korea. Russia's humiliation was complete; but the Triple Intervention had only been partially avenged, and the Japanese have long memories.

Which did not fail them in 1914, when Britain declared war on Germany. As Britain's ally, Japan promptly seized the German leased port of Tsingtao and every German-held island in the Pacific. France's turn would come next.

But not immediately. First, in 1915, while the rest of the world was preoccupied with Germany, Japan launched her second unprovoked attack on China, was swiftly victorious and marked her victory with a list of 21 demands to which the Chinese were required to accede promptly. Whereupon the British and Americans stepped in and virtually stripped Japan of the fruits of her second Chinese war. It was 1895 all over again; and worse was to come.

In 1921, Japan's alliance with Britain was due for renewal.

Britain had already indicated that it was her intention to renew, and Hirohito's visit (as Crown Prince) to England had been such a success that the Japanese were confident that it would be renewed. After all, had not the Prince of Wales been his constant companion? Had not King George V himself been positively paternal? Had not Lloyd George, the Prime Minister, been both deferential and flattering?

But the Japanese had not given sufficient consideration to the role now being played in world affairs by America who, for the cost of a mere hundred thousand lives, was claiming to be the predominant victor of World War I. And America was displeased with Japan.

Displeased not only because of her recent adventure in China (for which, since it had lately had the good sense to become a Republic rather than an Empire, America now nursed an especially tender regard) but also because Japan was proving truculent on the subject of naval limitations. In point of fact, was even demanding the right to build the same tonnage of capital ships as America herself. Exerting all of its post-war influence, Washington therefore persuaded Whitehall to renege on the promised renewal of the Anglo-Japanese Alliance. The Japanese were outraged.

Washington, however, had not finished demolishing Japan's pride. In 1924 it included the Japanese in the category of 'orientals' virtually banned from immigration into the United States. To have her would-be emigrants to California banned was loss of face enough to Japan; but to have them labelled orientals, as if they were mere Chinese, was intolerable.

Every Western nation, it now seemed to the Japanese, had the right to settle where it wished; they were denied the right because they were yellow. Every Western nation had had for centuries the right to seize foreign territory and colonise it; they, in the so-called interests of world peace, were denied it.

No wonder their Prince Konoye had recently written that 'Pacifism is by no means necessarily identified with justice and morality.' And how proper it was that he had also insisted upon 'the abolition of economic imperialism, and of discrimination between the yellow races and the white'.

By 1924, therefore, Japan (though by no means forgetful of France's thirty-year-old slight) had become obsessed with the idea that she was the victim of an Anglo-American conspiracy to keep her navy less prestigious than theirs, and to deny her the right of colonial expansion. Reminding herself that Britain's colonies studded the surface of the world, and that America's record in relation to the Mexicans, the Panamanians and the Hawaians, to name only a few, was no more selfless than its recently acquired passion for the Chinese, Japan began to seethe.

China became the focal point of her rage. China was Japan's sister civilization. In decay and disarray it was to Japan she should be looking for rescue from her own corruption, Soviet ambitions and Western exploitation. China needed development, and Japan was the one nation entitled to help develop it – and, in the process, to provide herself with a huge colony for her would-be emigrants and a huge market for her exports, which the onset of the world depression had already decimated.

In 1931, therefore, Japan embarked on her third invasion of the Chinese mainland, describing her substantial campaign in Manchuria merely as an Incident, so as not to provoke the League of Nations unduly. At which America baldly declared her action to be a war of aggression and persuaded the League of Nations (of which it was not a member) to follow its example. Aware of the fact that this example might well be followed, Japan decided that, if the League of Nations were so 'rude' as to criticize her by name, she would leave it. She was criticized by name, and the rudeness of it infuriated her.

Preferring the million square miles of China she had virtually occupied, and the vast new market for her manufactured goods that she had thereby acquired, to international approbation, Japan ostentatiously resigned her membership of the League.

'What guarantee is there,' Matsuoka demanded of the League in his final address, 'that what you call world opinion is not mistaken? We Japanese are resigned to undergoing a period of tribulation. Certain people in Europe and America are seeking to crucify Japan here and now in the twentieth century.'

The period of tribulation that followed was China's, however, not Japan's; Manchuria being transformed into a puppet state and one Chinese city after another being put to the sword. Nanking fell on 7 December, 1937, after resistance as stubborn as Shanghai's had been. In the ensuing month, the 100,000 Japanese victors murdered and tortured to death 200,000 Chinese surrendered soldiers and civilians, and raped some 20,000 women. The western world was outraged.

*   *   *

15

Not everyone in Japan approved this policy of blatant aggression. Some even warned that it would lead to war with the United States and Britain. The militarists first silenced this body of opinion by assassinating its spokesmen, and then, adopting Hitler as their mentor, made adherence to their own philosophy obligatory. Any contrary opinions were branded 'wrong thinking'; and wrong thinking attracted the instant attentions of the Thought Police, whose methods were arbitrary and brutal.

Hitler's subsequent Blitzkrieg did nothing to undermine the overweening confidence of the militarists. Britain was on the brink of defeat, Europe had already succumbed, Russia had been invaded and America was palpably anxious *not* to go to war. There was no adventure that Japan could not now risk.

Should she so wish, and despite her Neutrality Pact with Russia, signed only months before, she could seize Siberia – and proposed doing so provided only that Hitler's march on Moscow did not falter. Or she could tighten the Navy's noose round the throat of Hong Kong (at whose border Japanese marines were impatiently awaiting the order to advance) and snuff out its life as a British colony. Or, easiest of all, she could at last avenge herself upon France, the third of 1895's insolent interventionists, by seizing its helpless colony in Indo China. Barely bothering to camouflage aggression as diplomacy, she persuaded the governor of northern Indo China (who could hope for no support from either Occupied France or its German masters) to allow her access to that province. And then, abandoning her plan to invade Siberia, because Hitler's offensive had stalled in the snow just outside Moscow, she began to move her massive Manchurian-based army southward, and brazenly occupied the whole of Indo China.

Three days later, Hitler agreed to the formation of a Tripartite Pact by which Japan's fate became inextricably linked with that of Italy and Germany. Implicit in that Pact was the understanding that, using Indo China as her spring board, Japan would immediately go to war with Germany's arch enemy, Britain. Japan, however, delayed – to discover whether Britain and America would offer her sufficient inducement to stay out of Hitler's war.

Churchill, preoccupied by the onslaughts of Germany and Italy, left the decision to Roosevelt; and Roosevelt decided that America, Britain and Holland should compel Japan's withdrawal from China and Indo China by denying her those supplies of oil, iron ore and

16

scrap iron without which both her economy and her military machine would founder.

By late 1941, Japan thus found herself opposed by a second Triple Intervention a thousand times more deadly, and ten thousand times more provocative, than the first.

It left her with three options. To accept Roosevelt's terms, and die of shame. To ignore them, and watch her factories and war machines seize up. Or to reject them, go to war and take by force the oil and iron she needed. The question was – the question to which we in Malaya might have to provide part at least of the answer – which of those options would Japan exercise?

* * *

That was the story we *could* have been told. But we were fed nonsense; and perhaps it mattered little, because we were soon to learn the truth for ourselves, and were doomed to defeat anyway – not least because the Japanese had been told a much more compelling story.

* * *

Entitled READ THIS ALONE – AND THE WAR CAN BE WON, a Japanese booklet left the Emperor's soldiers (to each of whom it was issued) in no doubt as to why they must fight, whom they must fight and how they must fight them.

'The New Restoration of the 1930's has come about in response to the Imperial desire for peace in the Far East,' it began. 'Its task is the rescue of Asia from white aggression. Already Japan, the pioneer in this movement, has rescued Manchuria from the ambitions of the Soviets, and set China free from the extortions of the Anglo Americans.'

Having thus set the scene, the stage directions for the coming invasion of Malaya followed, succinct and explicit.

'Treat the natives with kindness,' the booklet commanded, 'but do not expect too much of them.'

'You may be killed in action,' it conceded, 'but don't die of disease.' Clearly, to allow oneself to die of disease was wrong thinking in its most reprehensible form. The author of the booklet, having given the matter further thought, reverted to it almost immediately. 'Do not,' he instructed, 'fall ill.'

17

The booklet was read by soldiers packed into the unventilated holds of ships that were sailing slowly towards Malaya through 120 degrees of tropical heat: it reminded them, though, that it was not only they who were suffering. 'Be kind,' it exhorted, 'to the horses.'

Nor would heat and disease be the sole dangers they would have to face once the voyage was over and the beach-head taken. 'If you discover a dangerous snake,' they were adjured, 'you must kill it. You should also swallow its liver raw, and cook and eat the meat. There is no better medicine for strengthening the body.'

Finally, as we who were already in Malaya had so often been told, there was the vexed subject of the jungle – into which, in our six wearisome months of training, we had ventured only once. About a mile. Just enough to demonstrate to us how disagreeable it was, and why our High Command had decided to meet any future invader either on Malaya's narrow roads or in the rubber plantations on either side of them. Where we would kindly not damage the trees because the sultans wouldn't like it. (Nor apparently did Hirohito, who enquired anxiously, once it had been decided to go to war, whether Malaya's rubber plantations would be damaged. He was doubtless re-assured to learn that the Japanese Army intended to advance down Malaya's narrow roads only in small units led by a few tanks. 'That way,' he was told, 'there should be little danger of damaging the rubber forests.')

READ THIS ALONE was fatally perceptive on the aforesaid vexed subject of the jungle. 'By jungle is meant dense forest,' it said. 'This type of terrain is regarded by the weak-spirited as impenetrable, and for this very reason – in order to outmanoeuvre them – we must from time to time force our way through it. With proper preparation, and determination, it can be done.'

As if that simple truth were not damaging enough to our chances of victory, the booklet then drove a final nail into our coffin. 'If a man can pass,' it observed 'so can a motor vehicle. If the road is too narrow, cut a way through. If there is a cliff in the way, let forty or fifty men in a bunch haul you up it.'

Haul you up it, indeed! *We* had been conditioned to believe we'd done well if we succeeded in cajoling back on to the road a truck bogged twenty yards into a perfectly flat plantation. In all their planning, though, the Japanese were (and are again today) infinitely more positive than we. We aimed merely at halting them: they aimed at nothing less than our destruction.

'To check the withdrawal of enemy forces,' every third class

18

private in the Japanese army read, 'one of your principal aims should be to outflank and gain control of catchment areas, wells and springs to his rear.' It was basic tactics like that that destroyed us.

And so, from mere tactics, to their morale.

'The long voyage, the sweltering march – all have been for this. When you encounter the enemy, after landing, regard yourself as an avenger come face to face at last with his father's murderer. The discomforts of the long sea voyage, and the rigours of the march, have all been but months of waiting for this moment when you may slay your enemy.

'Here before you is the man whose death will lighten your heart of its burden of brooding anger. Should you fail to destroy him, you may never rest in peace – and the first blow is always the vital one!'

And now came a morsel of that cheap invective that had been our staple diet. But it was only a morsel; and it came at exactly the right place in a heavy meal. 'Westerners,' the booklet jeered, 'being very superior people, very cowardly and effeminate, have an intense dislike of fighting in rain, mist or darkness. Night, though excellent for dancing, they cannot conceive of as a proper time for war. IN THIS, if we seize upon it, lies our great opportunity. The final realities of our holy crusade will come on the battlefield ahead.'

From Tokyo, General Tojo broadcast even more succinctly. Vowing that Japan had done all in her power to avert the war upon which she was now embarked, reminding his captive audience that in 2600 years Japan had never been defeated, he promised his fellow countrymen, 'Final victory.'

CHAPTER TWO

>>>>>>><<<<<<<

Getting to Know Them

ACCORDING TO the war histories – even the Japanese war histories – our little battle, which started on a river bank at Muar and ended in a rubber plantation at Parit Sulong, was a gutsy and splendid one; but to those of us who fought it, our side of it was a shambles. Constantly deprived of the initiative, and devoid of tactics, we fought more like rats than heroes.

The Imperial Guards never ceased to bewilder us with their swiftness and daring; never failed to cut us off from re-supply and reinforcements; and never hesitated to strike first. We merely reacted – until the second day at Parit Sulong, when came the only incisive order we ever received: 'It's every man for himself,' we were told.

Sauve qui peut is normally the most dispiriting of injunctions, but to some five hundred of us – the suvivors of two battalions and one battery of Australians, and a brigade of completely untrained and terrified Indians – it was downright exhilarating. We were surrounded, exhausted, ravenous, parched, written off and reduced to a few rounds each of ammunition, but at last we were free of the dead-hand of a command whose wits had for weeks been paralyzed. All we now had to do – each of us relying upon no one but himself – was to break out of our encirclement by the apparently uncountable and ferocious Japanese.

For some reason, we never doubted that we would. To where exactly? To China, if we so desired. Or India. Or Australia. Or Singapore – which was about two thousand miles closer than the other three and would involve rather less swimming. After all those months of being trained not to think, to do only what one was told, one was at last at liberty to make up one's own mind – indeed was obliged to do so, because no one else of any rank any longer had any intention of doing it for one.

I dashed from the firing line to an almost burnt-out truck, pushed aside the three charred corpses of the men who had been part cremated inside it, and found a map. On the hundred yard dash back to the line bullets kept splatting into the trunks of rubber trees beside and behind me. The white latex oozed, and my bravado with it. But I still had visions of myself escaping to Ayer Hitham and swimming to Sumatra. In less than three days, however, I was to find myself (along with seven others) in Japanese hands, about to be shot.

*   *   *

The hours between the decision to break out and the moment of our capture contribute nothing to a story whose theme is the inextinguishable daring and explosive energy of the Japanese; but one must respect the laws of continuity.

Six of us decided, under cover of darkness, to head for Yong Peng. Yong Peng was about forty miles away as a crow might fly over the intervening swamps and jungle; but it should still be in British hands when we reached it, because it was a railhead. We set off from the firing line just before dawn, scuttling, passing a huddled group of over a hundred non-walking wounded who refused to encumber the non-wounded walkers. They wished us good luck and said they would surrender in the morning, when we had gone.

We then learnt our first lesson about the Japanese. Though as fiercely organised as ants, they are capable of an almost whimsical inconsistency. None of us should have escaped that relentless encirclement; the non-walking wounded apart, all of us did.

'I somewhat feel,' a Professor Mukai observed in 1980, 'that the Japanese, including myself, of course, lack tenacity of purpose. So, like staging a campaign, they make a lot of noise for a while, but calm down as soon as it's over. I don't think persistence is part of the Japanese disposition.'

Not exactly the way we would have put it as we crept through their lines in 1942; and not exactly the impression they have created among the industrialists of the rest of the world since August 1945; but a view they hold of themselves – with whose virtues and vices they are obsessed.

For the moment, though, it was *our* capacity for persistence that concerned us, not theirs. The following day, in the early afternoon, leech-bitten, bedraggled and close to collapse, we stood on a path that led, a mere mile away, we were assured by a wary Malay in sarong and tarboosh, to Yong Peng.

21

'Ada Japoon?' we asked him.

'Tidak Japoon,' he told us. So we'd done it. We had reached Yong Peng and it was still in our hands.

'I want two volunteers to go back the way we've come and bring out any stragglers,' rapped an officer who seemed suddenly to have forgotten that he had got this far only under our guidance, with our map and our compass, and without so much as a hint of an order from him. No one but the most pusillanimous would have taken any notice of him.

I was pusillanimous. Having been brought up never to cause others embarrassment ('Don't point, darling, you'll embarrass him'), I said I would go simply to spare him the embarrassment of having to go himself. Faithful to the strange tenets of mate-ship, Hugh Moore at once said he would go with me. 'I'll leave a guide for you,' the officer promised.

We left; we went back the way we had come; we found no stragglers interested in being led to Yong Peng; we returned to the track where the Malay had stood, but no guide awaited us; so we lay down and went to sleep.

A torch woke us, glaring in our eyes. An officer, a sergeant and two gunners from our own now defunct battery stared down at us. We staggered along the track, out of the jungle, into the rubber, out of the rubber, on to a road and stood at the top of a hill looking down at Yong Peng. Which was swarming with Japanese.

We set out for Singapore, more than a hundred miles away, our wits functioning only intermittently, conversation staccato. No food for four days. Only a quart of water in the last forty-eight hours. Water bottles empty. We would never make Singapore cluttered up with rifles. No bullets in them anyway. So we ditched them and grew careless and were observed by two Tamil rubber tappers, who sprinted away. Mindlessly we followed. We should have known better, because within minutes rifle and automatic fire was coming at us from three sides. The Tamils had betrayed us. The jungle being only a hundred yards away, Hugh and I took off, passing bullets on the way.

'Halt, those two men!'

Officer's voice. *Don't think, do what you're told.* We stopped and looked behind. Four men with their hands up. A soldier's duty is to escape. Turned towards the jungle again. A Japanese gentleman was barring the way, pointing what looked like a Bren gun. We raised our hands.

Herded together. Stripped of watches, fountain pens, wallets, identity discs, Hugh retrieved his wallet. I retrieved my paybook. Don't know why.

Prodded toward a shallow drain. Made to sit on its edge, six of us in a row, trussed up in shirts, shorts, boots and socks. Flexed wrists as they were bound. Had read that that was the thing to do in *Boys' Own Annual*. Reminded self only to give name, rank and number. Not even asked.

What followed lives in the memory like an old film, grainy and flickering.

A light machine gun was set up in front of us and a Japanese soldier lay behind it, squinting at us along its barrel. It didn't seem unfair. Unpromising though. A Japanese officer was standing by the machine gun with his sword held aloft. 'Very sorry,' he told us, 'all men die.' Hugh and I decided if we were to be shot we'd at least be shot at running. Unflexing wrists, found it fairly easy to slip one hand through bonds as per *Boys' Own*. Was busy untying Hugh's hands when the sergeant, on my left, betrayed us. Re-tied, re-untied, re-betrayed. Also denounced as Jap killer. True of all of us, except the sergeant, who had spent the war at the bottom of a slit trench. Hated him. Was about to slip hand from bonds a third time when the Japanese officer waved his sword. The machine gun opened fire.

Dead? Not dead! Machine gun firing over our heads. At stragglers fifty yards away. Hands high, two more join us in our ditch. Sergeant sobs for mercy. Japanese pack up machine gun, prod us on to feet, tie us together (from wrists to throat to wrists to throat) and march us off into the impenetrable jungle. The Japanese officer's map is blue-veined with tracks we never knew existed.

We pound along them, clearly heading for a rendezvous. Japanese uniforms not smart, but practical. Short Japanese legs tireless. Officer says anyone falls to ground, he shoot them.

We come to a road. Japanese suspect mines, Japanese right. Make us go first. Very sensible. An ambulance of ours the other side of the minefield. Riddled with bullets. Full of dead. Look at captors and think, 'Bastards.' Captors recognize look and thump with rifle butt.

Re-enter impenetrable jungle. Meet another group of Japanese, all angry. Just been fighting and maybe six of them (it's a long time ago and only impressions remain) are wounded. They lie side by side, neatly, across the track. A soldier comes up to each, bows, offers a lighted cigarette, and withdraws.

23

All the non-wounded Japanese soldiers then beat us up. Fists, rifle butts, bayonets in scabbards and one unsheathed sword. We duck, weave, stumble and trip one another, because still tied together; but somehow survive. Hugh's forearm shockingly gashed by the sword. Stumble on; but tied now in threes, the sergeant between Hugh and myself, one end of the rope from his wrists up round my throat and down to my wrists, the other via Hugh's throat to his wrists.

Explosions behind us. The Japanese wounded have killed themselves. No need; they were winning; no one was going to capture them. But they couldn't fight any more. Strange people. Our second lesson.

Come to another road. Japanese very wary. We all lie while they peer. I get a field dressing from one of the others and crawl to Hugh. 'Kurrah!' shouted the Japanese officer. (It is spelt KORA, but the Japanese pronounce it KURRAH.) Don't know what Kurrah means, so ignore it and bind Hugh's gaping wound. Japanese officer loses interest.

Cross road back into the jungle. Pound along until the sergeant falls to the ground. Officer asks will I carry him. Say no. He is shot. I am not sorry. (And was to remain unrepentant for twenty years, until I was given a bad trip on LSD by a doctor, with a nurse in attendance, as part of my research for a novel. Towards the end of the trip, when everything had become rather nasty, the sergeant appeared, a bullet hole in his forehead.

'Murderer!' he shouted.

'You were a coward and a traitor and they shot you,' I defended myself.

'You wouldn't carry me. I couldn't go on and you wouldn't carry me.'

'You were yellow.'

'I was *frightened*. I thought they were going to shoot me.'

Had the Japanese officer asked me then, I would have picked him up and carried him for an eternity. Twenty years too late, I had learnt that it is not a capital offence to be frightened.

'They *did* shoot you,' I reminded: and tried to crawl into the hole in his forehead so that I couldn't any longer hear him shouting, 'Murderer, murderer'. But just then someone gave me a shot of something – chlorpromazine, I think – and my trip ended).

Tied now only to Hugh, I stepped over the sergeant's body and we strode on. But more grimly. Wondering where the hell they were taking us, and for what purpose, since we were so demonstrably expendable.

In the distance, a burst of automatic fire. Instantly – like American footballers executing one of their complex manoeuvres at the end of a huddle — our captors sped into the jungle on either side of the track, fanning out as they ran, a wolf-pack drawn by the scent of blood. No words of command, no hesitation. In seconds they had vanished, leaving us in the care of only one of their number, who pinned us in a heap beneath the snout of his automatic rifle.

Within minutes they were back, having either encircled and destroyed the source of that crackle of gunfire – or found it friendly. They did not bother to explain which. Not to us: not even to the one they had left to guard us. It was all in a day's work to them; but to us their brief and practised foray had been dazzling. So perfectly choreographed, and so unbelievably economical. It was small groups like theirs, we realized then, that had confused and flung into endless retreat whole regiments of us, all the way down the Malay Peninsula.

We slept that night under the hut in which they slept. We discussed attempting an escape, but agreed that none should make the break until all were ready. More than five of us at a time were seldom ready; and one of us (inexplicably wearing tennis shoes) was never ready; but to abandon him to our captor's reprisals was unthinkable. So we rested that night, and derived considerable comfort from the fact that while we rested one after another of our equally weary captors had to stay awake to guard us.

Morning, and the flesh of one coconut between us. Time has blurred the chronology, even the sequence, of events. Except, it seems, that we were no longer tied together. From some of us, I remember, they took our boots, to replace their own, which were web-toed and made of canvas.

We march on, barefooted. Japanese aeroplanes keep flying low overhead. Pilots salute. Soldiers take off helmets and caps, untie headbands from black bristled skulls, and wave them. It's all so co-ordinated. They know exactly where they are, where they're going, what they're doing.

Reach a clearing. One hut. A Malay emerges. He has a meal waiting for our captors. They fill their mess tins and we and they withdraw fifty yards up the track. They give us nothing. The Malay looks at us from just outside his hut, as if to say, 'What else can I do?'

Well for a start, he can fill my water bottle. As I stand, one of our guards looks up from his rice, restive. To hell with him. I walk down the track to the Malay, thrust my water bottle at him and say, 'Ayer!'

It never occurred to me that I was taking a risk, still less that the Malay would refuse. I was British. The Japanese would naturally respect my demand for water. The Malay wouldn't dare reject it.

Yuji Aida writes in his book that, as one who fell into the hands of the British at the end of World War II, he glimpsed their 'unknown soul' and found it 'a frightening monster'. In Burma, he observed, they had somehow come to be accepted 'as a special kind of superior being, full of cold arrogance that arouses an enormous fear in people who are used by them'.

Professor Aida is a cultured man whose specialist field is European history: he still detests the British – of whom, by virtue of the demands of the EEC, I am no longer one. In 1942, however, all Australians were British; and doubtless it was my Britishness that moved me to ignore our captors and insist that the Malay ignored them too. I felt no cold arrogance toward him or them, and had no desire to be a frightening monster to anyone, but I never doubted that I was their superior.

I remember that the Japanese soldiers sat apart from us, their packs off, their helmets and caps off, their belts with the heavy pouches and grenades off, their flies undone and their trousers agape (it was hot, and that was sensible; but gaping flies do not induce a sense of awe in those who witness them). Their rifles were leaning against a banana tree, and they were scooping rice into their mouths from close-held mess tins.

I remember thinking that they looked brutalized with their savagely cropped skulls. I remember feeling no doubts that they would lose the war, because we were British. History had taught us that wars were things the British always won. So it was probably as an inevitable victor that I found it in order to disregard our captors and go in search of water. What concerns me today is the vivid recollection of myself, just twenty-one years and two days old, thrusting a water bottle at a man old enough to be my grandfather, and insisting that he fill it.

'Ayer!' I had said – water – as confident he would oblige me as I was that the Japanese would not shoot me. But many Americans and Filipinos *were* shot for attempting to obtain water. Neither my elderly Malay nor I was shot, however; and on reflection, while absolving myself on the charge of racist arrogance, I plead guilty to a certain blithe, almost frivolous sense of confidence of a kind then common to so-called Britons.

However contemptible that quality (and Aida detested it) it is, on the one hand, no longer a British attribute, and it did, on the other, prompt centuries of Britons to take outrageous entrepreneurial risks. Today it is Aida's race, the Japanese, in whom this quality of confidence is most evident; and it was one of their most brilliant businessmen, Masaya Miyoshi, who recently assured me that Japan's vanquished competitors in the exports war 'lack risk-taking policies'.

In 1945 it was what Aida called 'an appalling fact' of his imprisonment in Burma that 'we found ourselves beginning to hold the British in awe'. As early as 1942, however, every Allied soldier had begun to hold the Japanese in awe; and what the Japanese victor of 1942 and the Japanese victors of today have in common is the confidence to be daring.

I returned to my fellow prisoners with my full water bottle.

'You stupid bastard,' Tennis Shoes rebuked me, 'you could have got us shot.' To make amends, I handed him the water bottle first. Our march resumed; but only its more bizarre memories remain – and again they are in the form of clips from a movie in which I see myself portrayed by someone I no longer know, and my companions as youths who no longer exist.

We reached another road, where a battalion of Japanese were re-grouping after what must have been a bloody encounter. We were herded into a corrugated iron tool shed on the verge. It was deep enough to accommodate us only if we huddled together, and so low that we had to squat. It was oven hot and I thought myself lucky to be the one who crouched nearest its opening.

Until a Japanese officer approached – tall, flushed, drunk and smouldering. His open-necked shirt was unbuttoned to the waist, his jack boots glistened, his hand gripped the hilt of his sheathed sword and his eyes were restless.

'You!' he said, peering down at me. 'How old?'

I told him, and he commented that I was a baby, that Japanese soldiers were at least 24. His brother, who had just been killed, was 24. A baby at war was no good. Being a prisoner was no good. Drawing his sword, he offered to release me from both bad conditions. I had only to kneel before him and he would cut off my head. He was neither discourteous nor overbearing, and it seemed perfectly natural for me to say, 'No thank you.'

27

By which he was so suprised, even disturbed, that he repeated his offer, but more clearly, lest I again misunderstood the kindness he was offering me.

Again I declined, aware of the fact that I was disappointing him. Shaking his head in dismay, he lurched off. Had he been so inclined, he could have decapitated all seven of us.

We moved on, through jungle, until we reached our fourth road – beside which, in a small clearing, was a hut, a shed and a chicken coop. We were stuffed into the chicken coop, a sentry at its entrance staring at us balefully. Tennis Shoes was unhappy with his position in the coop. To shut him up I agreed that we should change places.

We heard trucks approaching, then heavy machine gun fire all round us. A bullet penetrated the wooden side of the coop and blasted a hole in Tennis Shoes' thigh. He was dragged out of the coop and bayoneted. Then we and the survivors of the ambushed convoy were herded into the shed, about thirty of us in a shed ten feet by ten at the most, all of us sprawled over a pile of copra.

There was a strong smell of coconut oil, blood and, later on, gangrene. That night the silhouette of a Japanese officer appeared in the doorway from time to time. He carried a torch which he shone round the bodies sprawled over the copra. He upon whose face the torch finally came to rest was taken outside, questioned, tortured . . . and put to death.

In the morning our reduced numbers were packed into captured British trucks still sticky with blood. We were driven to a large bungalow, for questioning and the treatment of wounds. While Hugh was having his arm cleaned (and dressed with cellophane) a group of idle Japanese soldiers poured gasoline on a Chinaman's venerable, pig-tailed head, set it on fire and gave him a bucket of water to put it out. The water was boiling. Eventually the Chinaman died.

After the destruction of Hiroshima, a Japanese poet wrote that some of the victims had made their way to a field to bury their 'roasted heads of bacon in the dust of agony'. It is not only atomic bombs that roast heads; it was not only the Americans who roasted them.

The Japanese medical officer who treated Hugh's arm made it clear that he disapproved of soldiers who surrendered. In the Imperial Japanese Army no one surrendered. Not even its doctors, who fought like everyone else, for which purpose they carried swords.

The Headquarters officer who interrogated us was equally unimpressed by our somewhat smug resolve to reveal no more than name, rank and number. When I declined to tell him to which unit I had been attached, he told me that it was the 65 Battery of the 2/15 Field Regiment — adding, for good measure, that our O.C.'s name was Major Julius, and that Julius had been killed on January 22 near the Barkri cross-roads. Their Intelligence in those days – garnered from Japanese photographers, mining engineers, restauranteurs, businessmen, sailors and bankers – was extraordinary. Nowadays it is no less extraordinary; but it is provided by the data-processing computers of powerful trading companies rather than the reports of individuals.

We were transported, those of us who were not Indians (whom they hoped to convert to the Japanese cause) to Kuala Lumpur, and marched to the gates of its gaol. The gates were flung open and we were herded inside where hundreds of others, mostly British, but a few Australians, milled around in a small courtyard. The gaol was called Pudu: within it our captivity and our inquest into its causes would begin. The captivity would end three years and seven months later, and is now mere history: the inquest into its causes goes on, because today they have brought Japan a victory to which not even she can have aspired when she went to war in December, 1941.

CHAPTER THREE
❯❯❯❯❯❯❯❮❮❮❮❮❮❮

The Sixteen Petalled
Chrysanthemum

WHETHER WE LIVED OR DIED during the thirteen hundred disagreeable days that followed was of small concern to our captors – until early 1945, when it was ordained, should our release appear imminent, that we were to die.

Nevertheless, two thirds of us were to survive the years of starvation by gorging ourselves on hatred; and it was to be Hirohito himself, inspired by the fate of Hiroshima, who pre-empted the order for our liquidation by speaking to our captors with what his subjects called 'The Voice of the Crane'.

Happily, we foresaw none of this as we squatted in the courtyard of the one-time female quarters of Pudu Gaol, attempting to reconcile ourselves to captivity and asking ourselves how such a thing could have come to pass.

The debate raged for weeks, but it quickly became evident that on one point at least there was unanimity – which was that, in absolutely everything we had been told about the Japanese, we had been sold a pup; that someone must have known the truth and advised his political masters of it; and that those in the know had been lying to us.

As indeed they had. Before Hitler began distracting and hypnotizing the world's statesmen, in 1933, it had been Japan, and only Japan, whom Britain's defence experts had envisaged as the potential enemy.

To them the Japanese had seemed anything but small, myopic, ill-equipped and frightened of the dark. On the contrary, as early as 1930 they had warned the British Government that Japan could 'without warning, inflict crushing blows on us from which we should with difficulty recover'.

The advent of Hitler, and the consequent likelihood of a war with

Germany, had horrified the British Admiralty. The Royal Navy, weakened by years of disarmament, had become overstretched. It would have been hard pressed to defend Hong Kong and Singapore against the Japanese Navy alone; against Germany in the North Sea and the Atlantic as well (not to mention Italy in the Mediterranean, now that Mussolini's rape of Abyssinia had gone unpunished) the Royal Navy could have achieved almost nothing in Far Eastern waters.

By 1937, Australia and New Zealand had become extremely anxious. In the event of war, Australia had enquired, would Britain be able to send a fleet to defend the Far East?

Why not station part of a fleet in Singapore even in peace-time? New Zealand had suggested.

Neither Dominion had been prepared to contribute a penny toward the cost of this aspect of Imperial Defence, of course, but both were determined constantly to remind Britain of her Imperial obligations; and it was then that the lies began.

If the Japanese should go to war with the British Empire, the British Government declared, a British fleet large and strong enough to contain the Japanese Navy would instantly be despatched to the East – even though Britain might at the same time be involved in a war in Europe.

Worse, in 1938 Prime Minister Chamberlain of Britain had sought to dispel the nagging doubts of Australia's Prime Minister by insisting that: 'The idea that, in the event of war, we might not be able to defend our overseas possessions is entirely false.' Chamberlain had known at that time that the Admiralty would have been able to despatch only one capital ship eastwards to deter an entire navy, but he had not hesitated to lie. And when Lieutenant General Sir William Dobbie, GOC in Malaya, had reported that *his* command was impressed with the performance of the Japanese in China; that he personally believed (contrary to expert opinion) that the end-of-year monsoon season could well be the time they would choose to invade Malaya; and that Singapore's air force was inadequate, he had promptly been relieved of his command.

Nevertheless, by 1939, far from rejecting the idea that Britain 'might not be able to defend her overseas possessions', Chamberlain's Government had come to accept the idea that they could *only* be held with the active co-operation of the United States of America – which co-operation seemed most unlikely to be forthcoming. The Dominions, however, were never apprised of this dismal fact.

Thus, by the time Italy had entered the war and France had surrendered, Singapore had become a naval base without a navy, and the Malayan Peninsula had become virtually indefensible. Chamberlain, however, had confided none of this to the Australian government; and his successor, Churchill, had merely asked Canberra to send one army division and two squadrons of aircraft to help strengthen Malaya's land and air defences.

Doubtless Chamberlain believed his lies justified, and Churchill could have cited the exigences both of war and of diplomacy to justify the despatch of British, Indian and Australian troops to a colony that was doomed. In Pudu, however, knowing nothing of these matters, we waxed vehemently unlyrical about the idiocy of our High Command.

We also agreed that, however ill-informed and badly led we had been, we could somehow have done better: could have played the Japanese at their own game, for example, and travelled light, lived off the land, fought in small, flexible groups instead of battalions and brigades, and attacked instead of waiting to be attacked. But in this we did ourselves an injustice, because we had been locked into a system that permitted nothing of the kind; because the Japanese had been trained to do it, and we had not; but most of all because they had had a staff officer called Lieutenant Colonel Tsuji, and on our side there was no one to match him.

*   *   *

Masanobu Tsuji is that rare creature in Japan, a man of mystery. In a society where both gangsters and great industrialists are household names, where everyone has his niche, and is neither envied it nor ever expected to depart from it, Tsuji is conspicuous because he achieved great things and then, twice, vanished.

Ask them to where he vanished at the end of World War II, and the Japanese smile almost conspiratorially and say they don't know. Ask why he vanished, and they still don't know – though Tsuji himself, in his autobiography, claimed that he was ordered to lose himself, and hints that it was in South East Asia that he did so.

Between August 15 and September 8, 1945, when the Americans came and occupied Japan, many officers and NCO's in the Japanese army were transferred, with different ranks, and under assumed names, to other units — presumably to protect them from Allied prosecutions. Only Tsuji was ordered to lose himself. There is much evidence to suggest that, had he not, he would have been hanged; but there is little to explain why a mere Lieutenant Colonel should have been ordered to spare himself the fate that so many of his seniors – from General Tojo, his long time Prime Minister, to General Anami, his last Minister of War – either stoically accepted or escaped only by committing suicide.

Why, having eventually returned to public life and become a member of Japan's new democratic Diet, he suddenly vanished a second time is a mystery. Asked about this, today's Japanese smile more broadly, because this time Tsuji has remained lost.

So what happened to him? Without exception his compatriots declare that he was shot. By whom? They shrug and suggest the Viet Cong, almost as if they have conspired to insist that Masanobu Tsuji was shot, but having agreed the bare bones of the story cannot be bothered fleshing it out, except to explain that he was a brilliant man who planned the most stunning campaigns of the Second World War — the conquest of Malaya, Singapore and the Philippines.

Seven years before Japan hurled herself into World War II, Tsuji had graduated with great distinction from his Staff College and been appointed tutor to Prince Mikasa, the Emperor's youngest brother. He had become something of a Court favourite and was honoured with gifts not only from Prince Mikasa and his brother, Takeda, but from Emperor Hirohito himself – and in those days gifts embossed with the fourteen petalled chrysanthemum of a royal Prince, or the sixteen petalled chrysanthemum of the Emperor, were to the Japanese what relics of the true Cross would be to a Christian.

Assigned the task of collating all the intelligence garnered from South East Asia since Japan's vast network of agents had been set up in 1934, and of planning twin campaigns in which the Imperial Japanese Army would challenge the entrenched might of Britain and America, Tsuji had set up Unit 82 in Taiwan Island and gone to work.

His basic strategy, since enemy forces were scattered along the Malayan Peninsula and among the Phillippine Islands, was to use a mere eleven Japanese divisions 'to attack with surprise and with our strength concentrated' and 'defeat the enemy units one by one'.

Tsuji not only devised the unorthodox tactics that enabled this strategy to be implemented, he even laid down a timetable to which it should adhere. Malaya and Singapore would fall in less than a hundred days from the outbreak of war; Manila in less than sixty; Java in less than a hundred and thirty; and Rangoon in less than a hundred and seventy. Only as to the Philippines was history to prove him apparently optimistic; and that was not his fault but General Honma's.

We, squatting on our hunkers in a packed little prison courtyard, may therefore have felt we could have done vastly better than we did, but Tsuji, as he planned our defeat, had never doubted that Malaya and Singapore would fall by mid March at the latest. That history should have proved him apparently pessimistic was not his fault but General Yamashita's.

A month ahead of schedule, then, it had come to pass, we in Pudu first being made aware of it when, from the neighbouring barracks, came a full throated rendition of Kimi Ga Yo, Japan's national anthem. Then a banner was strung across the courtyard announcing that the Singapore garrison had surrendered.

We chose not to believe it. For most of our lives we had heard that Singapore was impregnable; and we knew that it was a small island to which maybe 50,000 invincible Britons had withdrawn and as many loyal Indians. It was impossible that the Japanese could so swiftly have conquered all of Malaya below Yong Peng, transported their forces across the easily defended waters of the Causeway to secure a foothold on the island, advanced inland to capture the heights that dominated the city, and forced all those men (upon whom we had been relying for our early release from the squalors of Pudu) to surrender, a mere twenty-four days after the débâcle at Parit Sulong.

But when the Japanese bombers ceased their daily run southward, and Japanese tanks were clearly heard clattering northward towards Burma, we were forced to accept that the impossible had happened. General Yamashita's 60,000 men, having outflanked and outwitted our original 130,000, had finally outfought what was left of them.

In Japan the press urged that the advance must go on, through Burma and India to Asia Minor, there to link hands with Germany. In Pudu we were told that we must henceforth call Japan 'Dai Nippon', or Great Land of the Rising Sun; refer to Singapore as 'Shonan', or Light of the South; and change our watches, if we still had them, to Tokyo time. Naturally we did none of these things, although we did compromise with 'Japan'. Omitting the 'Dai', we began to call it Nippon, because it appealed to us to refer to the all-conquering Japanese as 'Nips'.

*　　*　　*

34

Only time would reveal how humiliatingly complete Yamashita's victory had been. Assigned five crack divisions, most of the Army's available tanks, the nation's best artillery, mortar and machine gun units, and all the bicycles and boats his men might require, he had been so instantly successful that he had dispensed with two divisions and defeated us with only three.

Those who commanded us, on the other hand, had so seldom allowed us to come to grips with Yamashita's three divisions that we had killed only 3507 of them – about one for every forty of us who surrendered.

It was allegedly Tsuji, however, who enabled Yamashita to bluff General Percival – a kindly man – into surrendering so prematurely on 15 February. At a time when the defenders of Singapore had vast quantities of ammunition and food available to them, Yamashita's arsenal was almost empty. So Tsuji, it is said, employed once again the terror tactic that had earlier compelled the surrender of the remnants of Hong Kong's hapless garrison. The tactic was pitilessly and publicly to rape and murder; and rather than see Singapore hold out a minute beyond 15 February – on which day an Imperial emissary would arrive to witness the capitulation – Tsuji was prepared to try it again.

Not that he seems to have needed much encouragement. One of Yamashita's divisions was comprised of tough veterans of the China war recruited from the coalmines of Kyushu. They were, as Tsuji would subsequently observe, 'quarrelsome and apt to commit acts of violence and plunder. 'Yet there was nothing,' he would add, 'to be said against that.' And when, to Yamashita's fury, that division committed atrocities in Penang, it was Tsuji who had sprung to their defence, and Tsuji who never forgave Yamashita for insisting upon court-martialling the offenders.

It must have been with mixed feelings, then, that he set out with an experienced team for Singapore's Alexandra Hospital and there supervised the butchering of 230 patients and 93 doctors and nurses – thereby convincing Percival that failure to surrender immediately, as Yamashita demanded, would mean hundreds of thousands of civilians being 'put to the sword', as Yamashita threatened.

Thus, with no loss of face to the Japanese Army, Singapore had fallen and the Emperor's representative had not been kept waiting. The Army had killed more of the enemy than the enemy had killed of the Army; but Tsuji – who wore cuff-links embossed with the fourteen petalled chrysanthemum, and drank sake from a cup

35

embossed with the sixteen petalled chrysanthemum – had twice been snubbed by Yamashita. Once when his tactical advice was rejected, the second time when his intercession on behalf of the Penang offenders was disregarded.

It was perhaps a blessing for six million Australians that Tsuji was so proud and influential a man, because he immediately began intriguing to deprive Yamashita of the Tokyo triumph he deserved and to have him relegated to his original unprestigious command in Manchuria instead. Had he not, Yamashita's wish to proceed at once with Admiral Yamamoto's plan to invade Australia would almost certainly have been granted; and Australia, at that time, had nothing with which to oppose him.

*   *   *

Flushed with victory, but unaware of Tsuji's conniving, our guards boasted that soon they would be in Australia, raping our women and killing our men. It was not difficult to hate them. Nor, in those first months of captivity, was it difficult to sustain our hatred; a trickle of newcomers from the jungle constantly refuelled it.

A twenty-year-old had stayed behind with one of the wounded at Parit Sulong who was his friend. A hundred and thirty of them, and he with them, had surrendered. They had then been tied up, bayoneted and thrown into heaps for incineration. But neither he nor his friend beneath him was dead; and his friend had moaned. So the Japanese had tossed the boy's body into a deep drain and killed his friend. Three weeks later the boy was captured a second time, and sent to Pudu. The bayonet wounds in his back had healed, but his eyes were dull with horror.

There were too many stories like that, none of them denied by the Japanese, who claimed that those who surrendered were so dishonoured as to be fortunate when they were subsequently put to death. That, they explained, was bushido. We were to hear a lot about the code of bushido in the next three and a half years, but were never, to our hosts' disgust, to be converted, difficult though it was to dispute the sincerity of those who preached it. None of them had surrendered to us; and their wounded had even chosen to kill themselves rather than delay their comrades' advance.

All the same, it was to come as something of a shock, four decades later, when Wataru Tajitsu – perched like an ancient child on one of Mitsubishi's huge armchairs – told me that Japan had vanquished the world in the trade war of the 1960s to the 1980s by running its industries 'in accordance with the rules of bushido'.

I had instant visions of captains of Mitsubishi vessels committing seppuku because they had docked late, of Mitsubishi pilots turned Kamikases and crashing their Mutsubishi freight planes on to the decks of rival tankers, of Mitsubishi employees by the thousand hurling themselves to their death off the summit of Fujiyama because Mitsubishi annual profits had grown by only five per cent instead of the stipulated six.

'You know my history, don't you?' I at once asked Mr. Tajitsu. He waited for me to elaborate. 'I surrendered to the Japanese Army in Malaya,' I told him.

'Very sorry,' he said — which, from the polite mouth of a Japanese, means, 'Too bad.' But he seemed in no way shocked. 'Before the war,' he explained, 'if the President of one of Mitsubishi's companies found it was not doing well, he would resign. Immediately after the war, that Mitsubishi spirit saw a decline; but now it's in the ascendant again.'

Nothing about killing themselves. On the other hand, their export offensive since the war had been, and is still being waged very much according to the Tsuji principle of attacking unsuspecting positions with concentrated strength and picking off enemy units one by one.

It occurred to me, however, that Mr. Tajitsu's bushido might not be the bushido of the Imperial Japanese Army. He was a very old man who would have been in his thirties at the time when the Army had begun to usurp the role of the Japanese government in 1931 – and the Thought Police to suppress any anti-militarist feelings. Had the Army distorted not only its government's foreign policy but its own Samurai code as well?

I sought out Shichihei Yamamoto, a distinguished critic and essayist who, in August 1945, in the Philippines, had been so obsessed with bushido that he had hesitated to accept the Emperor's order to stop fighting. When eventually he had done so, and been put in an American prison camp, he had refused to speak to those inmates of the camp who had been captured before hostilities ended. Much of the time since the war's end he has spent investigating the truth about the bushido of the Imperial Japanese Army compared with that of the Samurai.

At great length, and with great patience, he explained that the gift of China's culture to Japan had been beneficial in almost every way – save that it had left the Japanese with an inferiority complex. Time passed and they evolved a defensive philosophy, the gist of which was that no one could legitimately succeed to an emperor's throne by means of usurpation, regicide or conquest; and judged by these criteria, the Chinese had had not a single legitimate occupant on their Imperial Throne for centuries! Indeed, the one true emperor in the world was Japan's, whose dynasty had reigned since time immemorial.

From this somewhat grandiose position it was only a short step, after the Meiji Restoration had endorsed Commodore Perry's intrusion into Japanese affairs, to the altogether more exalted position that, the Imperial line having sprung from the loins of a goddess, every subsequent emperor had been divine.

Thereafter, serving the Emperor would take precedence over every other obligation in feudal Japan; every school child would daily worship from afar; and, as industrialization and the depression combined to wreck Japan's agricultural economy, hundreds of thousands of farm boys would be prompted to join the Army. Where it was easy to persuade them that it was indeed their dearest wish to die for the Emperor; that the spirits of those who died in battle would indeed fly to the Yasukuni Shrine, there to share the divinity of the Emperor himself; and that the sixteen petalled chrysanthemum engraved on the butt of their rifles was proof that the weapons were indeed a personal gift (like Tsuji's sake cup) from Hirohito to themselves.

Thus was effected the Second Restoration, whereby Hirohito became a god, the Army his instrument, the war a holy one and the capture of even one of his soldiers so unthinkable that none of them was ever instructed what questions he should refuse to answer should the enemy interrogate him.

The fact that in practice it was largely junior officers who thereafter interpreted the Emperor's divine will, and imposed it on a cowed government and a docile nation, was neither here nor there; so intoxicating was the theory of the Second Restoration that even those who exploited it accepted as irrevocable its basic premise that they must die rather than allow Hirohito's army to be insulted or his reputation sullied.

These, then, were the men into whose hands we in Malaya, and the garrison of Hong Kong, had fallen. Within the next four months, as they swept apparently invincible through the Dutch East Indies, the Philippines and Burma, they would net hundreds of thousands

38

more. Because we had surrendered, they took no pains at all to understand us: because it was essential to our survival, we took such pains as were necessary to understand them.

Addressing the House of Commons after the fall of Hong Kong, Anthony Eden accused them of 'nauseating hypocrisy' in their exaltation of bushido. Rather, he said, they had 'perpetrated against their helpless military prisoners, and the civil population, the same kind of barbarities as had aroused the horror of the civilised world at the time of the Nanking massacre of 1937'.

Eden, however, was wrong. Not even the Japanese have ever denied that the Nanking massacre of 200,000 Chinese civilians in 1937 was atrocious; but by 1942 the concept of bushido had been so distorted, yet so profoundly inculcated, that the Imperial Japanese Army (which is not to be confused with the Kempeitai) could justify atrocities committed in its name not only without a trace of hypocrisy, but even with total sincerity.

CHAPTER FOUR
>>>>>>><<<<<<<

'I am the Only Man who Must Apologize to His Majesty'

THERE WERE superficial differences by the score between them and us. We pushed a saw, they pulled it. We said, 'Come here,' and gestured with the first finger of a hand held palm upwards: they used all the fingers of a hand held palm downwards. We read the horizontal lines on the page of a book from left to right and top to bottom, the pages themselves from the front of the book to the back: they read vertical lines from top to bottom and right to left and the pages themselves from back to front. We hate crocodiles and regard their tears as a symbol of hypocrisy: they regard the crocodile as a symbol of courtesy. We stood to attention with fists clenched; they with the fingers outstretched. We nodded at people; they bowed. We used four letter words to let off steam: they, having no obsenities in their language, either shrieked such ungratifying epithets as 'bakayaru', which means nothing more than 'fool', or lashed out with fists, boots, rifle butts and anything else that came to hand.

They required us to bow to them, sliding our hands down the front of our thighs as our bodies became rectangular. Naturally we declined. Britons didn't bow. Even our monarch expected only an unostentatious duck of the head – unless one was a woman. But we refrained from mentioning that lest our guards insisted that we curtsey.

It was necessary, of course, to defy them. Only defiance enables a captive to retain his pride; and it has to be as consistent as it is uncomprising or it becomes self-indulgence. It was also necessary to hate them, because it would otherwise have been too easy to die.

Unfortunately, habitual defiance corrodes humility, and prolonged hatred corrodes sanity. Each of us who came home has since had to consider whether the price paid for self-respect and survival was too high. The question is a recurring one.

For me it recurred most recently when I visited Osaka to inter-view Kenosuke Matshushita, the 88-year-old founder of the Electric Industrial Company and National Panasonic, and one of the world's richest and most powerful industrialists. Half way through our meeting it dawned on me that I was in the presence of a great man; and I was surprised. Great men are rarities, and I had not expected to meet one in Osaka.

Professor Aida would have been unsurprised by this vestigial Anglo-Saxon arrogance, but I had thought better of myself – having learned my lesson, I had imagined, when I was astounded to learn that Joan Sutherland came from Woollahra, a Sydney suburb where my grandparents lived, which made it, in my opinion, the least likely breeding ground for a prodigy. Yet indisputably Sutherland, the coloratura genius, had been born there. It had been a sharp lesson to me. Which I had forgotten when I went to Osaka.

The Matsushita organization had further surprises in store for me. When I was shown into a car by two of its executives and an exquisite receptionist, the executives said good-bye in the Western fashion, but the receptionist bowed until her hair hung round her face like a glossy veil. She remained bowed until my car turned a corner 300 yards away. Courtesy is one of Japan's many virtues, even at a distance: rudeness is abhorred.

'I do hope,' said Yuso Hatano, of the Japanese Embassy in London, before I went to Japan but after he had learnt of my war-time experiences, 'that while you were a prisoner my people were not, ah, too . . . rude to you?'

I hastened to assure him that they could not have been ruder; nor I to them; and regretted only that he was too polite to tell me how rude the Americans had been to him when, in his fifteenth year, they flattened his home town of Osaka. We laughed – which was some-thing I had never done with a Japanese before, even though I had spent the best part of four years in their company.

To them, as Colonel Tsuji tartly observed, we prisoners of war 'looked like men who had finished their work by contract at a suitable salary, and were now taking a rest from the anxiety of the battlefield'. This, though, is precisely what surrendering implies. Without being so tactless as to say it outright, men who surrender are suggesting; 'Look – we've run out of ammunition, food and hope, so we're going to stop trying to kill you, and in return you will promise not to kill us. Instead, you will provide us with adequate food and lodging until the war ends, when you will discreetly repatriate us if you have won, or our side will welcome us home as heroes if we have won.'

It is a ludicrously illogical system; and the Japanese never saw any sense in it. Nor did I. To this day I do not understand why they didn't shoot us when first they captured us. Having refrained from doing so, however, I confess I would rather they had treated us thereafter (as Mr. Hatano would have put it) less rudely.

In Pudu the months passed, the bloom of youth vanished from the faces of my companions, we developed beri-beri, experienced the first of hundreds of attacks of malaria and dysentery, and were told by the Japanese that the Dutch East Indies had fallen; that Rangoon had fallen; that Burma had fallen; and finally that the Philippines had fallen.

We were not told that, just as Hong Kong's Fort Stanley had been persuaded to surrender prematurely by the screams of five nurses being raped and then bayoneted atop a pile of corpses, and Percival to surrender prematurely by the massacre of the staff and patients at Alexandra Hospital, so were the defenders of Corregidor encouraged to surrender, again at Tsuji's instigation, by the fate of 8000 compatriots and Filipinos who perished or were murdered on a death march from Bataan.

From the rape of Nanking in 1937 to the murder of American airmen at Fukuoda after the war had ended, Hirohito's warriors regularly committed atrocities; but atrocities notwithstanding, the conquest of the Philippines was a stunning victory which cost the United States a garrison only a few thousand smaller than Singapore's – and 6000 greater than the total of her dead in World War I. Washington decided that the American counter-offensive would be launched from Australia, which the Japanese had not invaded only because Tsuji had exerted all of his considerable influence at Court to thwart Yamashita's desire to do so.

*   *   *

Ironically, in a society that aspires to harmony and despises individualism, this kind of internecine rivalry – these feuds, dichotomies and schisms – have always been an element in the national dynamic of Japan. From the beginning of the twentieth century until 1941, for example, there existed a venomous schism between those who wanted to seize territory from Russia and those who wanted to seize it from colonised South East Asia. From wherever it was to be seized, Japan's army and navy would have to do the fighting; yet *their*

42

rivalry exceeded even the rivalry of the Strike North Faction and the Strike South Faction.

Again, as one 'incident' followed another in China, during the thirties, a rivalry to the death developed between the Army in Manchuria and the government in Tokyo. As Secretary of State Stimson would put it, in a cable to his observer at the League of Nations, 'The military chiefs and the Japanese Foreign Office are evidently sharply at variance as to intention and opinion.'

Similarly, during the Pacific War, a dangerous rivalry developed between the Army, which had become the government, and the Peace faction, which, as early as June 1942, had foreseen calamitous defeat for Japan unless she negotiated a favourable settlement while she still had an abundance of conquered territories with which to bargain.

Most recently, in the days of post-war reconstruction, implacable rivalries have existed between one steel-maker and another, one car-maker and another, one maker of television sets and another. Not for the Japanese was the industrial answer to this problem to be the Western one of mergers and safety in numbers. Instead, each firm fought the other to the death, each producing more and more goods tailored specifically to the demands of a domestic market that could pick and choose; and when this domestic market was saturated, each firm sought fresh markets overseas, where it did battle with foreign as well as Japanese competitors.

Representing all these manufacturers, businessmen and exporters today is the Keidanren, an organization so powerful that its decisions are frequently of more importance to the rest of the world than those of either the government or the Diet; and therein is found the most recent of Japan's dichotomies.

A pragmatic race, the Japanese not only accept as inevitable the existence of rival factions within their national structure, they exploit them so that they work to Japan's advantage.

Thus, arraigned by the League of Nations for waging war against China, successive Japanese governments were able to plead that they were doing all they could to restore peace, but the Army had momentarily become unmanageable – the Army meantime insisting that all it awaited was explicit instructions from its government. Year after year, the League of Nations (like Stimson) was thereby so befuddled that it deemed it positively undiplomatic to press the Japanese government too hard. Meanwhile, the Japanese armies pressed ever deeper into China.

Similarly, in 1981, when the United States of America discovered that its annual trade deficit with Japan had reached a terrifying fifteen billion dollars, the Keidanren smoothly accepted Washington's demand that Japan's exports to America be voluntarily curbed, and her imports from America substantially increased; but added that this was a decision for Government. And Government expressed its sympathy with the suddenly penurious Americans; but explained that the Keidanren had suggested increased Japanese imports rather than reduced exports. Rather curtly it then added that America and Europe should pay more heed to the Japanese consumers' demands and start sending them what they wanted rather than complain about Japan's reluctance to buy foreign goods.

'But what could the West and the Americans sell you?' I asked Mr. Tajitsu, unable to think of any manufactured product that the Japanese did not make more cheaply and better than any of their foreign rivals.

He pondered the question; and then, with the faintest of smiles, said, 'Britain could send whisky, and America chocolate!'

Thus, by exploiting a propensity for double thinking, can the Japanese achieve an acceptable consensus, the effect of which is to reduce one nation's demands to another's semantic absurdity. Like judo, however, it is not an art that is infallible; and during the Pacific War its practice led more than once to disaster — the worst disaster being the Battle of Midway.

*　　*　　*

While the Army had been stealing all the headlines in China, from 1931 onwards, the Navy had not only lacked a starring role but had even been humiliated by a treaty that limited its strength in capital ships to three fifths of either Britain's or America's.

Thus inhibited as to capital ship construction, it had concentrated on the construction of such new-fangled and less prestigious vessels as aircraft carriers – of which, by the time the decision had been taken to go to war, Japan had more than America.

If Admiral Yamamoto, the Navy's Commander in Chief, had ever been unaware of the significance of this untried species of warship, the British were about to enlighten him. In November 1940, twenty antiquated bi-planes took off from the flight deck of the Royal Navy carrier *Illustrious* and lumbered across the

44

Mediterranean to Taranto, where the Italian main fleet, one of the most modern and beautiful in the world, lay at anchor.

The twenty bi-planes sank or crippled more than half of the sleek Italian battleships and returned to *Illustrious*. The significance of this resounding victory was not lost on Yamamoto, who knew his planes to be neither antiquated nor lumbering, and whose complement of carriers would make possible an even greater victory. In January 1941 he ordered plans to be drawn up for a similar attack on the American Pacific Fleet in Pearl Harbour. He approved the plan in April, eight months before it was put into effect, and his pilots began to train assiduously.

The attack, as history has taught us, was stunningly successful, except that, when the Japanese bombers struck, Pearl Harbour's aircraft carriers were not at anchor but at sea, where they escaped destruction. There were some Japanese strategists who were impatient to lure those American carriers, and the remnants of America's Pacific Fleet, to their destruction in a battle with a numerically superior Japanese Navy. There were others who warned that a Japanese victory in such a set-piece battle was not inevitable.

'The Pacific War was started by men who did not understand the sea, and fought by men who did not understand the air,' Mitsuo Fuchida, one of Japan's Pearl Harbour heroes, was to complain of the Army and Navy. For four centuries the cannon had decided every naval action, and it was always within the cannon's range that battles at sea were fought. 7 December 1941 changed that forever. While America's Fleet was being destroyed in Pearl Harbour, the nearest Japanese cannon had been hundreds of miles away. Battleships, with their massive guns, no longer signified; and if there remained any naval strategists who doubted it, they should very soon have been convinced by the fate of Britain's mighty *Prince of Wales* and *Repulse*. Both were despatched, with almost contemptuous ease, by torpedoes launched from 28 Japanese bombers.

Admiral Nagumo's air staff was therefore wholly correct when it argued, after Pearl Harbour, that 'Our next step must be an all-out effort to destroy the enemy's carriers. And as a means of luring the enemy (carriers) out, invasion operations should be undertaken against Midway Island and Kingman's Reef, 960 miles south-south-west of Pearl Harbour.'

Prone as ever to conflicting views and damaging rivalries,

45

Naval General Staff chose to ignore Naval Air Staff's irrefutable logic, and pushed its own plan to invade Australia.

But even this plan was scuttled by the *Army's* jealous claim that it was unable to provide the ten required divisions. They might have been available to Yamashita, but Yamashita had been despatched to Manchuria. What the Army wanted was to attack Russia from the rear as soon as the Germans launched their Spring offensive against the Soviet Union.

Thus thwarted, but determined not to lose the initiative, Naval General Staff planned merely to isolate Australia by occupying Eastern New Guinea, the Solomons and all the islands from New Caledonia to Fiji. With those in Japanese hands, it would be impossible for the Americans either to set up, or to maintain, bases in Australia.

Thus widely committed, the Combined Japanese Fleet seemed unlikely ever to become available for the crucial battle (with America's aircraft carriers) advocated by Naval Air Staff. What made it available was another Japanese weakness, pride.

On 18 April, 1942, Colonel Doolittle's small force of planes took off from the flight deck of an American task force, eluded the Zeros sent out to intercept them, scattered a few symbolic bombs over a handful of Japanese cities, and then, lacking the fuel to return to their carrier, crash-landed in China. As one Japanese commentator remarked, it was 'not so much a Doolittle as a Do-nothing raid'.

To which the official response was one of quite disproportionate fury. Tokyo had been bombed. The Emperor had been insulted. Those American pilots who had been captured must die. The sacred home islands and the Emperor's death-defying servicemen must never again be exposed to such an insult. America's carrier force must therefore be destroyed. The Midway plan was on again!

Two hundred ships and seven hundred planes would assemble secretly in the area while an apparently small invasion force would tempt the unsuspecting Americans to the rescue of Midway Island. Midway, of course, should have fallen months earlier, when first it was attacked. Having underestimated the valour of its defenders, however, the Japanese had for once failed to prevail and (with that peculiar inconsistency we had noticed at Parit Sulong) lost interest. Now they planned to capitalize on that initial failure. Their next attempt would lure America's refurbished Pacific Fleet, plus its supposed two remaining carriers, to their destruction.

Submarines and carrier-born bombers would first soften up the

American cruisers and carriers, and wipe out the air defences of Midway Island; then the battleships would move in for the kill. Incredibly, those who were fighting Japan's war at sea had still not learned all the lessons of the air. Nevertheless, against an American Fleet whose battleships lay on the bottom of Pearl Harbour, whose cruisers and destroyers were significantly outgunned and whose carriers were outnumbered, the Japanese had little, it seemed, to fear.

In the event, they reaped none of the rewards they had expected for daring and superior strength, and paid a frightful price for those other qualities that, from time to time, have operated to their disadvantage.

Because of inter-service rivalry, the battle took place later than it should have done; and in the meantime another naval battle had been fought in the Coral Sea. This battle had been a victory for neither the Japanese nor the Americans, though each had claimed it as such; but it *had* put an end to the Japanese hopes of seizing Port Moresby, it *had* sunk one of Japan's aircraft carriers, and it *had* cost the lives of 77 of Japan's comparatively few naval pilots.

Because of Japanese tendency to inconsistency, Midway Island had escaped the occupation that befell every other isolated American base; and, in the intervening months, both its land and air defences had been strengthened.

Because of her tendency to succumb to overweening pride – the Victory Disease as it came to be known in Tokyo – Japan not only believed her Purple Code to be unbreakable but her tactics to be invincible. She would prepare a vast, sea-borne ambush for the Americans whose Fleet would rise to the bait, rush out of Pearl Harbour, be destroyed and leave New Caledonia, Fiji and Hawaii defenceless. After which, British naval power in the Indian Ocean and the Bay of Bengal could be destroyed, and Ceylon invaded. India would fall while the Germans took northern Africa. Japan would join hands with Germany in the Middle East. Australia and New Zealand would have to accept the inevitable, bowing, to what Tojo called, 'Japan's real intentions'. Most of South America would fall to Japan. America would surrender to Japan and Britain to Germany. When she was ready, Japan would start another war, against Germany, and make the world hers alone.

Had daydreams been the sole ill-effect of the Victory Disease, it might not have mattered; but there were other effects. For example, in the war games conducted to examine the feasibility of the Midway plan, the Presiding Officer, Rear Admiral Ugaki, constantly overruled the umpires when they made decisions incompatible with an overwhelming Japanese victory.

The carriers *Atagi* and *Kaga* had taken nine hits between them, the umpire ruled.

Three, said the Admiral.

Atagi and *Kaga* were sunk, the umpire ruled.

Atagi was only slightly damaged said the Admiral.

Similarly, it never occurred to the Japanese to consider that the data upon which they had based their Midway plan might have changed; but it had. First, their Purple Code had been broken, so that it was the Americans who would set the ambush in the seas around Midway. Second, the carrier *Yorktown*, which the Japanese believed they had destroyed in the Coral Sea, was ready to fight again. And third, Midway had been reinforced (with troops, bombers, anti-aircraft batteries, motor torpedo boats and twenty submarines) so that (with it and *Yorktown*) America had the equivalent of two carriers more than the Japanese had calculated.

Nevertheless, thanks to Taranto, the Japanese had so far outscored the Americans in every one of their naval-air clashes around the Solomons; and although the element of surprise now lay in America's favour, the only real surprise to the Japanese would be that the Americans were *not* surprised. Japan's combined Fleet still had a full complement of battleships, where the Americans had none; and Japan's carriers still outnumbered the Americans by four to three plus Midway Island.

So the Japanese carriers launched their bombers on Midway, and found its airfield innocent of planes. While its Brewster Buffalos fought gallantly, if hopelessly, its bombers stayed out of harm's way until the enemy returned to his carriers. Then flying boats from Midway shadowed the Combined Fleet. And the Combined Fleet's search planes, which were not equipped with radar, were unable to find the American Fleet. But the American carriers launched air attack after air attack on the Combined Fleet, causing little damage but restricting the Japanese to defensive manoeuvres, which exhausted their fighter planes of fuel so that they had to return to their carriers for re-fuelling.

Now the last of Japan's weaknesses made its contribution to disaster; and where rivalries, inconsistencies and the Victory Disease had merely proved embarrassing, this final weakness – a hatred of making decisions, of being denied a consensus, of having to improvise – proved fatal.

Admiral Nagumo had to decide whether immediately to send all his unescorted bombers against the American Fleet, part of which had just been sighted; or whether first to recover the bombers and escorting fighters now making a second attack on Midway, retire briefly while he re-armed and re-fuelled, and only *then* attack the Americans.

Aware that his Fleet had thus far, and without too much difficulty, fought off the attack of no less than forty unescorted American torpedo bombers, and shot down most of them, Nagumo elected to be dilatory. His four carriers were crowded below decks with fully armed, fully fuelled bombers; but he delayed launching an attack on the Americans; and was himself attacked!

Within hours three of his four carriers, along with all their planes and most of their pilots, were gone, and *Hiruyu*, his fourth carrier, was soon to be badly damaged. Nagumo then decided to engage the American Fleet with his two battleships, three cruisers and twelve destroyers. Very sensibly, the Americans declined this surface challenge and resumed their attack from the air. *Hiruyu* was completely disabled and had to be scuttled. The Combined Fleet being now defenceless, the much vaunted Midway operation was abandoned. Its purpose had been to destroy America's capacity to wage war in the Pacific: its effect had been to shatter Japan's principal weapon of defence, and to sign the death warrant of every Japanese soldier then fighting or garrisoned in New Guinea, the Solomons, the Carolines, the Philippines, Burma, Saipan and Okinawa.

'But how can we apologize to His Majesty for this defeat?' one of Admiral Yamamoto's staff officers asked him when the news reached him on the bridge of *Yamato*, the mightiest battleship afloat.

'Leave that to me,' said Yamamoto, whose plan to invade Australia, had it been implemented, might well have averted the stalemate on Guadalcanal, the aborted invasion of Port Moresby, the fearful war of attrition along New Guinea's Kokoda Trail, the costly battle of the Coral Sea and the catastrophe of Midway itself. 'Leave that to me,' he said. 'I am the only man who must apologize to His Majesty.'

The truth, it would seem, is that Midway was the fault of no individual but of the Japanese temperament – the strengths of which are manifold, but the flaws in which produce chronic rivalries, unpredictable lapses of concentration, fatal delusions of invincibility and an incorrigible aversion to any departure from an agreed plan.

War, of course, is transitory. Even defeat is transitory. But national psyches tend to be immutable; and just as the West must respect the strengths of the Japanese psyche, so must the Japanese acknowledge its flaws. Otherwise a Japanese historian might one day have to paraphrase Commander Fuchida's epigram that 'The Pacific War was started by men who did not understand the sea, and fought by men who did not understand the air,' so that it will read, 'The export war was started by men who did not understand themselves, and fought by men who did not understand their rivals.'

Should the Japanese in the 1990s decide that the economic world could be theirs (as they decided that the terrestrial world could be theirs in 1942) they will risk an economic Midway no less catastrophic than the Midway of which Yamamoto so selflessly declared, 'I am the only man who must apologize to His Majesty.'

CHAPTER FIVE
>>>>>>>><<<<<<<<

'Do not Come Home Alive'

OUR GUARDS TOLD US nothing about Midway for the excellent reason that they knew nothing about it. Not even Tojo, the Premier, was told anything at the time, he being an Army man, and this being a naval disaster. Several months were to elapse before Tojo, the man allegedly running the war, was advised of the defeat that meant that Japan could no longer win it. More than a decade was to elapse before the Japanese people learned the truth about Midway.

Indeed the Japanese Navy – which, even among us prisoners of war, had a reputation for decency and honesty – lied so shamelessly from the Coral Sea Battle onwards that Mr. Chamberlain and our Intelligence Officers seem, by comparison, to have been veritable George Washingtons.

Of the Coral Sea Battle, which had probably been a draw (albeit America could afford its losses and Japan could not) the Navy declared that it had been a glorious victory; but of Midway, which had been a débâcle, the Navy first said nothing, and then declared it a calamitous defeat for America. And the Japanese believed it.

'Tojo number one,' our guards gloated. 'Churchill number ten.'

'Nai, nai,' we argued, 'Churchill number one, Tojo number two hundred.'

Curiously, they never took exception to this flagrant example of wrong thinking – seemed almost to respect it, in fact – and equally strangely we intuitively avoided being rude about their Emperor.

We knew nothing then about the fanatical bond that existed between every soldier and his divine Tenno; but some instinct imposed upon us an unfailing discretion where Hirohito was concerned: we never mentioned him. In contrast, and rather touchingly, the Japanese – miners, peasants, mechanics – referred almost affectionately to our king, whom they called Georgie Six. We should have recognized it as courtesy; but the unremitting need to hate them precluded that.

51

So . . . 'Tojo number one,' they bragged when victories were proclaimed. Or, 'Tojo presento', when, as a reward for a job we had tricked them into believing had been well done, they gave us a cigarette. It was invariably one of their own cigarettes, but still they said, 'Tojo presento'.

Yet just as Midway was the worst thing the Japanese proclivity for dissension brought them during the war, so was Tojo himself the worst it had brought them before the actual outbreak of hostilities. In any other country he would have been lucky to have been given a division to command: in Japan he was given an Empire.

A runt in his school days, he had been conditioned to despise everything pleasant and to apply himself instead to duties that were unpleasant; and the Triple Intervention had stuck in his fifteen-year-old craw. He became a soldier.

Like all the Japanese, he had welcomed the treaty of friendship negotiated with Britain and was no less delighted when, two years later, Japan decided to attack Russia – which it did while its diplomats talked peace in Moscow.

Hideki Tojo did not fight in the war against Russia and found promotion in peace-time depressingly slow. He went to Staff College; served as a military attaché in Switzerland and Germany; and returned to Japan via America, whose people he despised. He favoured the idea of colonising Manchuria; approved the assassination of Premier Hamaguchi, who favoured friendship with China; was given command of a brigade in 1934; and in 1935, because he was reliable and uncontroversial, at a time when the Army had become frightened of its own young hot-heads, he was promoted to major general and posted to Manchuria to command the Kempeitai (which, not to put too fine a point on it, was the Japanese equivalent of Himmler's Gestapo).

While Major General Tojo made of the Kempeitai the vicious organization that South East Asia would soon learn to loathe, a Lieutenant General Itagaki was Chief of Staff to the volatile army that virtually ran the new puppet state of Kwangtung, which previously had been Manchuria.

In Tokyo, in 1936, another series of assassinations removed many of the Army's opponents, and so enraged the Emperor that he rightly described the assassinations as a mutiny.

Itagaki, greatly taken aback by Hirohito's fury, ordered Tojo to root out any mutineers who might yet lurk in the officer ranks of the Kwangtung Army. Tojo applied himself to the task with the humourless passion for which he was notorious. His reward was Itagaki's post in Kwangtung.

By now, government and army were on ever widening courses. Government sought respectability and prosperity; the army sought respect and conquest; and the army could bring down any government simply by ordering whichever of its generals was the Army Minister to resign, and refusing to nominate another general to succeed him.

Meantime, at his Chief of Staff's desk in Kwangtung, Tojo had added the Chinese in general and Chiang Kai Shek in particular to the list of those he detested. The list was headed, of course, by the Russians.

While the Japanese Army in China contrived incident after incident to fuel the war fever of its people at home, Tojo never ceased to lecture his subordinates about the real threat from Russia. This conduct flouted the policy of the government, whose servant he allegedly was, yet such was the Army's power that, instead of being dismissed from his post and retired, Tojo was moved sideways and made Inspector General of the Air Force.

By 1940, when Admiral Yonai had become Prime Minister, the Army was once again contemplating assassination as a means of achieving its political ends; but instead General Hata, the War Minister, resigned and brought down Yonai's government.

Prince Konoye then became Premier and General Tojo was nominated by the Army's General Staff as his Minister of War. As such, he reinforced the Kwangtung Army and ordered it to be ready to invade Russia once Hitler had rendered the Soviet Army harmless.

When Hitler's Russian offensive stalled, however, Tojo agreed to exploit the Navy's recent penetration of northern Indo China by making Kwangtung's divisions available for the invasion of southern Indo China – provided, he insisted, 'if need be, we also accept war with Britain and the United States of America'.

When Roosevelt retaliated with an embargo on the export to Japan of oil, iron ore and scrap iron, Tojo was made Prime Minister – not because he was the best man for the job but because his fanaticism suited the Army, which his record persuaded the Emperor he would keep under control.

A short, scrawny man with a fierce moustache and glinting eye glasses, he had no friends, was nicknamed The Razor, looked ludicrous in his ill-fitting uniform and, most unfortunately for Japan, was determined not to avoid war.

Under his and Konoye's aegis it was decided that the China Incident should be hurried to some kind of satisfactory conclusion so that all of Japan's energies could be devoted to a drive through South East Asia to Asia Minor. To that end, the Japanese people were to, 'rid themselves of selfish thoughts' and 'cultivate a scientific spirit'.

'We cannot tell what is in store for us,' Tojo told one audience, 'but we must go on to develop in ever-expanding progression.'

Such was the credo – mordant and doom-laden – imposed upon the formidable race with whom we (who had only expected to fight Nazis) had found ourselves at war. Yet were one not assured that one was reading the credo of the late Lieutenant General Hideki Tojo, virtual dictator of war-time Japan from October 1941, until April 1944, one might easily imagine oneself listening to the concluding words of a speech by a Japanese premier to the Japanese people of today.

Except, perhaps, that today's Japanese seem to have too much humour to swallow such rhetoric as 'we must go on to develop in ever-expanding progression'. Instead, smiling wryly, they refer to their 'bicycle economy' – which must be kept moving or those who ride it will fall off!

* * *

It was on bicycles, one is reminded, that their infantry harried our infantry whenever it was obliged to retreat, which was constantly. Whole battalions of them, riding four or more abreast, taking absolutely no precautions, squeaked and rattled down Malaya's trunk road in hot pursuit of those who staggered southward on foot, *their* motor transport long since shot up at road blocks, or bogged down in the rubber.

The Japanese themselves had comparatively few trucks, but those they did have they cherished. 'Motor vehicles get through by determination,' their implacable little booklet told them. 'Force your way ahead, even if you have to carry the thing on your shoulders.'

As their prisoners, we were constantly dismayed by the burdens the Japanese thought each of us could carry on our shoulders. 'One man one,' they would bellow as two of us carried their 250 pound bombs from one dump to another. 'One man one,' they would shriek as we staggered under the burden of 40 foot lengths of water-filled bamboo thick as a man's thighs. 'One man one,' they would scream about railway sleepers, lengths of rusted railway line, two hundredweight sacks of rice and boulders spawned by Gibraltar. And if we demurred, or failed to obey, they bashed us.

It seemed so gratuitously brutal; yet they themselves laboured under the injunction: 'Motor vehicles get through by determination. Force your way ahead, even if you have to carry the thing on your shoulder.' And they were slapped, beaten and kicked almost as often as we were bashed. Even fourteen-year-olds in the Youth Colonist Corps in Manchuria were slapped and beaten, quite often with shovels, always by other fourteen to eighteen-year-olds. For their brothers in the Army, however, discipline was both merciless and senseless.

'My squad leader slapped me on the face,' the narrator of the novel *Fire on the Plain* recalls, his offence being that he had been discharged from the hospital to which he was sent with tuberculosis, after only three days. Since he had taken five days' rations with him, the hospital had profited by getting rid of him so soon, and his squad leader had then been obliged to feed him. So the squad leader first slapped him, and then ordered him back to the hospital – whose doctor had had the forethought, in such an event, to warn him that he must kill himself.

It was not an unfamiliar situation to members of the Imperial Japanese Army. 'Once you're on enemy territory,' their instructors had constantly told them during their training, 'be prepared to die an honourable death. Do not be afraid of combat; and do not come home alive.'

None of our guards expected to go home alive. Their souls would go to the Yasukuni Shrine, and their ashes would go to their parents; but they would not go home. 'All we can do,' one of them wrote, 'is go on fighting, and win, win, win. We are no longer ordinary human beings. We are wild animals, barbarians.'

Every soldier had to memorize the whole of the 1940 Imperial Rescript if he wanted to become a First Class Private. It had an introduction, five articles and a conclusion, and it went on interminably. But a good Japanese soldier would eventually learn every word of it by heart.

His squad usurped the part in his life previously played by his village and his family, neither of which he would ever see again. His village spirit was forgotten, as was the delicate social fabric of his home: his squad was all that mattered now.

Above everything, of course, he worshipped the Emperor; but he had done that ever since his school days, when he had worshipped at a distance and boasted that his dearest wish was to die for His Majesty. Respect, however, was not confined to the Emperor. He had to respect every superior from the Emperor downwards; and even fellow privates were his superiors if they had been in the service a day longer than he. Any lapse in the paying of such respects earned him a slapping at least. He paid his respects to his superiors and seniors by doing menial tasks for them.

As well there were his military duties; and, every evening, roll call. For this the squad had to be smartly dressed, but it seemed to be a point of honour with every sergeant to find at least one man improperly dressed, and to beat him.

'Turn to the East,' the sergeant would order, and the squad would to face an Emperor upon whose countenance they had never been allowed to gaze, who lived in a palace more than a thousand miles away.

'Worship the Imperial Palace! The Supreme salute!' the sergeant would bellow. They would bow low, horizontally, palms of hands flat on taut thighs. 'Return to attention. About face.' Fifteen men would turn about.

'Respectful recitation of the Five Imperial Doctrines.' Fifteen voices would gabble the articles in the curiously hoarse and breathy manner upon which the Army insisted. Often it sounded like turkeys gobbling; at other times, like beagles barking.

'First,' they would chorus, 'the soldier makes it his destiny to be patriotic. Second, the soldier observes the rules of etiquette. Third, the soldier respects martial courage. Fourth, the soldier values truthfulness. Fifth, the soldier remains austere.'

Then their sergeant would dismiss them, and they would bow to him saying, 'Thank you for your trouble.'

Thus were Japanese soldiers daily reminded of their duties in a ceremony they found irksome only because it so often led to a slapping. Today, in all their huge factories, they stage almost identical ceremonies.

Matsushita's Electric Industrial Company is typical. Round the world it has 150 factories making 10,000 products and employing 110,000 men and women, In every factory a morning meeting is held, at which everybody wears the company uniform and is encouraged to speak his mind. In all its wholly Japanese factories, the employees – standing in well-drilled rows – recite the company creed.

'Through our industrial activities,' the creed proclaims, 'we strive to foster progress, to promote the general welfare of society and to devote ourselves to furthering the development of world culture.'

Instead of the Army's Respectful Recitation of the Five Imperial Doctrines there is the work force's respectful acknowledgement of the Seven Spirits of Matsushita. Which are:

The Spirit of service through industry:

The Spirit of fairness:

The Spirit of harmony and co-operation:

The Spirit of struggle for the sake of progress:

The Spirit of courtesy and humility:

The Spirit of assimilation: and

The Spirit of gratitude.

Basically the two ceremonies differ only in that the former was conducted by a draconian sergeant. Should an officer have attended the former, however, as well as the draconian sergeant, his inspection of the squad would have made an always anxious time positively menacing.

He would have picked on any enlisted man and asked him, 'What are you doing?' And the enlisted man would have been required to reply, 'Something bad' – and for that he would have been slapped.

Japanese soldiers knew no moments of light relief during their war. Our guards lived as austerely as monks, and seemed almost ashamed that they were safe with us, rather than dying in Burma, which they called Birrima.

Leave, concert parties, films, visits from celebrities – none of these were for them. Just the endless paying of respects, the inescapable duty to die, not to go home, the constant slappings, the inhuman obligation to treat subject races and Western captives 'severely', and the strait jacket of etiquette. Little wonder they bashed us who looked 'like men who had finished their work by contract at a suitable salary and were now taking a rest free from the anxiety of the battlefield'; who talked endlessly of going home, and treated them with no respect at all.

That is not to say that we were overtly disrespectful. Overt disrespect invited a bashing to or beyond the point of death, and we, unlike them, had no intention of dying. So one learned, if one was tall, not to stare down at them, but just over the top of their heads. If one was of medium height, one met their eyes, not contemptuously but blankly. And if one was compelled to salute, or bow, one did it as if it were an involuntary reflex – not in the style of the interned English lady who wrote on the wall of her cell, 'Was bashed today for not bowing in a sufficiently servile manner. In fact, a rather casual nod.'

To the Japanese, whose every physical courtesy can be judged both by the manner of its execution and the degree of its sincerity ('Seven bows is enough, nine is too many!') our calculated indifference became – like our rejection of death – positively bemusing. In the end they accepted it.

Driven back upon themselves, the only entertainments available to them were squad conversations (always in the softest of voices, always seated in the same pattern, every position in which indicated a subtle gradation of superiority) or singing songs. Like:

> *See the sky opens over the Eastern Sea.*
> *The Rising Sun climbs higher, radiant in its flight.*
> *The Spirit of Heaven and earth is throbbing with vigour.*
> *And hope dances through the eight islands of Japan.*

We used to sing: *We're off to see the Wizard, the Wonderful Wizard of Oz*, and our foes and allies in Europe sang of a whore standing by a lamp post.

At Matsushita's factories, the work force sings:

> *A bright heart overflowing*
> *With life linked together –*
> *Matsushita denki.*
> *Time goes by but as it moves along*
> *Each day brings a new Spring.*
> *Let us bind together*
> *A world of blooming flowers*
> *And a verdant land*
> *In Love, Light and a Dream*

It is their company song. Westerners at work don't sing anything any more. They rarely even whistle. They call the Japanese wage slaves and robots, which is ridiculous. When Japanese industrialists consider it advantageous to employ robots (rather than men and women who sing, and whose hourly wages are today exceeded only by those paid in America) they install the real thing. As long ago as 1980 they were using 6000 of them – or about twice as many as the rest of the world put together. By 1982 they had 100,000 of them, and were installing more every month.

*   *   *

58

An escape was organized by two of the Malay Volunteers – white men who had worked in the country before the war, spoke the language and had native contacts up and down the Peninsula. They had arranged safe houses all the way from Kuala Lumpur to the coast, and at the coast a boat in which to sail to India.

They took several others with them the night they escaped, and the Japanese recaptured all of them within hours because not only were informers well paid but non-informers were savagely punished. The escapees were held for some time: then taken to a cemetery and shot.

It is arguable, though, that their execution was intended less as condign punishment than as a compliment to their daring. The Japanese, some three years later, executed six captured members of the raiding party from Australia that had sunk a number of vessels in Singapore Harbour.

They were prosecuted by a Major Kamiye, who summed up the case against them by saying: 'With fine determination they infiltrated the Japanese zone. We do not hesitate to call them heroes. It was fortunate for us that we thwarted their plan, but when we examine their motives, and share their feelings, we must spare a tear for them. Their victorious spirit recalls the daring enterprise of our heroes of the Naval Special Attack Corps who died in May 1942 while making their attack on Sydney Harbour.

'The same admiration and respect shown by the Australian government and people for our heroes must be shown by us to their heroes standing before us. They must have left Australia aflame with patriotism, and with the trust of the entire Australian people resting on their shoulders.

'The last moment of a hero must be dramatic. Heroes cherish their reputation above all else. Respecting them as we do, we acknowledge our responsibility to crown their last moments with the glory that should be theirs. By doing so we will ensure that their names will forever be remembered by the people of Britain and Australia.

'In those circumstances,' he concluded, as only a major in the Imperial Japanese Army of 1945 could have, 'I consider that each of the accused should be awarded a sentence of death.'

On 7 July, 1945, their hair cropped and their beards freshly shaven, they were each given a last cigarette, allowed to shake hands . . . and beheaded. It was, says the official Japanese transcript of their trial, 'a sublime fate' for men who were the very 'flower of

59

chivalry', and an example to all Japanese soldiers if they were still 'to win the war'. Five weeks later their Emperor acknowledged that the war was lost.

*   *   *

Lately I have wondered whether our group was spared (after our capture outside Yong Peng) simply because we became unworthy of execution the instant our sergeant screamed for mercy. Or was it because they momentarily lost interest in us, as they had done when they let us escape from Parit Sulong?

I asked Shichihei Yamamoto if he could explain it. He was, after all, a veteran of the war in the Philippines who had believed in the distorted Bushido Code of the time and would almost certainly have had us executed had he led the squad that captured us. He suggested that our captors might never have intended killing us – were simply taking the sort of precautions to which they had become accustomed in China, where captured soldiers were apt to bear-hug the Japanese – and pull the pin of a grenade.

He did not look as if he believed it, though; and I certainly did not. According to our guards, the one thing that had terrified them in China was the black scorpion. It infested the plains and even the woodwork of the peasants' huts – which they explained, was why they still opened doors with a boot!

I think they didn't shoot us because, once our sergeant screamed for mercy, we probably were no longer worthy of their bullets or bayonets, and certainly not of their swords. But it would have embarrassed Mr. Yamamoto to say so. He had been reluctant to give himself up for twelve days after his country's surrender; and an officer colleague of his, Lieutenant Hirowo Onada, had stayed alone in the jungle and refused to give himself up for thirty years.

To Japan's post-war generations, however, veterans of World War II are old men whose opinions no longer matter, and whose code of executions and death they wholly reject. All of the scores of them to whom I have put the question have agreed that they would fight to defend Japan; but none has said that he would kill himself to escape capture. In the classic days of bushido – that is, before the fanatics of 1931 to 1945 corrupted it – they point out that a samurai could always surrender; and that the cleverest feudal lord of all was the one who habitually persuaded his rival's warriors to defect before the battle had even begun. Modern Japan, it would seem, has

60

inherited the worthiest of her martial virtues and discarded those that the rest of the world finds reprehensible. They are, as one is frequently told when visiting Japan, a pragmatic race.

'Be resolved that Honour is heavier than the mountains, and death lighter than a feather,' our guards were exhorted. 'Duty should weigh with us as the mass of a lofty mountain. Against it, our lives are as light as a swan's down.' Their children and grand-children would not dispute this : but they would interpret Honour and Duty quite differently.

CHAPTER SIX

>>>>>>>><<<<<<<<

Nippon Number One

'YOU MUST DEMONSTRATE to the world the true worth of Japanese manhood,' *Read This Alone* instructed. 'The implementation of the task of the Showa Restoration – which is to realise His Imperial Majesty's desire for peace in the Far East, and to liberate Asia – rests squarely on your sholders.'

To an army that knew little of geography, and nothing at all of liberty, the concept was awesome, the language grandiloquent. To us, the Imperial Japanese Army seemed to consist entirely of sadistic, humourless thugs. Aware at last of the intolerable stress to which they were incessantly subjected, one can only remember them – nuggety, indomitable and prone to tempestuous rages – with compassion and incredulity.

Our future, which we never doubted, was victory and a joyous return home. Their future, which they were never allowed to forget, was violent death. Employing imagery as chilling as it was nihilistic, *Read This Alone* described their future thus:

> *Corpses drifting swollen in the depths of the sea.*
> *Corpses rotting in the mountain grass.*

Only the Imperial Japanese Army would first have promised its servicemen a premature death and then stripped death of any imagined dignity by portraying it in verse as a process of bloating and putrefaction. The verse concluded:

> *We shall die,*
> *By the side of our lord, we shall die.*
> *We shall not look back.*

It is with some humility that I recollect that we, their enemies, sought no such poetic inspiration. Throughout my undistinguished military career, I was given to quoting from only three poems – *The Owl and the Pussycat, Winnie the Pooh's Winter Hum*, and the *Song of the Shirt*.

62

Pussy said to the owl,
You elegant fowl,
How charmingly sweet you sing,

I was apt to intone when a guard screamed too loudly. And I found *Pooh's Winter Hum*, which began, *The more it snows, tiddly pom*, and ended, *How cold my toes, tiddly pom, are growing*, very comforting in the tropics.

Only when our hosts became unbearably tiresome did I indulge in the more lachrymose, *Stitch, stitch, stitch, In poverty, hunger and dirt;* but each of them must have infuriated the Japanese, who were compelled to envisage themselves as corpses drifting swollen in the sea or rotting in the mountain grass.

Yet when dysentery and cardiac beri-beri began to kill us off, and the crudely crated corpses of our comrades were carried past them, they invariably sprang to attention and bowed. Then they would march us out to work, and bash us because we did it badly.

We also stole anything not actually embedded in concrete, and sabotaged anything that might conceivably be of use to them. In this we were successful not so much because we were clever at it (although we were; and grew so much cleverer that it was marvellous to watch) as because petty theft was alien to our guards, and sabotage seemed to them a perilous and unlikely enterprise for a breed as cowardly as we had proved to be.

As a consequence, we returned to the gaol one evening having poured boiling pitch down the barrels of three 25 pounders and stolen a field radio set, which we stuffed into an empty rice sack. We passed the bulky sack from one to the other while we were being searched, and it was not discovered because nothing so defiant was ever expected of us.

In all the years of our captivity our guards never understood us, and to this day all sorts of influential Japanese like to confess their countrymen's ignorance of the mentality of other people, which they present as a kind of childish but far from reprehensible inadequacy. In fact it is a conscious uninterest which could lead them to misjudge their rivals no less calamitously in the decades ahead than it did between 1931 and 1945.

Quite soon Japan will be the richest industrial nation in the world, with a per capita income higher even than that of America and a Gross National Product much larger than its present ten per cent of the Gross National Product of the world. How Europe,

63

Russia and the United States of America will react to that novel situation should be as fascinating to the Japanese nation today as was winning the export war to the Japanese industrialist of yesterday: but, on the contrary, it seems almost unconcerned.

Atypically, Masaya Miyoshi, Executive Director of the Keidanren, was not unaware of the problem as it had crystallised by November, 1981. 'Until the late sixties,' he said, 'the West was both our model and our target. Then came many things – Vietnam, Watergate, the oil shocks, the recession – and we lost faith in the western model. Now, in the eighties, when we have exceeded the target, we're beginning to think that we can become the world's model.

'And that's dangerous. Already too many Japanese are saying, "Now we are the top nation," and becoming over-confident, like those army officers we had before the war. It's very dangerous; but I think we can control it. I think we can control it this time because we are aware of the danger of destablizing the world's economy.

'This time our responsibility is to avoid such destabilization, and instead to stabilize – to become a stabilizing factor. But to do that we need a leader. And we Japanese avoid putting ourselves up for leadership because to assume its mantle is presumptuous; and unless you're a very old man you can't afford to be presumptuous in Japan.

'Our Keidanren President, Mr. Inayama, for example, is only 78 – much too young to presume to leadership! So men like Mr. Inayama, or our Prime Minister, always seek a one hundred per cent consensus before they say, "This is my opinion. This is the solution we must adopt for the problem." '

Had Tsuji been a European, or an American, his post-war autobiography would have been entitled *How I Won the Malayan War*. Because he was Japanese, he called it simply *Singapore*, and in it was scrupulously careful to ascribe his plan not to himself but to the whole of Unit 82, and its success not to General Yamashita but to the valour of three divisions of the Imperial Japanese Army.

With the Keidanren as its Unit 82, post-war Japan has won a score of victories no less significant than the capture of Singapore. From the annihilation of the British ship-building industry to the decimation of the British motor-cycle industry; from the domination of the world's steel industries to the defeat of the American automobile industry; the Japanese advance has been one of sustained brilliance.

It has reached the stage today, in fact, where only three counter-measures can prevent it from becoming the destabilizing element that Mr. Miyoshi said it must not become. Yet another massive hike in the price of oil could do it: the imposition by the rest of the industrial world of massive anti-Japanese tariffs could do it; or the Japanese themselves could do it: but that would require an inspired leader.

By their very nature, however, they are unlikely to produce such a leader. The counter-measures, if they come, are much more likely to be American inspired, and to take the form of any such economic collaborative weapon as will adequately inhibit the Japanese industrial machine.

Yet such a weapon will be regarded by the Japanese as nothing less than a third Intervention. Economically, it might succeed: politically, it can only fail. The Japanese will simply seek other ways to feed their 120,000,000 mouths and perpetuate that state of prosperous self-esteem to which they have become accustomed. This is the dilemma of the late twentieth century.

*   *   *

Our stolen radio told us the truth about Midway and the turning tide of war in Northern Africa and Russia. It did not, as I recall, tell us about the three midget Japanese submarines that penetrated the boom protecting Sydney Harbour, fired their torpedoes at some of the choicest sitting targets in the history of naval warfare, missed them all (because their torpedoes were defective) and were instantly sunk.

Nor did it tell us that, in a mood of quite unwonted chivalry, the Australian government retrieved the bodies of the Japanese submariners, cremated them and despatched their ashes to Vladivostok – whence the Japanese Government was able to retrieve them because a state of neutrality existed between Russia and Japan.

For us, in Pudu, few events in the war were to be more significant. A feeling had grown among us that we would be executed once our work in Kuala Lumpur was done. Against that day, we had armed ourselves with grenades and sticks of dynamite stolen from the ammunition dump in which we were forced, from time to time, to labour.

To postpone that day, we had devised go-slow techniques of which even the Trade Union movements of Great Britain or Australia would be proud. But we knew in our hearts that neither our go-slow nor our arsenal would avert our execution: they would merely delay the inevitable.

Instead, all eleven hundred of us – Australian, Dutch and British – were moved to Singapore and accorded the status of official prisoners of war as a token of Hirohito's gratitude for the ashes of six of his submariners. We were not surprised; but we were reminded that one may never take Japanese reactions for granted.

When my fellow prisoners had pissed in thousands of metal boxes containing mortar bombs (because mortar bombs dislike moisture) before removing them from the bowels of the one-time British ammunition dump, and loading them on to lorries, the Japanese had neither noticed the operation nor taken any measures to prevent it. Perhaps they had not believed that so few men could piss so prodigiously. More probably they were having one of their well-known lapses in concentration. It did not surprise us.

When they drove the lorries all the way to Port Swettenham and loaded the bombs on to ships (which were then to sail all the way to New Guinea, where the bombs would be unloaded and carried all the way down the Kokoda trail, only to fail to explode) it did not surprise us.

When their Emperor equated our eleven hundred lives with the ashes of a mere handful of Japanese sailors, it did not surprise us. All that suprised us was that our compatriots, whom now we joined in a huge camp on the northern tip of Singapore island, disbelieved almost everything we told them about the Japanese, of whom *they* had seen almost nothing.

Since the war was won in 1945, the Western world has been no less deaf to, or disbelieving of, the words of those who were taught by long experience what it has never understood at all. To it, in the main, the Japanese are either a race of sadists or a hundred million drudges. The truth about them is very different.

CHAPTER SEVEN

>>>>>>><<<<<<

'This War Last One Hundred Years'

IF WE WHO HAD BEEN CAPTURED up-country, and incarcerated in Pudu Gaol, looked to the Japanese like men taking a rest from the anxiety of the battlefield, those who had surrendered in Singapore, and marched to Selarang Barracks at Changi, must have looked like holidaymakers on a package tour, even though package tours had not at that time been invented.

The tens of thousands of inmates of Selarang Barracks and its acres of semi-parkland had set up theatres, night clubs, orchestras, university courses, unarmed combat classes, debating societies, football and rugby teams and hospitals.

One Australian battalion (whose commanding officer imagined himself an antipodean Erwin Rommel) drilled regularly at his behest, using dummy rifles and taking no pains at all to conceal from the Japanese the fact that it was preparing to assist the Allies whenever they re-invaded.

Food was adequate, epidemics and skin diseases (to which we at Pudu had long been prone) were virtually unknown, forced labour was almost unheard-of and the camp's worst enemies were generally agreed not to be its renegade Sikh or infrequent Japanese guards, but its own senior officers, who had retained their passion for being saluted. For many of its inhabitants, unfortunately, the dream was about to end. Transported to Thailand, they were to endure a nightmare instead – their bodies becoming skeletal and their eyes glowing in deep, ape-like sockets.

The story of the Thailand Railway is too well documented to merit repetition; and anyway there is little about it that I can remember. Except being told that peace-time plans to build it had invariably been abandoned because they involved so huge a loss of life!

Except becoming so hideous that I threw away the triangle of mirror I had acquired in Changi rather than continue to look at my face as I shaved with a year-old blade:

Except the stench of custard pie ulcers on one's legs, and the daily terror of having them scooped out with a spoon:

Except the stick-like corpses, and the pyre upon which they were cremated:

Except the Japanese shrieking, 'Speedo, more speedo', and the interminable bashings:

Except viaducts a hundred feet high, cross-stitched to the cliff face, tier upon tier of teak clinging uneasily to sheer rock: and bridges just as high, tottering across river gorges. Hand-made all of them, every inch of them, by us:

Except the Imperial Japanese Army testing the finished bridges by sending fully laden trains across them. Fully laden with us. It reminded me of the Sydney Harbour Bridge – which its designers tested before its opening by parking steam locomotives on it from one pylon to the other. As a child I was taken to see it by my father – and had longed for the lot to plunge into the harbour:

Except – most significant of all – a Japanese officer one day telling me, 'This war will last a hundred years, Mr Braddon. I'm afraid you will never go home.'

That must have been no later than November, 1942; but it meant that Japan's hopes of a swift victory over America and Britain had already faded in the minds of those who controlled her propaganda.

Some of them, indeed, had never anticipated final victory. Admiral Yamamoto, for example, would never promise more, on behalf of the Navy, than, 'In the first six to twelve months of a war with the United States and Great Britain, I will run wild and win victory upon victory. But then, if the war continues, I have no expectations of success.'

Nor were any of those who were actually planning the coming war against the United States and Britain unaware of the fact that even Yamamoto's promised success depended upon Germany and Italy tying up most of the Royal Navy and part of the US Navy in the Mediterranean and the Atlantic. Should Germany's war effort falter (or worse, collapse) Japan's would also fail.

Be that as it may, Yamamoto and his navy had indeed run wild for six months; and might have run wild for twelve had his plans to invade Australia been accepted; but the Coral Sea Battle and Mid-way had put an end to that. Thereafter, Yamamoto had had 'no expectation of success', and, being Japanese, was probably not too appalled, while on a tour of inspection in New Guinea, to find himself the victim of an aerial ambush in which, eventually, he died.

Not even Tojo had contemplated war with unequivocal optimism. At a liaison conference five weeks before the attack on Pearl Harbour he had allowed an adjournment after no more had been agreed than that Japan had only three options. Options two and three had both meant war; but the first option had been to forget America's insulting challenge and work for perhaps twenty years to make Japan America's industrial equal instead.

In the language of the day, this first option had meant that Japan must 'sleep on logs and drink gall' until finally she achieved victory of a non war-like kind. In the event, she had plumped for options three *and* one. First she went to war and then, from August 15, 1945 until about 1960, she slept on logs, drank gall and built the new Japan which soon will not merely have equalled, but will have actually surpassed the industrial achievements of the USA.

The third option having been exercised on 7 December, 1941, Pearl Harbour was bombed, Singapore was captured and Yamamoto's navy 'ran wild' until the following June. But the Marquis Kido, Lord Keeper of the Privy Seal and, (despite his unprepossessing looks) a man of great influence in the Emperor's court, had no higher hopes of eventual success than Admiral Yamamoto. While the rest of Japan gloated over its triumphs, Kido urged Hirohito, 'to grasp any opportunity to bring about the earliest possible termination of the war'.

There was little, in fact, that Hirohito could have done at that moment to terminate the war: divine though he was, he lacked executive power. His role was to approve the decisions of Tojo's dictatorial cabinet, and thereby cloak them in an aura of divine authority. Yet even Tojo was beginning to see the war in a different light by the middle of 1942.

Addressing a group of foreign correspondents in Tokyo – Germans, Italians, Russians, Asians and neutrals – he told them: 'Japan is prepared to fight for a hundred years until victory is won and our enemies are crushed.'

On Guadalcanal, the Kokoda Trail and the outskirts of Port Moresby, Americans and Australians had checked the hitherto irresistible Japanese advance. It was for purely military reasons, therefore, that Tojo had begun to envisage victory only in terms of a century of attritional war.

From anyone else the idea would have been 'wrong thinking' in its most treasonable form: from the lips of Tojo, it was to prove Delphic. By the end of the year we would hear it from the lips of even the most junior privates.

By then, though, there was little they said or did that could make life worse for us. Continuing merely to live had become our ultimate act of defiance. Either we were so foully emaciated that we weighed only as much as our bones and the discoloured hide that clothed them, and awaited death by dehydration; or we waddled along like vertical dirigibles, swollen to bursting point with the fluids of beriberi, and awaited death by drowning.

Not a few rejected the indignity of such a life, and, lying calmly down, folding bony hands across hollow chests, died. To the rest of us our guards said constantly; 'This war last one hundred years. You never go home.'

'You never go home either,' we retaliated; but *they* had never hoped to go home. More than anything, that was what exacerbated our relationship.

So the work in the cuttings, on the bridges and through the jungle went on – a delirium of bashings, ulcers, speedos, cholera, malaria, funeral pyres, beri-beri, monsoonal storms and perverse defiance.

The Japanese had driven occasional trucks up the path we had hacked to accommodate the approaching railway line. Each had had to be abandoned in chassis-deep mud – and their batteries had promptly been stolen to power our pirate radios.

It was thanks to just such an abandoned truck, and to a radio concealed in a battered concertina, that word reached our jungle camp that Italy had surrendered. Hitherto – lacking the battery from that truck – the radio had been silent about such things as the annihilation of General Horu's troops by Australian and American troops at Buna in New Guinea; the final defeat of the Japanese on Guadalcanal; the beginning of the Americans' island-hopping campaign that would soon blast out, burn out and starve out one Japanese garrison after another.

We did not even hear, as probably our guards had heard, that Tojo, in a speech to the Diet, had commented of the fighting in the last six months of 1942, that it had resolved itself 'into a persistent tug of war'. To both the Diet and the hundreds of thousands of men stationed on islands that could no longer be supplied, he had issued the warning: 'The real war is starting now.' But all our guards told

70

us was that the war would last a hundred years, and that we would never go home.

About Italy's surrender, on 25 July, 1943, we found out for ourselves; and vowed to stay alive if only for the pleasure of seeing her two Axis allies follow her splendid example.

'We must prepare for the worst,' the aristocratic Kido told his Emperor when the King of Italy placed his subjects' fate in the hands of Marshal Badoglio – who promptly capitulated to the Allies.

Panic stricken lest their Emperor followed the example of Italy's King Umberto, Tojo's junior officers made it instantly clear that they would tolerate no Badoglios in Japan. It apparently never occurred to them that their panic could have been inspired only by the realization that their war was lost.

Certainly there were grounds for panic. Germany was clearly heading for a defeat which would allow the Americans and British to bring their total strength to bear upon Japan. And the British had already begun a campaign to recapture Burma, using short lines of communication from India while the Japanese had to send munitions and men through a sea swarming with American submarines and along a railway line through Thailand that was incomplete.

'No slackening of our effort can be tolerated,' Tojo broadcast.

'Speedo,' screamed our guards.

'The time has come for the Japanese people to adapt themselves to the present war situation,' Tojo told his docile listeners – and introduced a seven day week of war work for the entire nation.

'Yazume nai,' our guards shrieked. No rest. 'Byoki nai.' You are not sick. 'All-u men work! Speedo!!'

So the railway line was finished, with one out of every three of its white labourers dead, and an even worse proportion of its indentured Asians. As Japanese troops trundled north, Allied bombers blew up the bridges we had so laboriously constructed; and, several thousand miles to the south east, a huge American task force plastered the Japanese forces on Tarawa and Makin with so much explosive that by comparison the bombing of Berlin seemed not immoderate.

It was November 1943 and our task was completed. Churchill and Roosevelt met in Cairo, where they agreed that Japan was to be stripped of every territory she had ever seized since 1905. In a moment of apparently unpremeditated idiocy, Roosevelt also proclaimed the doctrine of unconditional surrender, taking no account of the fact that the so-called Restoration of Showa had rendered the

71

Imperial Japanese Army psychologically, and legally, incapable of any kind of surrender.

'It is undeniable,' Tojo told the leaders of those puppet states of which Japan was to be stripped if defeated, 'that the nations of Greater East Asia are bound by indissoluble ties of blood'; but Japan had been a brutal master, and his audience was unimpressed. As one Burmese politician would put it, after the war: 'If the British sucked our blood, the Japanese ground our bones.'

Roosevelt recognized Chiang Kai Shek as the leader of China's post-war government; and induced Stalin to promise to attack the Japanese armies in China within three months of the defeat of Germany.

'The real war is starting now,' Tojo told the Diet.

'Looking over the future trend of the world,' Kido confided to his diary, 'I believe that we must serve and cultivate our real power in the state for about one hundred years.'

He continued with a flight of wishful thinking in which China and Russia fought on Japan's side until the Anglo-Saxons grew weary and agreed to a favourable peace. More realistically, Hirohito told his ingratiating adviser that the war was lost.

The American Pacific Fleet was now colossal. Aircraft carriers had been launched by the dozen, and battleships too. It was as if Pearl Harbour had never happened. That Midway had happened to Japan's navy, however, was incontrovertible.

The Marshall Islands were attacked – Kwajalein by five Americans to each of the Japanese defenders, and Eniwetok by eight Marines to every three Japanese. Both islands were pounded almost to extinction by Admiral Nimitz's enormous armada before the Americans swarmed ashore.

Unable to reinforce any of his South Sea garrisons, Tojo decided to resume the offensive from Burma, and ordered 155,000 men to advance into India. The Japanese onslaught was first contained, then repelled.

'Now is the time to capture Imphal,' Major General Tanaka nevertheless ordered his battered division. 'Our death defying infantry group expects certain victory when it penetrates the enemy's main fortress. The coming battle is the turning point which will decide the future of the Greater East Asia War . . . For that reason it must be expected that the division will be almost annihilated.'

72

As an inducement to individual valour, Tanaka further ordered that: 'Rewards and punishments must be given on the spot.' To which end, and 'in order to keep the honour of his unit bright, a commander may have to use his sword as a weapon of punishment, exceedingly shameful as it may be to have to shed the blood of one's own soldiers on the battlefield'.

Reinforcements had arrived, however, and Tanaka was not prepared to believe that General Slim's forces at Imphal and Kohima were invincible against the heroism of his own and the other divisions of General Kawabe's army. 'On this battle rests the fate of the Empire,' he proclaimed. 'All officers and men – fight courageously!'

The battle was lost; but not because the five divisions involved fought anything but courageously. 'I know of no other army that could have equalled them,' wrote General (later Field Marshal Lord) Slim. We, their prisoners, had seen them going up the railway line in their thousands, paying us no more attention than modern travellers pay airport workers. One in three of us had died. Already more than half of them were dead and Kawabe, recalled to Japan in disgrace, had been replaced by General Kimura.

In the twelve months that followed, the rest were to be decimated. And those who survived were to go into that captivity which Aida would find so intolerable. In Japan, meantime, the newspapers were tacitly acknowledging the fact that all was not going well by running stories, editorials and even advertisements about the Hundred Year War.

*   *   *

We returned to Singapore from Thailand, and a few months later 7000 of us were marched into Changi Gaol. That was all that the segregation (and, in some cases, defection and liberation) of the Indian troops, plus death, and transportation to Borneo and Japan, had left of our original 130,000. We were confined in Changi Gaol to facilitate our execution, should the need for it arise, and to build a military aerodrome in the meantime.

After the railway, the aerodrome was not so much hard as tedious work, and it was even worse constructed than the line through Thailand. The layman might think that there is little one can do to sabotage the construction of an aerodrome, but there is

73

plenty, and it's easy. One simply clogs up all its essential dry-course drains. Changi aerodrome, as constructed by us, was a menace to aviation. Vastly different though it doubtless is today, I prefer not to land on it.

It was not laziness but integrity that made our guards such ineffectual supervisors. Incapable of shoddy workmanship themselves, it never occured to them that people who looked so busy as we did could be doing so little so badly. The last laugh, however, appears to have been with the Japanese. That same integrity that enabled us to build them a truly terrible aerodrome in 1944 has made them immune ever since to the western disease of industrial strife. Today, as then, they work with care and zeal.

'Workaholics', the western world calls them, as if they were the victims of an anti-social disease. Since the 1960s 'workaholics' is the penultimate in a long list of epithets, all of them as self-justifying and self-defeating as those of 1941 which alleged the Japanese to be short, myopic, ill-equipped and frightened of the dark.

To explain away its ever-increasing inability to compete with Japanese exporters, the western world has successively described them as the fortunate beneficiaries of American generosity, those most likely to succumb to communism, wage slaves, robots, parasites on the back of the American taxpayer, workaholics and protectionists: to believe any of it unreservedly is to indulge in self-delusion.

Magnanimous though America indubitably was in victory, she intended Japan to become no more than a defenceless industrial rival to Britain in South East Asia – as which she would be an importer of such technology and raw materials as America might choose to sell her. Meantime, she was to abjure re-armament, refrain from trade and commerce with her one-time largest market, China, and be grateful for the privilege of sheltering under America's defence umbrella.

Having expected much worse, Japan complied absolutely with the conqueror's demands. Defeat in the war to which the Meiji and Showa Restorations had so inevitably led her had obliterated the concept of the Imperial Way and revived the concept of a shogunate. Her new shogun was Douglas MacArthur.

Before ceasing to be divine, however, Hirohito had given his people his final Imperial command – that they should endure the unendurable, eat stones and drink gall, and rebuild Japan. That rebuilding began the instant MacArthur's shogunate ended. So shattered was Japan's economy that in 1955 few westerners thought it could ever become viable, and none envisaged it as a potential threat.

The great reconstruction nevertheless began, and was marked from its inception by managerial innovation and daring, on the one hand, and labour's flirtation with communism on the other. The West took condescending note of the flirtation, but failed entirely to observe the innovations and the daring; and the Japanese labour movement – finding the stridency and assertiveness of communism alien to its innate sense of harmony – quietly abandoned its flirtation and embarked instead upon a policy of collaboration with management.

With whose blessing, house unions were formed which negotiated the best pay and work conditions compatible with the continuing prosperity of the company. Employment, it was mutually accepted, was for life. Demarcation disputes did not exist. Promotion, in almost every case, would come with seniority. Bonuses would be paid, according to profits, twice yearly. An employer's loyalty was to his work force, as once the Emperor's had been to his servicemen. Each company had to compete with every other company producing the same goods. Quality control became as much an imperative to the man on the factory floor as to the President of the company for which he worked.

The formula succeeded. Those who were so recently alleged to have been mere wage slaves have long since surpassed the hourly earnings of the work force of Western Germany and Canada, and will soon surpass those of the work force of the USA. To the impartial observer, the so-called 'robots' of the Japanese work force reveal qualities of integrity, good humour and pride – none of which is mechanical. They also celebrated the fortieth anniversary of Pearl Harbour with an economic victory over America so complete that Washington instantly sued for peace.

'Export LESS,' begged the US Trade Secretary, 'and import MORE.'

'Rearm!' some Congressmen demanded, choosing not to remember that it was at the behest of the USA that Japan foreswore war and wrote perpetual disarmament into her constitution.

'Buy OUR beef,' America demanded, disregarding the fact that for every ton of American beef Japan imported Australia would have to export one ton less.

But the Australian government would NOT accept a cut in

her beef exports to Japan of 7000 metric tonnes, Canberra announced.

It was the wrong way to talk to the Japanese, who promptly ordered 7000 tons of American beef. Which made very little impression on America's 1981 trade deficit with Japan of fifteen billion dollars.

Within the next seven days, New Zealand, Brazil, China, Canada, Spain, Egypt, Russia and the Arabs were likewise either nagging or holding out a begging bowl. Within a month, the American automobile industry, whose world supremacy had been unchallenged for half a century, abdicated sourly in favour of a Japanese rival only half its age, but with a thousand times its confidence.

*   *   *

In October of 1941 the fathers and grandfathers of Japan's present day work force had had three options available to them, and had chosen the one that had led them, five weeks later, to war.

As early as 5 June, 1942, that option had been varied by Tojo. The new option would not produce the inevitable victory he had promised the nation in his broadcast of December, 1941; it would achieve victory by default – but only after a hundred years of fanatical resistance.

In spite of which, Japan's capacity to wage war, even to survive, would be virtually destroyed by August 1945, and it would need the voice of the Emperor himself to persuade his servicemen to stop fighting, his subjects to start sleeping on logs and drinking gall, and his nation to set off on an industrial marathon at the end of which Japan would be the winner, America the runner-up and the rest of us . . . also-rans.

Asked when he thought that day would come, Mr Tajitsu, the elder statesman of Mitsubishi's banking organization, laughed almost merrily and clasped his two tiny but slightly arthritic hands like an excited child.

'Number one, number four, number two?' he speculated cheerfully, 'that's a difficult question.' But suddenly the smooth old face lost its blandness and the hands parted, to gesture earnestly. 'Military-wise we are probably number four,' he said, rubbing his left thumb between the thumb and first finger of his right hand. 'Economic-wise, number two. And city-wise Tokyo is number one. But probably we should most concern ourselves with the duration of our stay, economic-wise, as number two.'

He admitted that Japan's trade surplus might seem to the rest of the world to be selfish. Possibly too selfish. 'Probably it's true that the West is frightened,' he conceded, 'but the government is thinking about it.'

With which the agitated massaging of his thumb stopped, and his expression of anxiety cleared. Torn between the Mitsubishi desire to export to that organization's maximum ability, and his banker's awareness of the economic anguish of America and the West, he had propounded an exquisitely Japanese solution. Government, who could change little, and would prefer to change nothing, would think about it.

America would protest that that was inadequate, of course. Then government could say that really the problem was the Keidanren's. To which the Keidanren would eventually respond that, while it sympathized, it could do nothing. And all the time the marathon – which both America and the West wanted to abandon – would continue, and Japan's pace quicken.

'Nippon number one,' our guards on the aerodrome confidently proclaimed, even when silvery B-29s began regularly, with complete impunity, to inspect our slovenly handiwork from a height of 40,000 feet.

'Nippon number two hundred,' we responded automatically, trying not to let our guards see us glancing gleefully up at that magical, silvery symbol of our enemy's imminent destruction, cheerfully ignoring the fact that the Japanese had said they would shoot us rather than see us released. Or rather, their bullying minions, the Koreans, had hinted that that was what the Japanese had told *them*. Anyway, a disagreeable prospect; but we would improvise something when the time came. For the moment, just don't look up too blatantly – it aggravates Nippon. And don't even mention B-29s – except as the Boundary Rider, which he doesn't understand.

*　　*　　*

How much he understood we could never assess. Was he so dim-witted that he actually believed the *Syonan Shimbun* when it said that the Imperial Japanese Army in Burma had lately embarked on an offensive to the *east?*

Could he have been so ignorant of geography in 1942 that he

really believed that New Guinea was part of the Australian continent, and that Japanese troops had therefore been hell-bent down the Kokada Trail to Sydney? (The fact that I, and 998 others out of every 1000 of us, could not have told *them* where Okinawa was, or Tokyo for that matter, was irrelevant. Australia was part of the British Empire and therefore cartographically red and important: Japan was neither British nor red and therefore of no geographical significance whatsoever.)

Did one's average Nip not understand that? Did he not also know that proud Tojo had been forced to resign as Army Chief (though he retained the War Office and the Premiership)? Did he not care, a little while later, that Tojo was forced out of office entirely? He seemed not to. In fact, for once, he joked with us about it. 'Tojo finishu,' he told us with a grin.

'Tojo number two hundred,' we intoned ritually.

'Hai,' he laughed. No one, in either Japan or its armed forces, it seemed, was sorry to see the departure from public life of the humourless, merciless and hitherto omnipotent Razor. Ironically, Imperial General Headquarters announced the capture of Saipan and the annihilation of its substantial garrison on the day of Tojo's abdication. We had known of it for some time, and been curious as to how our guards would react to the killing of so many of their soldiers and the suicide of so many of their civilians. They did not react. As ever, we had failed to perceive how differently a man thinks when he is told to go away and die, to think of himself only as one whose destiny it is to float bloated in the sea or lie rotting in the grass.

Not even we, though, could deny his sincerity. Nor, after Saipan, the sincerity of his civilian brothers and sisters. Nor, after their bloody defeat at Imphal, the gate-way to India, when 270,000 men began their doomed 'advance to the east' through a torment of bullets and disease, could we doubt their cussed valour. Imphal may have been Japan's worst defeat of the war – a worse defeat even than Stalingrad had been to the Germans – but the demeanour of our guards did not change. Had our pirate radios not assured us to the contrary, our guards' demeanour would have convinced us that Japan was still the land of the triumphant Rising Sun.

Neither more nor less arrogant than they had ever been, they continued, each dawn, to march us to the aerodrome (for which they no longer had any planes), to bash us for working too slowly, and to march us back to the gaol each dusk.

Where, at last, at every roll call (or tenko, as they called it) they made us give orders, and number off, in Japanese. Bad news did not make them conciliatory. After a year of unrelieved disaster, and with the prospect of a worse year to come, they sought no post-war favours and suffered no doubts. They could no longer win, of course, but equally they could never lose. Not while a single one of them, or of those doing war work at home, was able to fight. As long as one of them lived, Japan was invincible – and there were a hundred million of them, fighting a hundred year war.

Though history was to prove this sublime war-time confidence misplaced, their response to almost every post-war crisis would be no less calm. 'Shock' is the word they apply to any crisis, and to them its connotations are dire. Nixon's abrupt policy of detente with China, the Arabs' savage quadrupling of the price of oil, the recent world depression, the latest hike in the price of oil – all of these were labelled shocks.

The Nixon Shock and the Oil Shock are phrases as familiar to today's Japanese as Dunkirk is to Britons or Pearl Harbour to Americans. But they are the only race of whom it can be said that they meet today's economic disasters with the same obdurate confidence as they displayed in the face of war-time's defeats. Justifiably proud of themselves, they may even now have started once more to think of their victorious homeland as Dai Nippon.

CHAPTER EIGHT

>>>>>>><<<<<<<

'We are not Barbarians'

INTERESTINGLY, although the Imperial Japanese Army on Singapore made no attempt to ingratiate itself with us in 1944, it equally made no attempt to avenge its ill-fated compatriots in New Guinea, the Marianas, the Philippines, Burma and Saipan.

Unfortunately, the same cannot be said of Japanese forces generally. In Borneo, for example, 2006 prisoners of war were sent on a series of marches from which only 150 were to survive. The others died the way 7000 Americans and Filipinos had died in 1942, when Major General King's 70,000 fever-wracked troops surrendered at Bataan to 110,000 Japanese. King had asked them, 'Will our troops be well treated?'

'We are not barbarians,' the Japanese interpreter had rapped back.

But barbarous is the only word to describe the treatment of King's men as they marched a mere 60 miles into captivity. Subsequently the indigenous population had been treated so abominably that Shigemitsu would describe their fate as 'a reproach that cannot be blotted from our memory'. And Allied aircrew captured anywhere in the fast-shrinking Japanese Empire were still being put to death; Chinese prisoners where habitually executed (usually by Japanese recruits, for whom this obligatory bayoneting was their initiation into the Holy War); and more than 3000 Chinese, Koreans, Russians and others were murdered in the course of chemical and biological 'experiments' conducted by General Shiro Ishii's special unit at Harbin.

Yet in a way these murders are easier to understand than the self-restraint of our captors in Malaya who must have known that, at Rabaul, 100,000 Japanese had been abandoned by Tokyo to fight or starve to death. The few who were captured unconscious constantly attempted suicide, when they revived in an American or Australian hospital, by pulling out drips, tearing open newly stitched wounds and even (when their hands were tied) trying to bite off their tongues.

At Bougainville, the few survivors of the 6th Division had withdrawn into the highlands and were attempting to grub a living from the forest while continuing the fight as guerillas. Those who survived longest would resort to cannibalism. In the end, almost all of them would die of fever.

In Burma, Slim's XIV army had killed tens of thousands of those who had sought to invade India via Imphal and Kohima. In the retreat that followed, starvation, disease and the monsoons had killed tens of thousands more. Our captors knew it. They also knew that, though relentlessly harried and shockingly emaciated, their comrades in Burma fought on, the wounded being told to commit suicide, and shot if they refused, the feeblest of the non-wounded being drowned in raging torrents, and the last 65,000 of them being re-grouped and, at the instigation of the ubiquitous Colonel Tsuji, ordered to defend Rangoon to the death.

On the island of Biak – stepping stone to a dozen other islands – 10,000 Japanese had retreated into caves. Using flame throwers, the Americans had cremated them.

On Saipan – a German colony Japan was awarded after World War I – 30,000 soldiers, outnumbered two to one, had died; and 15,000 civilians had elected to die with them. Of the civilians, more than 10,000, at Tokyo's behest, had withdrawn to the northernmost tip of the island and brained their babies before hurling themselves – mothers, fathers and older children – from the high cliff tops into the rock-strewn sea.

At Guam, 18,500 of the 20,000 Japanese defenders had been wiped out by 55,000 US Marines; and at Tinian, 8748 Japanese had been killed by almost twice that number of US Marines.

On the Philippines, and in the seas around them, 200,000 of Hirohito's soldiers, pilots and sailors had been ordered to achieve a strategic victory by destroying Nimitz's enormous fleet of 840 vessels and killing more Americans than Washington would be prepared to continue sacrificing. Roosevelt, the theory was, would then forget his doctrine of Unconditional Surrender and agree to a negotiated peace.

Our guards knew all of this, even if they were not told that, in the event, the Japanese Naval Air Arm had lost almost half its 1000 planes before the land and sea battles for the Philippines even started; and that those pilots who survived had destroyed themselves in the first kamikase raids of the war.

'Give us of the Combined Fleet a chance to bloom as flowers of death. This is the Navy's earnest request,' Admiral Nagasawa had begged in answer to his Commander in Chief's do-or-die order from Tokyo.

'We are throwing our entire strength into the impending battle,' Admiral Toyoda had advised his subordinates. 'You are expected to render your life to the beloved fatherland, fighting courageously and tenaciously in order to achieve the task assigned to you.'

The lesson of Midway well-learnt, the Americans had sunk four battleships, four carriers, thirteen cruisers and twelve destroyers; and the Japanese Navy had ceased to exist. Once Leyte, Luzon and the lesser Philippine islands were recaptured, and the garrisons on Iwo Jima and Okinawa destroyed, Japan's home islands would lie open to invasion.

By the end of 1944, 65,000 Japanese had been killed on Leyte; and, despite all the skills of 'Tiger' Yamashita – recalled from the oblivion to which Tsuji's malicious intrigues had consigned him in 1942 – much worse was to come on Luzon and the remaining Philippine Islands.

In one year, then, some 300,000 of Hirohito's servicemen had died, and 2,000,000 more (occupying Korea, China, Indo-China, Thailand, a corner of Burma, Malaya, Singapore and the Dutch East Indies) awaited the same fate.

It was against that background that Japanese soldiers and airmen who had sought no quarter, and been ordered to kill prisoners rather than allow their liberation, had sent thousands of them on death marches and executed almost every flier who fell into their hands.

Conversely, after the starving survivors of Saipan's main garrison had staged a final suicide attack, and after 10,000 civilians had killed themselves, more than 900 Japanese soldiers had surrendered, and 10,000 civilians as well. Similarly, 1250 out of 20,000 defenders had been taken alive on Guam; and another 250 out of 9000 on Tinian.

Compare that total of 2400 Japanese soldiers with the 350,000 odd Allied soldiers who surrendered to the Imperial Japanese Army in 1942, however; compare the stupefying bombardment each of them had endured (before the fighting even began) with the minor air raids which were our lot; compare their post-war prospect of eternal shame with ours of a rapturous welcome home, and it is arguable that *their* capture signified little more than that of those found unconscious on New Guinea's beaches and jungle trails.

Equally, of course, it is arguable that they surrendered because they were sick of the inhuman code of the Second Restoration; but those who so argue must first explain the loyalty to that code of the Japanese mutineers in a prisoner of war camp in Australia; of 85,000,000 Japanese who, armed only with bamboo spears, were prepared to resist the planned Allied invasion in 1945; of the army in Tokyo in the last hopeless days of the war; and of Corporal Shoichi Yokoi and Lieutenant Hirowo Onada, who fought epic one-man wars long after their compatriots had accepted defeat.

* * *

Though 1253 of Guam's Japanese garrison of 20,000 had omitted to obey orders and die in battle, only 1250 of them had actually surrendered in 1944: Corporal Soichi Yokoi and two others had withdrawn into the jungle and hidden instead.

Yokoi's two companions, Minegawa and Ito, would surrender a mere sixteen years later; but Yokoi, who had long been living on his own by that time was not so readily to be seduced into disregarding that section of the Battlefield Commandment entitled *Regard for Reputation.*

'Those who know shame,' it declared, 'are strong. Have regard for the honour of your homeland and endeavour to live up to its expectations of you. Die rather than experience shame as a prisoner. Do not die in ignominy.'

Accordingly Yokoi, a tailor in civilian life, dug himself an underground bunker; camouflaged it cunningly; made tools with bits of metal from the debris of war, made snares, ropes and clothing out of jungle fibres, bamboo and the inner bark of the pago tree; made medicines and ointments out of the gall bladders of eels and the oil from copra; fed himself on fish, roots and berries; kept himself fit with daily exercises; kept himself clean with a daily bath in a nearby stream; and spoke to no living soul for 28 solitary years.

Though he was certain that he would be killed if the Americans captured him, (but only after his eyes had been gouged out and his nose cut off) it was not fear that stopped him surrendering. He would not surrender because he wanted to die a soldier.

Haunted by the ghosts of comrades killed in that final battle which he had chosen to survive, he prayed regularly to their angry

83

spirits in the dark solitude of his underground lair where his most cherished possession was his rifle – on whose butt was engraved the Imperial chrysanthemum.

The years became decades, but his faith in the Imperial Way was never to falter. In the Philippines, Hirowo Onada endured a similar ordeal by solitude for two years longer than Yokoi; but Onada, as an officer, was intellectually better equipped to fill the endless hours than the little tailor, and had more to fear from the rabid Filipinos than did Yokoi from the amiable inhabitants of Guam. Let Yokoi's story, therefore, serve them both – the more so since Onada, on his return to Japan, was able to present himself in a more attractive light than the austere and guilt-ridden corporal.

It was only after 28 years that two natives of Guam, brothers-in-law who occasionally fished the stream where Yokoi fished, caught a glimpse of a strange figure wearing a jacket and shorts of unusual texture and design, and with a head of neatly cropped hair. They stalked him, pounced on him, tied his hands behind his back and took him to their house, where they fed him while someone went for the police.

'What is you name?' one of them asked him.

'Yokoi Shoichi,' Yokoi replied – and, having broken the silence of half a life time, could not stop talking.

Taken to hospital, he revelled in hot water, good food and the visits of local dignitaries. Though undernourished, he was as fit as an adolescent, but more than ever troubled by the ghosts of his dead comrades, who kept him awake at night with words he was unable to understand.

Told of the atom bomb, he asked was it Japanese?

And was President Roosevelt still alive? he wanted to know; and even when he was told that Roosevelt was dead, remained convinced that one day the Americans would take him from the hospital and execute him.

Ito and Minagawa were sent from Japan to speed his rehabilitation. 'I am going to be killed,' he told them. 'Will you die with me?'

A special Japan Airlines plane was sent to bear him home, 'I should have come home dead,' he told the hostess as the plane taxied toward a reception committee on the Tokyo tarmac. He descended from the plane, shook hands with the Minister of Welfare, and was led to a microphone.

'Yokoi Shoichi,' he announced bleakly, 'reporting back from Guam, shamefully alive, to explain how the war was lost.' And then, mindful of the Army's injunction always to take care of one's health, added flatly, 'I am well.'

At his subsequent Press Conference he barked like Tojo himself – as indeed everyone had done in the days of the Imperial Japanese Army. But that army had been demobilized for almost thirty years, and those to whom he spoke found his delivery both difficult to understand and almost offensive.

'Japan lost the war because she had no weapons to fight with,' he barked. 'There were insufficient weapons to go round, and no aircraft. That was the reason. Not because we lacked spirit.' And banged the table with his fist.

Were they to read Yokoi's words today, there are many Americans who surrendered in the Philippines, Britons and Australians who surrendered in Malaya and Singapore, Canadians who surrendered at Hong Kong, and Dutchmen who surrendered in the East Indies who could not put it better. Yokoi spoke for us all, but almost immmediately withdrew from our international fraternity into unequivocal Japaneseness, declaring, 'I have brought back the rifle given to me by his Gracious Majesty the Emperor. I now return it to his Majesty. I am deeply ashamed at my failure to have served him.'

'Can we honestly say,' his biographers would later ask, 'that we have produced a Japan worthy to receive this new citizen?'

Shichihei Yamamoto, when asked that question, had no doubts. 'Yokoi and Onada would both have found it very easy to return to life in Japan. There remained so much that was Japanese. As a people, we have always been controlled by traditional ways of thought rather than new ways like bushido. Bushido only began to evidence itself in the *eighteenth* century. It was not formulated by law until 1890, at the time of the Meiji Restoration. But the traditional way of thought has existed since the thirteenth century. It underlay bushido. It underlies all Japanese thinking. It was to that security that Yokoi and Onada returned in 1973 and 1975.'

He talked also of those who, unlike Yokoi and Onada, had allowed themselves to be taken prisoner before the end of the war. 'Those of us who survived the war, and were then ordered to report to the nearest American unit, were put into camps where we met others who had surrendered before the war ended. We refused to talk to them, even to acknowledge them.' He inhaled deeply on his cigarette. 'But now I feel that those who surrendered before the war ended were wise.'

85

The cigarette between his fingers suddenly forgotten, his lively expression became almost melancholy, as if remembering a youthful, long-forgotten Yamamoto who barked orders, slapped faces, was indifferent to the murder of Filipino villagers and treated compatriots who had surrendered like cowards and traitors. Yamamoto, the philosopher with long iron-grey hair, was clearly unable to identify with Yamamoto the one-time shaven-skulled knight of bushido. It would probably not console him to know that few of today's 60-year-olds, of whatever race, can identify with the smooth-cheeked killers they were during World War II.

*　　*　　*

Defiance of the captor being a coinage common to all prisoners of war, it was perhaps inevitable that the Japanese would spend more of it than anyone else. In Section B of the Federal Detention Camp on the outskirts of Cowra, in Australia, there were 1104 of them, who decided in 1944 that their lost self-respect could only be repurchased with their lives.

None had surrendered as we had surrendered, with hands high and an irrational optimism, and all had been treated with immense consideration by their Australian guards (who were doubtless aware that we in Malaya would pay the price of any brutalities they might inflict on their incomprehensible wards). Loathing the stigma of captivity, almost every Japanese had assumed a false name. They never even asked one another about their family or military backgrounds; and they positively dreaded meeting anyone who had known them in less shameful days.

All of them had been nursed back from unconsciousness (had they not been unconscious, they would have blown themselves up; had they not blown themselves up, a comrade would have shot them) but none doubted that he had become a non-person for whom there was no longer any family, homeland, honour or future.

An added shame was the scrupulous fairness of the enemy administration. Every Japanese soldier had constantly been assured that capture meant torture and death (it was one of the things that had made it easier for the IJA, as we called it, to maltreat its prisoners and execute captured airmen) yet here they were, in rural New South Wales, comfortably housed, well clothed, well fed and never slapped.

They learnt the fearful fate of Saipan's defenders and civilians;

and new prisoners from New Guinea told them that the last of Japan's troops there (upon whom the camp had been relying to invade Australia) were trapped and starving.

If ever that invasion had come, it had been their intention to rise up and die as they killed as many Australians as possible. Useless to have survived (those who had survived the Russian captivity, in 1905, had found themselves social outcasts for life back in Japan); but to have died assisting their invading comrades would at least have brought them death without ignominy.

Now, however, there could be no invasion, and Japan itself was facing destruction. 'We'll be treated like dirt,' they told one another. Which mattered to them, as Professor Aida was so indignantly to point out, much more than having their heads chopped off or being tortured.

They therefore rioted, attempting either to scale the high barbed wire barricades and escape, or be shot. One hundred and thirty-one were killed. Those who escaped hanged themselves, or threw themselves under trains. The death toll passed two hundred. But four hundred rioters survived, and another five hundred had neither escaped nor rioted.

'The way of the samurai is the way of death,' the more fanatical now began to remind those who had hesitated the first time. An atmosphere of near frenzy affected everyone, even the sentries – who, in the words of the official history, became 'alert and tense'.

Some of the sick lined up beneath a convenient rafter and, encouraged by their friends, hanged themselves, one after the other. Others said, 'We apologize for our inability to join you,' and, facing north, where the Palace lay, gave three banzais before accepting a razor blade and slicing open their carotid arteries.

While the unfit killed themselves, their comrades collected baseball gloves, blankets and strips of cloth, to help them scale the barbed wire, and improvised weapons with which to kill Australians.

That night, they set fire to their huts; a bugle sounded; they charged the wire; the searchlights came on and the sirens wailed; the Australians fired high at first, and then, when their warning was ignored, more purposefully; the attack was checked; and an Australian interpreter urged them to desist over the Public Address System.

'Listen carefully, you Japanese prisoners who have just rioted. As soldiers, we respect the bravery you have shown, but most of you

87

have now fallen. Further resistance is futile. No man who raises his hands will be fired on or punished.'

One group of Japanese responded by swarming up an observation tower and killing the sentry. They were all shot by the sentries in the remaining towers.

The few who escaped found themselves cold and overawed by the vastness of Australia's outback. In the Japanese manner, they suddenly lost all enthusiasm for their venture and allowed themselves to be rounded-up, confident that they would be taken back to the camp and executed.

One way or another, 234 Japanese died (including 31 by suicide, and 12 in the huts that were set on fire) and 108 were wounded. Only three of their captors had been killed and three wounded. To the astonishment and dismay of the surviving rioters, there were neither executions nor reprisals. Confounded, Cowra's Japanese returned to the shameful comfort of their non-life while we, 3000 miles away, continued shamelessly to build a decidedly slip-shod aerodrome.

CHAPTER NINE

>>>>>>>><<<<<<<<

'A Stepping Stone to the Future'

As 1944 GAVE WAY TO 1945 we told ourselves that Easter would surely see our liberation. We had told ourselves the same thing every New Year's day since 1942 (and vice versa), but we forgot that: we would be home, at the latest, by Easter.

In Tokyo, Toshikasu Kase, a member of the Foreign Office, wrote in his diary, 'This is the year of decision. We have lost the war . . . There is only one question left: how to avert the chaos attendant upon disastrous defeat: how to achieve the reconstruction of a Japan so defeated?'

In Changi, the Imperial Japanese Army put it the same old way. 'This war last one hundred years,' they assured us as complacently as ever – and invited us thenceforth to address each and every one of them as 'Master'. Which we omitted to do, Master being a word that came unnaturally to our lips. Apart from an occasional bashing, the Imperial Japanese Army did not press the matter. Unlike bowing, addressing people as Master was not an everyday Japanese courtesy.

Though a quarter of a million Japanese had already lost their lives in the fruitless defence of the Philippines, the Army fought on, and the Navy allowed its marines to behave atrociously in Manila.

Though Iwo Jima and its 21,000 strong garrison fell at a cost of less than a third of that number of Americans, the Army fought on.

Though the US Air Force now launched massive raids on Japan from fields on Iwo Jima, and though there was so little oil in Japan that the training programme for pilots had to be abandoned, the Army not only fought on, but posters went up in every Japanese city proclaiming:

A Hundred Year War

Never has Great Nippon known defeat.

The present difficulty is but a stepping stone to
the future.

Rally round the Imperial Throne and fight on,

for this is a HUNDRED YEAR WAR.

'In this hour of her peril,' wrote Marmoru Shigemitsu, the
Foreign Minister, 'Japan must tread the path of honour. If we do not
stray from that path, Japan may fall, but she will rise again.' The
seeds were being sown for what, by 1967, *The Economist* would
describe as 'the world's most intelligent system of planned economy'.

Meanwhile, Japan was launching ships made of wood; but as fast
as she launched them American submarines torpedoed them; and
we were being forced to plant castor oil and peanut bushes, from
whose crop oil was to be distilled; but as fast as they approached
fruition we chopped their roots and killed them.

March came, and at Meiktila in Burma the last fifty Japanese
defenders jumped into a lake and drowned themselves. Late March
and April brought air-raids on Tokyo such as the militarists could
never have envisaged, either when they had insisted on going to war
or when they had imposed a mandatory death sentence on captured
fliers because Doolittle had disturbed the Emperor.

In one incendiary raid after another the Americans transformed
Tokyo and other cities into a roaring inferno. As they fled their
flaming homes, seeking the sanctuary of parks and rivers, the
Emperor's subjects also burst into flames, or died of asphyxiation
when they inhaled the roasting air. Almost a quarter of a million
perished; and even the Imperial Palace – to which every Japanese
from Osaka to Singapore, from Mukden to Rangoon, still daily
bowed – was eventually burnt to the ground.

The Allies, though, were less concerned with the fate of their
civilian enemies than with the treatment by the Imperial Japanese
Army of their captured compatriots. Accordingly, Shigemitsu began
to make appropriately diplomatic utterances on the subject in the
Diet; but neither the Diet nor the Japanese people was in the mood
for such conciliation.

Why, Shigemitsu was challenged, did he object to the term
'American devils'? And why should enemy prisoners be better

housed and fed than the Japanese, of whom the American B-29s had just burned to death hundreds of thousands? And anyway, the Army snarled, there was no truth in the enemy's claims of atrocities. Such claims were lies, invented to slander Japan.

As to which Shigemitsu would subsequently lament, 'The Army at the front withheld the truth'; but Hirohito's response was both more immediate and robust. The mistreatment of prisoners of war was, he said, 'a serious breach of duty that reflected shame on the Army' – whom he thereupon instructed, 'to put the matter right'.

As was its wont, the Army took no notice at all of the Foreign Minister's words, and not much more of the Emperor's – which were attributed (as always when he said anything not entirely to the Army's liking) to bad advice.

That the Army 'withheld the truth' is now as well known to the world as eventually it became to Shigemitsu; but the extent to which it denied what it knew to be the truth is breathtaking.

Of the 235,473 British and American prisoners of war in Axis hands in Europe, four out of every 100 died. Of the 95,134 British, Australian, Canadian, New Zealand and American prisoners of war in Japanese hands in South East Asia (the rest were Indian Dutch, Indonesian and Filipino) 28·65 out of every 100 died – an unforgivable proportion of them on marches they were never intended to survive, as targets for bayonet practice, as the victims of capricious but elaborately staged executions, or like garbage in an incinerator (which was the fate of the Americans imprisoned on Palewau. They were herded into three air-raid shelters into which buckets of kerosene and lighted torches were also thrown. Those who attempted to escape were machine-gunned and bayoneted as they burst through the flames).

The Emperor having spoken, the Army allowed us a distribution of a few of the Red Cross parcels which had been regularly des-patched to us since February 1942, but delivered, in my experience, only thrice. In some camps there may have been a few more deliveries, but nowhere more than half a dozen. One parcel a month was despatched from home for each of us in captivity. Most of us received one fortieth of one parcel on three separate occasions over a period of three and a half years.

On its return voyage, in April 1944, the vessel that had just delivered our parcels was sunk by an American submarine and some 2000 Japanese civilians, who were being repatriated, were drowned. Conveniently overlooking the much vaunted desire of every

Japanese to die for his Emperor, and suppressing the fact that all Japanese then resident in Singapore were members of a remarkably pitiless occupation force, Shigemitsu lodged a formal complaint.

Shigemitsu was arguing *post hoc*, of course, and largely for the benefit of a Western audience, but he did his 2000 fellow countrymen on the *Awa Maru* a disservice when he portrayed them as the innocent victims of America's war. It had always been their war, and a holy war at that – in the prosecution of which, even as the *Awa Maru* was sailing for Singapore with its token cargo of Red Cross parcels, the Army, in the person of its Vice Minister of War, was making rather less generous provisions for our future.

'Prisoners of war must be prevented from falling into enemy hands by all means available,' the Vice Minister ordained in a telegram to every camp commandant. In that oblique language to the use of which the Japanese are prone, the telegram further instructed that, in the event of an enemy attack, prisoners of war should be 're-located' (where their compatriots' bombs were falling) 'kept alive' (and worked until the last moment) when they should be 'set free' (and 'Emergency measures should be taken against those with an antagonistic attitude'). Which meant that we were to be shot.

*   *   *

We, of course, knew nothing about the Vice-Minister's telegram, nor anything about similar orders for our disposal awaiting promulgation from Field Marshal Terauchi's East Asian headquarters. We merely knew – with that almost feral instinct common to all who live close to death – that, come the glorious day of Mountbatten's invasion, our captors intended killing us.

It is not to the credit of either of the two captive colonels who successively commanded us in Changi Gaol that they made no contingency plans for a break-out, or for a counter attack, or even for a siege from which Mountbatten himself would eventually retrieve us. It is also an indication of the weariness that had overtaken us that we omitted to make our own contingency plans. When the time came, we would have a go. Until then, it was better not to think about it.

Not so the Koreans in our midst, who by now were becoming anxious about their unsavoury performance as our guards. In all sorts of small ways (by turning a blind eye, issuing a furtive warning, soliciting friendship) they were seeking to curry favour.

I took notice of only two. The first impressed me with his assurance that the Socialists in Korea would take over the whole country as soon as possible after Japan had been defeated. The second terrified me because he had almost persuaded one of my friends to help him steal a Japanese bomber and fly it to Darwin.

'Where they'll promptly be shot down by the entire Australian Air Force,' I protested to one of their confidants.

Fortunately the plan fell through.

Each of us had survived so many dangers that it seemed unreasonable now to expect further good fortune. Upon most of us a kind of wariness had descended. I even gave up thieving. Not in obedience to any conscious decision but rather – having just declined an invitation to participate in the sort of robbery from a Japanese workshop that would normally have delighted me – because it suddenly occurred to me that I had exhausted my quota of luck.

Whether we would have been interested to learn that the entire civilian population of Japan was as desperately hungry and weary as ourselves, I cannot say. But I suspect not. Undiluted hatred for everything Japanese was still what most sustained us. The news that a Korean guard had just shot himself was more joyous to us even than the BBC's report of the capture of Iwo Jima. At last one of them had acknowledged what *we* had known all along – that they were doomed to defeat. We looked forward to the suicide of the entire Imperial Japanese Army. We even hoped to watch it.

*   *   *

We now knew that only Okinawa lay between the home islands of Japan and their invasion: so did our captors. We knew that Kimura's armies in Burma had been destroyed: so did our captors. We knew that Germany must soon surrender and Okinawa be invaded: so did our captors. We knew that Mountbatten planned to invade Malaya fairly soon: so did our captors.

Our totally dissimilar worlds were steadily merging into the one microcosmic world of Singapore. There, it seemed, we were to suffer a common fate – we at their hands, they at the hands of Mountbatten's army. So entrenched were we in our respective attitudes, however, that neither side made the slightest attempt to appease the other.

*   *   *

Okinawa was invaded on April Fool's Day. For once there was no resistance. The Japanese planned to lure the Americans on to a

93

killing ground of their own choice and there achieve a stunning victory. But from ashore, the sea and the air, they were hopelessly outgunned. Despite their valour, their kamikases and their ruthlessness, the campaign lasted only eleven weeks, and killed only 12,500 Americans. As against that, 110,000 Japanese soldiers and 75,000 Okinawans lost their lives, not all of them to the Americans.

Civilians in caves, taking refuge from shell fire, were ordered to vacate them in favour of the Imperial Japanese Army. They died in the open, under the American bombardment.

Whole families fled from the American advance, wondering how best to kill themselves. One family used a hoe, another a baseball bat, a third a pen knife, many others a boulder.

'I'll start with mother,' said the head of the family whose weapon was the pen knife, and severed her jugular. Then killed each of his children, and finally himself.

To kill one's family with a baseball bat, a hoe or a boulder is easy, but to kill oneself with a baseball bat, a hoe or a boulder is extremely difficult. The father of such families, his responsibility to them fulfilled, usually had to hang himself.

Other families, whom some envied, had been issued with a hand grenade. But grenades are capricious; and even though they sat close together, there was often a badly wounded survivor. Such survivors were usually clubbed to death by the nearest Japanese soldier, who would shout, 'Here's another,' as he wielded the butt of his rifle.

Schoolgirls were conscripted as nurses, and died in caves with the soldiers. Fathers scavenging for food for their families were seized by the Army and asked, 'Who is more important, your family or the Emperor?' Whichever the answer, they were executed.

Only the very fortunate found themselves in caves where they were offered milk laced with cyanide. They were the wounded. Upon drinking their potion, they were listed as killed in action and their souls became eligible for a better life at the Yasukuni Shrine in Tokyo.

Amid this inferno of fire and shell, the pain of hunger and the anguish of obligatory death, the Okinawans can be excused if they failed to notice Hitler's suicide on 30 April, and the surrender of Germany eight days later.

We noticed them, though; and so did our guards, who commented briefly, 'Deutzel number ten,' and carried on as if it didn't matter. What neither of us knew was that, led by the mighty battleship *Yamato*, the pathetic remnants of the Japanese Navy had sailed out of home waters to do battle with the US Navy at anchor off Okinawa. Engaged just off Kyushu, they had been sunk without trace.

Okinawa fell. The Allies met at Potsdam and formally demanded Japan's unconditional surrender. Russia, to Japan's consternation, denounced the neutrality pact of 1941. Japan's new Prime Minister, the octogenarian Admiral Suzuki, broadcast an apparently contemptuous rejection of the Allies' Potsdam Declaration. And fleets of B-29s ranged the skies over the Japanese homeland, putting one city after another to its ordeal by fire.

*   *   *

Abruptly, the Imperial Japanese Army demanded working parties of 100 for a task in Johore. We were not told the nature of the task, and we were stripped naked for a search before our party departed from Changi's Gaol. We therefore arrived at our new camp – an attap hut with two bamboo tiers on either side of a central aisle: a small compound and a guard house: all enclosed by a barbed wire fence – without a radio. We were isolated, vulnerable and fatally ignorant of the current state of the war.

Our task was to dig tunnels. The tunnels were short, had no exits and were designed to facilitate military ambushes, not the passage of trains. We dug them fifty yards or so into the flanks of clay hills. When the British invasion came, the Japanese proposed hiding inside them, camouflaging the entrances. Once the British had passed them, they would swarm out and attack from the rear.

Since it was unlikely that the Japanese would want our company in the tunnels, and even less likely that they would want us rushing off to warn our friends where they were hiding, it was not difficult to deduce that we would be shot within minutes of any Allied landing anywhere along the Malayan Peninsula. Without a radio to warn us when to make a break for it, we would have to rely on animal intuition: which, for the moment, told us not to worry.

Needless to say we dug bad tunnels, relying upon green pit props instead of seasoned timber to achieve the desired ill-effect. These began to rot at the tunnel's entrance long before the digging was completed. When they collapsed, so did the tunnel. We were always able to dig one another out; but given a decent preliminary bombardment, we felt confident that the Japanese would be entombed when the invasion took place in a few months time.

I have no idea why we thought it would be neither earlier nor later than a few months time; I do know that we were right. Perhaps there is an intuitive as well as a biological clock. And perhaps one's intuitive clock measures the chronology not only of time past but of events to come as well. In any event, we decided that September would be the time, in our vernacular, 'to shoot through'; and had the Emperor not insisted that Japan surrender in August, 6 September was in fact the proposed date for Mountbatten's invasion.

Meanwhile, I continued to take absolutely no risks other than those which were one's obligatory contribution to a bad day's work for a bad day's pay – at that time (when a coconut cost twenty dollars) thirty cents. I refused to help an English comrade abduct an amiable dog that belonged to one of our least amiable guards. So he abducted it on his own – which was very dangerous. But he gave me just as vast a helping of dog stew as he would have had I been his accomplice, so I presume he understood.

Before August 15 of that year, the only images I retain on the retina of my mind's eye of life in that camp are a tunnel collapse and not helping Ivor kidnap that dog. I have read in another man's diary that it was a comparatively pleasant time, and I can believe it: the weather in Malaysia at that time of the year is good, and the work we did was neither particularly taxing nor at all effective.

August 15, 1945, I remember because that was the day the maddest and most skilful thief in our midst announced his intention of slipping away from the tunnel to steal a radio. So we covered for him, and when we returned to camp that evening he returned with us, having deposited his stolen radio just outside the perimeter fence.

He had walked brazenly along the road to the Japanese Head-quarters in Johore Bahru, bowing en route to all passing Japanese (who had bowed back), had bowed to the Headquarters sentry (who had bowed back), had found a radio in an unoccupied officer's bedroom, bowed to the sentry as he left with the radio, and walked brazenly back to our camp, confident that any Japanese soldiers who saw him would take him for just another Australian electrician repairing a radio for the Imperial Japanese Army.

That night he crawled through the wire, plugged his radio into the power lines that ran between the telephone posts outside, took it into the latrine, switched on and tuned in.

Some quarter of an hour later someone near the guard house called out a soft 'Red light', which was passed down the line to the latrine, whence emerged our thieving friend. 'I've just heard the King,' he told us incredulously. 'The war's over. We've won.'

96

CHAPTER TEN

>>>>>>>><<<<<<<<

'An Unbearable Thing'

NO WORDS, IT SEEMED TO US, could have provided a better curtain line to the war; but we were wrong. In Tokyo, for six days and nights on end, words of such theatrical splendour had been uttered as to make the climax of our little drama seem pallid by comparison. To compare the two, in fact, is to compare the final episode of a soap opera with the last act of *Hamlet*. We had forgotten that the war had been global: that when the final curtain came down it was not on us, in Johore, it would fall, but on the Japanese Empire, in Tokyo.

In the last months of that war, one city after another had been incinerated by the huge formations of B-29s that flew low and unimpeded over Japan. From most of them, the children had been evacuated to the country, where they lived harsh, hungry lives, awaiting the Allied invasion. Those city dwellers who had relatives in the country had likewise fled the B-29s' constant raids. But the greater part of the urban population had had no alternative but to stay where it was and endure whatever befell it.

When the B-29s roared overhead, they took pointless refuge in community halls and schools, and attempted to exclude the leaping tongues of flame by stuffing windows and doorways with mats of straw.

When their communal shelters caught fire, they fled into the open incandescent air in small family units, mothers strapping on to their backs daughters, whose hair burst into flames, fathers carrying in their arms sons, whose cotton clothing burst into flames; their flight futile anyway because more often than not they were found next morning charred and shrivelled, even vulcanised together. Or, if they had reached a stream, boiled.

At other times, fire storms generated winds so strong that infants were plucked from their parents' arms, and vanished, flaming like meteors, into the inferno.

Down draughts sent sheets of fire skimming the surface of rivers

97

and lakes so that they seemed as flammable as gasoline, devouring oxygen and flesh alike.

Yet after each raid, in the short time when electricity was available, the loudspeakers in every street (and shop) would blare the Army's determination to continue the war, to prepare for yet another 'final battle' – but this time on the sacred soil of Japan itself.

A hundred million people, the loudspeakers and posters and newspapers inaccurately proclaimed, armed with bamboo spears, would rout the invading barbarians. Men, women, students and even school children were to fight to the death. More than 7000 planes would make their first and final flight when they sought out the enemy's fleet and plummeted on to its decks.

Leaving only a skeleton force in Manchuria, Japan brought home the bulk of the Kwangtung Army and, at the same time, sought Russia's good offices in her attempt to persuade the Americans that a negotiated peace was preferable to the frightful losses they would suffer in pursuit of the unattainable goal of unconditional surrender.

The Japanese government, led by the ancient and unpredictable Admiral Suzuki, did not know that President Truman had already bribed Stalin to enter the war, but it should not have been so ingenuous as to imagine that Stalin would resist the temptation of an almost defenceless Manchuria. By now, though, wishful thinking had become the government's only contribution to the nation's defence.

'Although we have no choice but to continue the war as long as the enemy insists upon unconditional surrender,' the Supreme War Council had agreed, 'we deem it advisable, while we still possess considerable powers of resistance, to propose peace through neutral nations, especially the Soviet Union, and to obtain terms which will at least ensure the preservation of our monarchy.'

The monarchy! There was the crux of unconditional surrender – which would leave the Allies free to depose the Emperor, thereby abolishing the whole imperial concept, which the Japanese called the National Polity. It could even result in the prosecution of the Emperor as a war criminal. Rather than that, his 'hundred million' subjects would fight till not one survived. Meantime, their government had sought Moscow's good offices, and Washington was awaiting its response to the Potsdam Declaration.

Which began: 'The time has come for Japan to decide whether she will continue to be controlled by those self-willed militarist advisers whose unintelligent calculations have brought its Empire to the threshold of annihilation, or whether she will follow the path of reason.'

Had those who formulated the Declaration been determined to *prolong* the war, they could have used no more effective language. Not only were the people of Japan powerless in the hands of the militarists, but the militarists – dubbed self-willed and unintelligent for waging war – would lose face to an even greater extent if they accepted the insult and stopped the fighting. What came next, though was worse.

'Following are our terms. We will not deviate from them. There are no alternatives. We shall brook no delay.

'There must be eliminated for all time the authority and influence of those who have deceived and misled the people of Japan . . . Stern justice shall be meted out to all war criminals . . . We call upon the government of Japan to proclaim now the unconditional surrender of all Japanese forces . . . The alternative for Japan is prompt and utter destruction.'

Neither Japan's Foreign Minister nor her Prime Minister chose to oblige those who had issued the Potsdam Declaration, for three reasons. First, they knew that the Army was determined to fight on; second, to have consented to the Potsdam demands would have been to invite their own instant assassination, and the Army's reversal of their decision; and third, they still hoped for Moscow's intercession on Japan's behalf.

Suzuki, therefore, stalled; but in the process let slip a word much stronger (because it was ambiguous) than either he or his advisers can ever have intended. Declaring that the government would 'maintain a discreet silence' on the subject of the Potsdam Declaration, he was quoted by the Tokyo Press as having said that the government would 'treat it with contempt'.

President Truman, in the words of Stimson, his Secretary of State for War, thereupon decided that the United States, 'could only proceed to demonstrate that the ultimatum had meant exactly what it said'. A less magisterial version of this turning point in history is that Admiral Leahy warned Truman that the policy of unconditional surrender would make the invasion of Japan inevitable, and inflict huge American casualties. Truman then proved himself to be made of sterner stuff than Roosevelt and General Eisenhower, who had succumbed, in the war against Germany, to the impulse to spare American lives.

That had been achieved by stalling the Allied advance upon both Berlin and Prague and leaving those two prizes to the Russians. In the case of Japan, Truman declined to take up either that option or the option of a negotiated peace. Remarking that he could do nothing to change the American public's demand for Japan's unconditional surrender, he said that the Joint Chiefs of Staff should proceed with their plan to invade Japan on 10 November.

But, as his advisers left his office, he turned to John McCloy, his cabinet secretary, and asked him what he thought. To which McCloy replied, 'Why not use the atomic bomb?'

Thus it was that on 6 August 1945, Hiroshima, a garrison town with the sort of red light district that Japanese garrison towns invariably attracted, was pulverised; and the most dramatic act in the drama of Japan's vicious but tragic war began.

*   *   *

From the days of her earliest and most momentous victories in World War II there had been those in Japan who wanted to seek an honourable peace. Marquis Kido had not been alone. There had even been those like Admiral Yamamoto who, though they foresaw early victories, had also foreseen inevitable defeat, and had wished not to go to war at all.

The Army had nevertheless had its way – not by argument but by coercion. The assassinations of 1936 were too well remembered, the Kempeitai and the Thought Police too powerful, the hate propaganda too successful and the public's veneration of the Emperor too ingrained to allow national debate – and Tojo had become Premier.

By June of 1945, however, only the Army's fanaticism and the people's devotion to their Emperor sustained what had self-evidently become a calamitous conflict. The Navy had vanished beneath the surface of the sea, the two Air Arms had been shot out of the sky, the Army had been scattered across South East Asia and China (where it could neither help nor, in the long run survive), every island jewel (not excluding Okinawa) had been snatched from the Imperial treasure chest, city after city had been reduced to ashes, there was no oil and little food (and no merchant navy with which to replace either, even had it been available) industry had ground to a halt, everyone wore a uniform of one kind or another, life was lived as if in a barrack, the sun – symbol of Nippon's greatness – blazed pitilessly over it all, and now the Bomb had fallen.

Typically, the Army promptly denied that such a weapon could be manufactured – yet made no effort to restrain Suzuki's government from registering a formal protest about its use.

As if aware of the Army's intransigence, Truman, in a broadcast from Washington, warned the Japanese that if they did not now accept the Potsdam terms (which he called 'our' terms) 'they may expect a rain of ruin from the air the like of which has never been seen . . .'

Now was the time for the men of the Peace Faction in Tokyo to speak out; but they continued merely to conspire. Braver than they, it was Hirohito who spoke up. The tragedy of Hiroshima must not be repeated, he told Suzuki's cabinet; and thereby began the solitary task of saving his nation and his army from self-destruction.

Unwittingly, the Russians helped him. Having procrastinated for weeks – having never, in fact, intended to promote the Japanese cause at all – they at last revealed their intentions. Foreign Minister Molotov summoned Ambassador Sato to his presence on 8 August and told him that as of 9 August Russia would be at war with Japan. As the Red Army began its onslaught on the depleted Kwangtung Army (which was soon either destroyed or transported to Siberia, where it would labour and languish for almost a decade) Hirohito ordered Kido to advise Suzuki that it was His Majesty's wish that the war be swiftly terminated.

Another atomic bomb lent added weight to words oppressive enough already to General Anami, the War Minister, General Umezu, the Army Chief of Staff, and Admiral Toyoda, the Navy Chief of Staff. Unable to accede to an ultimatum imposing unconditional surrender as well as defeat, they had hoped to extract no less than four major concessions from Washington. Now the Emperor's message, followed so swiftly by the destruction of Nagasaki, had made them apprehensive.

Their problem was that while Suzuki, Togo and Admiral Yonai were prepared to accept the Potsdam ultimatum (subject only to the proviso that the Imperial Polity be preserved, which Washington had declined to guarantee) *they* wanted three further concessions – that the enemy's occupation force should be nominal; that Japan should try her own war criminals; and that Japanese officers should demobilize Japanese troops. By so insisting, however, they split the cabinet, made any move to end the war impossible, disobeyed the Emperor and subjected Japan to the risk of more atomic bombs.

101

Defending the three extra conditions, General Anami said: 'We cannot pretend that victory is certain, but it is far too early to say that the war is lost.' The difficult part of his argument thus blithely disposed of, he proceeded less tortuously to more serious matters. 'Furthermore,' he said, 'our army will not submit to demobilization. Our men simply will not lay down their arms. And since they know they are not permitted to surrender, since they know that a fighting man who surrenders is liable to extremely heavy punishment, there is really no alternative for us but to continue the war.'

It was the kind of illogic to which only the Japanese could have subscribed; but an entire race had come to accept it as irrefutable. Then, as now, they believed that nothing unacceptable to Japan would be allowed by the fates to come to pass: or, conversely, that Japan was entitled to anything the Japanese wanted. Being divine, they had divine rights.

With his cabinet evenly divided, and unable to agree a compromise on a matter of such national importance, it would have been in keeping with precedent for Suzuki to resign and bequeath the problem to a successor. He declined to do so.

'I consider myself utterly unfit for the office of Prime Minister,' he had confessed in a speech to the Diet when first appointed. 'It is only because of the grave situation that I have accepted the Imperial command.'

Since then the situation had deteriorated immeasurably, but the old admiral knew that he had been appointed to extricate Japan from the consequences of her reckless war, and he was determined not to shirk that dangerous responsibility.

He was unpredictable and frequently eccentric, but he was also brave. That much he had proved when he led a destroyer squadron against the Russians in 1904. Nor, as a liberal in the 1930s, had he ever hesitated to oppose the militarists until assassination became the reward for such candour, and one of the 1936 murder squads had shot him three times. He had been spared the coup de grâce only because his loyal wife had begged that she be allowed to finish him off. As Premier in August, 1945, he was therefore under no illusions about the dangers confronting him. One false step and either the army would gun him down as a Badoglio or the Americans would drop a third atomic bomb on Tokyo.

Unable to put forward any agreed policy for the Emperor's approval, he took the unprecedented step of asking the Emperor to act as arbitrator. Accordingly, at ten minutes to midnight on 9 August, Suzuki and ten others sat at two tables on either side of the Emperor's stuffy air raid shelter while the Emperor sat at the head of the room. Behind the uniformed Emperor was a silver screen; in front of him a small table covered with a cloth of gold. His eleven subjects wore either morning clothes or uniforms.

Suzuki read the Potsdam Declaration; confessed the cabinet deadlocked; apologized for requesting the Emperor's presence; and called upon each of his ministers in turn to argue for or against surrendering in view of the fact that the Allies had declined to give assurances that the National Polity would be preserved.

Togo, the Foreign Minister, and Admiral Yonai were in favour of accepting the terms of the Potsdam Declaration, as, of course, was Suzuki, Generals Anami and Umezu, and Admiral Toyoda opposed acceptance unless their conditions about the National Polity, war criminals, a small occupation force and disarming of Japanese troops by Japanese officers were incorporated. Closely questioned by Baron Hiranuma, a Privy Councillor, each remained adamant.

'Your Imperial Majesty's decision is requested as to which proposal should be adopted,' Suzuki then begged. 'The Foreign Minister's, or the one with the four conditions.'

At two o'clock on the morning of 10 August, the Emperor gave his answer.

With his first quietly spoken words he dashed the hopes of Anami, Umezu and Toyoda. Not only did he declare that to continue the war would mean the annihilation of the Japanese people, he also made it clear that he no longer believed in the boasts of the militarists.

'Since the beginning of the Pacific War there has been a tremendous disparity between our calculations and the realities. Now I hear that the Army and Navy are preparing for a battle in the homeland. One of the main defensive positions is Kujukuri-hama. But there is a great difference between the advice of the Chief of Staff about the state of the defences at Kujukuri-hama and the observations of our chamberlains. They tell me that they are only one tenth completed. Also the production of aircraft is quite inadequate.

'In these conditions, how can we prevail, even in the homeland? If the entire population is killed, we can hardly hope to perpetuate the nation! It is my opinion that we must end the war, although that is an unbearable thing.'

103

It was unbearable also to see his loyal troops disarmed; 'but the time has come to bear the unbearable', he concluded. 'I give my sanction to the proposal to accept the Allied Declaration on the basis outlined by the Foreign Minister' – and left the shelter. It thus became the responsibility of the Cabinet to implement the Emperor's decision that Japan must surrender.

CHAPTER ELEVEN

>>>>>>><<<<<<<

'The Emperor has given his Decision'

THE CABINET MEETING to decide the wording of the message accepting the terms of the Potsdam Declaration was held at the Premier's official residence. At four in the morning of 11 August, after much haggling, this note was agreed. It accepted the Allied terms provided they did 'not comprise any demand which prejudices the prerogation of his Majesty as a Sovereign Ruler'.

'And if the enemy refuses to guarantee the preservation of the Imperial House?' Anami enquired, 'Will you go on fighting?'

'Yes,' said Suzuki.

That morning Anami ordered all senior members of the War Office to meet him and, when they had assembled before him, told them that the government, subject to the proviso about the national polity, had agreed to end the war.

'We have no alternative but to abide by the Emperor's decision,' he insisted, in an attempt to quell their immediate uproar. 'Whether we fight on, or whether we surrender, depends upon the enemy's response to our note.'

The hitherto unthinkable prospect of surrender had at last been posed as a likely reality; but Anami was still talking. 'You are soldiers,' his subordinates heard him say. 'You must obey orders.'

Anami's words meant the Army's death: a disgraceful death. A junior officer spoke for them all. 'The War Minister has told us that we must obey his orders. Is the War Minister even *thinking* of surrender?'

'Anyone who plans to disobey my orders will have to do so over my dead body,' Anami rapped back.

That morning, while Tokyo was being bombed yet again, President Truman and his advisors were studying the Japanese note, which hardly conformed to the late President Roosevelt's demand for unconditional surrender – a demand with which America's allies Britain and China, had concurred. They would have to be consulted.

Meantime, Suzuki's government had to decide how to prepare the exhausted people of Japan for *possible* surrender without so depressing them that they would be unable to continue the war should that become necessary.

Finally a statement was cobbled together for release on the afternoon news broadcast. It suggested that, although the enemy was employing a new and barbarous bomb, the Army would doubtless repel any invasion. 'But,' it continued, 'we must accept that the situation has become very bad. Nevertheless, the government is exerting itself to the utmost to ensure that our last line of defence is held, and to protect both the national polity and the honour of our race. The government expects that the nation will surmount the present difficult situation and preserve the polity of the Empire.'

There was no mention of the Potsdam Declaration, nor of the government's conditional acceptance of it; but there was the sort of hint that the populace, accustomed as it was to tortuous metaphors and an unusually ambiguous language, should have been able to interpret.

Doubtless the Japanese would have done so (particularly since they had already been apprised of Russia's entry into the war against them) had not the Army, with the War Minister's consent, deliberately muddied the waters of comprehension with a communiqué of its own that was blatantly bellicose.

'The Soviet Union,' the Army declared, 'had directed its armed might against the wrong enemy by invading Japan.'

In fact, the Soviet armed forces had merely begun to round up the hopelessly outnumbered Japanese forces in Manchuria; but the Army, like the Navy, had never hesitated to lie, for all that its samurai code proclaimed that a soldier always spoke the truth; and if its words were taken to mean that Russian soldiers had actually invaded the northern islands of Japan, so much the better for its plan to prevent the government from surrendering.

'Nothing remains to us,' the statement continued, 'but to see through to its conclusion this war for the defence of the Land of the Gods. Chewing grass, eating stones and living in the fields, we shall fight on, for in our death lies our country's one chance of survival.'

Desperate to counter the adverse effect this news statement would have on Truman, Togo's Foreign Office at once authorized the Domei News Agency to transmit, in morse, the text of its own note to America. Its concentration lapsing yet again, the Army, which normally censored all transmissions abroad, failed to block this vital message – which sped to the desk of every newspaper editor in the world.

Though unaware, in fact, of the Japanese Army's belligerence the American State Department replied firmly to Japan's equivocal note. From the moment of surrender, it advised, the authority and future of both the Emperor and the Japanese Government would be decided by the Supreme Commander of the Allied Powers, General MacArthur, alone.

It was by now mid-morning, Saturday, 11 August. As the Emperor summoned War Minister Anami to his presence, to reprimand him for allowing the Army to issue its inflammatory proclamation, fifteen junior officers met in the War Office bomb shelter to brand Suzuki, Togo and Marquis Kido traitors fit only for assassination, and to discuss plans for the occupation of the Imperial Palace and the protection of the Emperor from further 'bad advice'. Confident that they would have the support of both Anami and General Mori, who commanded the Imperial Guards, they expected their proposed coup d'état to transfer the reins of power into their hands. Washington's insistence that the Emperor's fate would depend on the whim of General MacArthur further inflamed their passion.

A group of B-29 crewmen held prisoners at Fukuoda were about to learn just how inflamed their passions were. Eight of them had already been executed: now eight more were taken to a field near Aburayama, stripped and, one after the other, butchered. Where the sword was used, it was used clumsily; but those were the fortunate victims. Others were treated like bulls in a corrida manned by a team of callous but clumsy toreadors. They were slowly beaten, stabbed and hacked to death. Though there were few fliers left in Japanese hands, there still some 350,000 prisoners of war in the hands of the Imperial Japanese Army: Fukuoda boded ill for them all.

Thus Sunday 12 August, was marked by intrigues and confusion. Togo wanted to comply with Washington's demands; the Emperor concurred; Anami reminded Suzuki of his promise to continue the war in the absence of an Allied assurance that would preserve the national polity; Suzuki agreed to insist upon such an assurance; the Imperial princes (suspecting that the Army might ask one of them to supplant Hirohito) pledged their support to the Emperor; the cabinet met, and fell into instant disarray; Togo stormed out in disgust at its rejection of an Imperial order; Suzuki proposed that clarification of its message be sought from Washington; Togo threatened that he would ask the Emperor to give Suzuki a second direct order to surrender; Kido first assured Togo that he would suggest that the Emperor brought pressure to bear upon the Premier, then reminded Suzuki that to continue the war, contrary to the Emperor's wishes, would cost the lives of millions of Japanese; Anami, at an early evening meeting with two of the conspirators planning the coup d'état, declined to commit himself, but in the early hours of Monday, 13 August, sent a message to his Cabinet colleague, General Umezu, to the effect that he was contemplating bringing pressure to bear on the Emperor to reject the Allied terms; Umezu told Anami's messenger that he was now in *favour* of accepting those terms; the Cabinet met once again; Umezu, though he now favoured acceptance of the terms of the Potsdam Declaration, voted *with* Anami and Toyoda against acceptance; the stalemate of 9 August, the Emperor's decision to the contrary notwithstanding, was repeated; and all the time the War Office grew more agitated and the plotters more bloodthirsty. They confronted Anami a second time and submitted their plan of attack for his approval. Anami stalled and left them, well aware that he had in no way dissuaded them.

Suzuki called a meeting of the Supreme War Council and failed to obtain that unanimous vote in favour of surrender without which he was unable to advise the Emperor that there was a consensus – that accursed rock upon which so many Japanese ventures have wrecked themselves.

'Inasmuch as we have failed once again to agree,' Suzuki then told the Council, 'I propose asking His Majesty for a second Imperial decision.'

'Will you give me just two days more before you approach the Emperor?' Anami begged – hoping in that time to talk his subordinates out of their proposed mutiny. Suzuki refused. Later, a naval officer repeated Anami's request: again Suzuki refused, pointing out that such a delay would see the Russians in Korea and northern Japan as well as Manchuria.

'General Anami will kill himself,' the naval officer warned.

'That will be very regrettable,' Suzuki bleakly agreed. Grateful though he was to Anami for not resigning (and thereby bringing about the fall of his government) he was prepared to sacrifice him. Aware as he was of the Army's plan to assassinate him if he persisted in his duty to the Emperor, he was even prepared to sacrifice himself.

Suzuki may also have declined to give Anami the two day's grace for which he had begged because the War Minister's motives were unclear. Certainly Anami appears to have shared his thoughts with no one in the government, and dared not do so with anyone in his own Ministry; but his subsequent words and actions have made them clear enough to posterity.

He had committed himself to his plan some hours earlier when, somewhat obliquely, he had warned Colonel Arao, one of his Staff officers, that he doubted that the forthcoming coup could succeed. He was far from confident, however, that the colonel had taken his point.

'I don't know whether Arao will interpret my remark to mean that I am opposed to the coup,' he later murmured, well aware that had Arao *mis*interpreted his remark, the plotters would find it that much the easier to enlist the support of General Mori of the Guards Division, General Tanaka, Commander of the Eastern District Army, and General Umezu, the Army Chief of Staff. Denied the two days he needed to keep those three in the government camp and discourage his junior officers from precipitate action, he went home to bed for two hours.

Tuesday, 14 August, brought the government two ominous pieces of news. First, that those inhabitants of Hiroshima who had at first appeared to be unscathed by the Bomb were now dying like flies; second, that millions of leaflets were being dropped from the bellies of American B-29s advising the Japanese people that their government had already accepted America's terms as laid out in the note of 11 August. Not only had many of thousands of civilians thus been fully apprised of the news at which their government had only hinted, but the Army had been warned that, if it was not to be opposed by a populace whose appetite for war had been destroyed by the prospect of imminent peace, its coup must start at once.

Of this latter danger Kido was swift to advise the Emperor, who immediately agreed to command a second Imperial Conference at which he would deliver (to his divided Council and deadlocked Cabinet) the Imperial decision for which Suzuki was begging.

It was as well he did. Needing only Anami's approval for their coup to be assured of success (because Umezu had again changed his mind and now favoured their proposed mutiny) the conspirators learnt that the War Minister was unavailable: along with his colleagues of the Supreme Council and the Cabinet, he was sitting in the Palace bomb shelter listening to the fateful words of his Emperor.

Dressed in military uniform, Hirohito sat before the same silver screen and behind the same small table covered by the same cloth of gold. Outside it was a sweltering morning; in the underground shelter it was so humid that the walls were streaked with damp. None of the councillors was formally dressed: on the contrary, they were as sweatily unkempt as they were embarrassed and apprehensive.

'I have listened carefully to all of the arguments opposing acceptance of the Allied reply to our note,' Hirohito told them. 'However, my own opinion has not changed. I have examined the conditions prevailing in Japan, and in the rest of the world, and I believe that a continuation of the war offers nothing but continued destruction.

'I have studied the terms of the Allied reply, and I have come to the conclusion that they represent a virtually complete acknowledgement of our position . . . In short, I consider the reply to be acceptable.'

He went on to acknowledge that there were those present who doubted the security of the national polity; that it would be difficult for the Army and Navy to submit to being disarmed and seeing their country occupied; and that he knew his people would willingly sacrifice themselves to preserve the national polity.

'But I am not concerned with what may happen to me,' he said. 'I want to preserve the lives of my people. I do not want them subjected to further destruction.'

He admitted that to see loyal soldiers disarmed, and loyal ministers punished as war criminals, was agonising; but insisted, 'As things stand now, the nation still has a chance to recover. I am reminded of the Emperor Meiji at the time of the Triple Intervention. But like him I must bear the unbearable and hope for the reconstruction of the nation.'

He expressed his willingness to join his people in that effort of reconstruction, his sorrow that so many had been killed, his grief for the bereaved and his anxiety about the future of those who had been maimed or whose homes and businesses had been destroyed.

He pointed out that surrender would be a shock for the nation and a source of dismay for his troops. 'If it is thought appropriate,' he said, 'I am willing to go before the microphone.'

Then he turned to Anami and Toyoda. 'The War Minister and the Navy Minister may not find it easy to persuade their troops to accept our decision. I am willing to go wherever necessary to explain it.'

His words left the General and the Admiral no alternative but to make themselves responsible for the obedience to his decision of the Army and the Navy. It was unthinkable that the Emperor should be insulted by having to justify to his troops a decision his government had asked him to make.

'I desire the Cabinet to prepare as soon as possible an Imperial Rescript announcing the termination of the war,' the Emperor ordered and, rising, left the room. As Anami made his way from the ruined palace he knew that the Army over which he presided had been consigned to oblivion and disgrace – by, of all people, the Emperor, in whose divine name it had committed millions of acts of valour.

*   *   *

While he and his colleagues proceeded to Suzuki's official residence, and his subordinates prepared to launch their coup, Anami could only despair. On the one hand, he had just been commanded to enforce the Imperial order that the Army allow itself to be disarmed while the enemy arrived unopposed: on the other, he had to persuade half a million hitherto victorious troups in South East Asia, and six times that number in Japan, not to kill themselves rather than surrender – a dispensation neither he nor they could ever have afforded their compatriots in New Guinea in 1943 as they died so pointlessly of hunger and wounds, the alternating flame and frost of malaria, and the blinding pain of typhus.

Kimura's armies in Burma had been dying just as pointlessly for more than a year and a half, hundreds of thousands of them, yet neither Hirohito nor a single Japanese soldier had ever suggested that they save themselves to help in the reconstruction of Japan.

The garrisons of Guam, Saipan, Iwo Jima and all the other islands had been offered no option to suicidal resistance. Not even the civilians of Saipan and Okinawa had been spared the fate prescribed by the Battlefield Commandment.

Were all of them now to be betrayed by their surviving comrades? Was the Imperial Japanese Army now to prove that, in

111

everything it had done in the 70 years of its existence, it had been insincere? Even to a civilian, to live without sincerity was shameful; but to the Army, not to die was insincere.

*　　*　　*

These were the irreconcilables tormenting Anami as he took his seat with his Cabinet colleagues to peruse the draft of the two Rescripts prepared for them by the Chief Cabinet Secretary and a one-time journalist from the *Nippon Times:* the first, the one Hirohito would broadcast to the nation; the second, the one to be broadcast to Hirohito's troops, ordering them to lay down their arms.

'The war will end even if I do resign,' Anami had demurred to those who suggested it. 'That is definite. And anyway, were I to resign I would never see the Emperor again.' And challenged by a War Ministry subordinate to explain why he had changed his mind, he had replied, 'The Emperor told me he fully understood how I felt, but, with tears in his eyes, he told me to persevere. I can no longer oppose his decision.' Then, lest anyone had misunderstood his position, he had added. 'The Emperor has given his decision, and we can only obey.' And had repeated his words of the day before. 'Anyone who wishes to disobey will have to do so over my dead body.'

Now, with eighteen others, his colleagues and their advisers, he sat at a table in the Premier's residence. Suzuki looked impassive and untired, despite his years; the others dishevelled and distraught.

They summoned representatives of the Japan Broadcasting Corporation and warned them that the Emperor would broadcast a Rescript the following day. They were to set up a room in the Palace for that purpose. The representatives of NHK were awestruck.

Next it was decided that the Emperor would record rather than broadcast the words of the Imperial Rescript; and after that came the matter of the Emperor's offer personally to address recalcitrant officers of the Army and Navy. 'I will guarantee the good behaviour of the Imperial Navy,' Admiral Yonai volunteered.

'And I speak for the Army,' said Anami, who then withdrew to the war Ministry where he addressed his heads of sections. 'The Army will obey the Emperor's command,' he told them. 'He offered to come here and speak to you himself. I replied that that would not be necessary. No officer in the Imperial Army will presume to know better than the Emperor and the government what is best for the country. The future of Japan is no longer in doubt. It will not be easy. You officers must accept that death will not absolve you of your duty. Your duty is to stay alive and help your country to recover, even if it means chewing grass, eating stones, and sleeping in fields.'

Stepping down from his dais, Anami returned to Suzuki's official residence and rejoined his colleagues round the table. They were perusing the draft of the Imperial Rescript – to which the War Minister took immediate exception.

As it stood, he complained, it implied that the Army had for months been lying to the country. 'The war situation grows more unfavourable to us every day,' it said. The Army had never even admitted that the war situation had *become* unfavourable! Unfortunately, no one could think of a suitable amendment.

Togo left them to it; and returned just in time to hear the unpredictable Suzuki announce that Japan must seek further clarification of the Allies' intentions towards the Emperor . . . and be prepared to fight on if they declined to compromise.

Anami suggested that the offending phrase, 'The war situation grows more unfavourable to us every day', be amended to, 'The war situation has not turned in our favour'. Incomprehensible though the distinction may be to Western minds, Anami was convinced that this amendment would render mass suicide by the Armed Forces, and mutiny by many of its officers, less likely.

All that sweltering day the Cabinet remained deadlocked. Several times during the afternoon the Emperor enquired, through a chamberlain, about the Rescript. Suzuki apologised for the delay. The haggling continued. And then, at seven o'clock, Admiral Yonai cracked.

'On the question of the phrasing of the Imperial Rescript,' he said. 'I would like to see it revised in accordance with the War Minister's desires.'

'Let it be done,' Suzuki ordered; and the phrase that had so offended Anami was amended to read, 'The war situation has not turned in our favour'.

*   *   *

Copies of the much corrected and unsightly draft were ordered for the Emperor's approval; and while they were being brushed on to the sort of thick paper suitable for a monarch's eyes, the Cabinet debated the best time for the transmission of his broadcast to his people. He was to record it that night.

*   *   *

A second debate was meantime raging between representatives of those officers of Anami's who favoured obedience to the Emperor's order, and seppuku as a gesture of shame for having failed him, and those who favoured disobeying their Emperor, because he had been ill-advised.

Those who advocated seppuku by the entire officer class argued not only that it was in itself 'a beautiful thing to do' but, in the circumstances, 'the only correct thing to do'. Those who disagreed – which they did out of no desire to spare themselves the agony that seppuku would cause them – argued that, by occupying the Palace, and cutting it off from all sources of corruption, they could 'assist the Emperor preserve Japan'.

'Don't you think this is a more beautiful plan than cutting open your belly?' one of them demanded of his opponent.

'Success in your plan *would* be more beautiful,' the latter concurred. 'But General Anami says there is no chance of success.'

In effect, success now depended upon the active co-operation of Generals Mori and Tanaka who, between them, commanded the loyalty of two divisions of Imperial Guards and all the troops of the Eastern District Army. Should this powerful force rally behind the conspirators, not only would the Palace be quarantined from further Peace Party infection, but Tokyo itself would be so securely held that neither the Army's outlying commands nor the Navy's few marines would dare intervene.

But the conspirators were emboldened to reject seppuku in favour of an immediate coup by the fact that a forged order had induced a second battalion of Imperial Guards to join the battalion already on duty in the Palace grounds. The Emperor, it seemed, was now cut off from his cabinet: later that night they would invade the Palace, surround NHK's studios, confront Japan with a fait accompli and continue the war.

*   *   *

Anami went home to change his sweat-stained uniform. There he was joined by General Tojo (whose son-in-law was one of the mutineers) and Field Marshal Hata. Making his first intervention into public affairs since his resignation in 1944, Tojo first observed that all Hirohito's war-time ministers would, of course, be tried as war criminals, and then said, 'What we must do when that happens is stand together. We must declare unequivocally our belief that the Greater East Asia War was necessary, that the war we fought was a defensive war.'

For his part, Hata, whose Headquarters at Hiroshima had been demolished by the atomic bomb, declared that he proposed giving up the rank of Field Marshal.

Anami, who had long since decided what he would do, made no comment to either and returned to the Premier's official residence to settle the time on 15 August when the Emperor's recording of the Rescript would be broadcast.

'At seven o'clock in the morning,' Togo suggested.

Anami demurred, pointing out that first it would be necessary to issue those orders to all overseas troops that would persuade them to lay down their arms when they heard the Emperor's Special Rescript to them. 'I therefore request that the Emperor's broadcast be delayed one day,' he said.

The longer the delay, the Director of Information pointed out, the greater the chance of violence, but every farmer in the land would long since have been at work in his fields if the broadcast were transmitted at seven in the morning: he suggested that the ideal time would be noon the following day. The Cabinet agreed.

*   *   *

As he read the carefully brushed copy of the Rescript handed to him by Kido, the Emperor suggested five changes. To save time, the Rescript's amendments were pasted on to the original document.

To Anami's delight, one of Hirohito's suggestions changed 'The war situation has not turned in our favour', to, 'The war situation has developed not necessarily to our advantage'. Grotesquely euphemistic though this has always sounded to Western ears, it probably did more than anything else to convince those who served outside Tokyo that they could honourably stop fighting – which was all that the Rescript purported to ask of them.

At eight-thirty that evening, while his capital buzzed with dire rumours of a huge enemy fleet in Tokyo Bay about to disgorge an invading host of vengeful barbarian rapists, Hirohito appended his signature and his Imperial Seal to the foot of a sadly blotched document unique in Japanese history. In the twentieth year of his reign (which, ironically, had been dubbed the Era of Enlightened Peace when he ascended the throne) at noon on the fifteenth day of August, the war upon which his advisers had insisted was to end in a surrender they had deemed unthinkable. Unless, of course, a coup could forestall it.

'I have heard nothing, and believe nothing, of a projected coup,' Suzuki assured an anxious Kido. 'The Imperial Guards are the last people in the world I would suspect.'

As if to confirm him in his confidence, Imperial Army Headquarters, among its daily quota of pronouncements, instructed NHK to announce on the nine o'clock news that everyone was to listen to an important broadcast the following day at noon.

At the War Ministry, Anami sat at his desk and composed the cable to all overseas troops which he hoped would procure their obedience to the Emperor's orders. Colonel Arao entered his office. Anami told him that he wanted the Army's young officers to do nothing 'foolish and heroic'.

'No seppuku, eh? You must help,' he instructed.

Having briefly reiterated this point, the War Minister returned to the Cabinet. Where a Foreign Office cable had to be signed by every member. The cable accepted in detail the terms of the Potsdam Declaration and advised that the Emperor had issued a Rescript to that effect. Via his embassies in Switzerland and Sweden, it would be transmitted to the United States, China, Great Britain and the Soviet Union. Anami signed without hesitation. Others read and re-read the cable before signing it, as if hoping to find some miraculous formula to avert the inevitable. When it was done, the Director of the Information Bureau drove through the blackout, along ruined streets, to the Palace – where the Emperor was about to record the Rescript.

As the Emperor entered the room in the Imperial Household Ministry that had been set up by NHK as a studio, all concerned bowed deeply. Apart from his chamberlains, not one of them had ever expected to gaze upon his countenance without being savagely punished. Nor, till that moment, would any of them have believed that the day would arrive when his sacred voice would be broadcast.

'How loudly should I speak?' the Emperor enquired uncertainly, approaching the microphone which stood in the centre of the room. The Director of Information assured him that his normal voice would be sufficiently loud. Without further ado, and adopting the strange, high pitch used for the delivery of Court Japanese, Hirohito read the long Rescript, concluding with the words, '. . . So that you may enhance the innate glory of the Imperial State and keep pace with the progress of the World.'

He looked at the Director of Information. 'Was it all right?' he asked.

'There were no technical errors, but a few words were not entirely clear,' he was told. He said he would like to make a second recording. As he did so, he sounded more nervous than he had the first time, and his voice was pitched even higher. He also missed a word.

'I am quite willing to make a third,' he immediately volunteered. All agreed that a third would be too great an ordeal for His Majesty – who then drove back to his Palace quarters.

NHK's technicians and officials, having decided that the first of the recordings was the one to be broadcast the following noon, bundled two copies of each recording into a pair of cotton bags which they left with a Palace official – who entrusted them to Yoshikiro Tokugawa, a chamberlain. Very sensibly, they feared to take the recordings back with them to the NHK studios lest the Army waylay their car and steal them; rather touchingly, they felt it disrespectful to remove the Emperor's recordings like thieves in the night. Tokugawa locked both bags in a safe in the office of one of the Empress's retinue.

With the Foreign Office's cable already winging its way to the victorious Allies, and the Imperial Rescript ready for transmission in twelve hours time, it seemed that nothing could now deny the exhausted people of Japan the peace for which they longed; but that was to reckon without the Army.

CHAPTER TWELVE

'A Broadcast of the Greatest Importance'

HAD WE KNOWN any of this as we dug tunnels into the orange clay hillsides of Johore between 10 August and 14 August, we would have laboured very uneasily. Some of us would even have bolted – and been caught and executed; and ten of us executed for each of them, because that was the rule of the Imperial Japanese Army.

Had we known that several of Anami's junior officers were asking why Japan should surrender when there were 350,000 Allied captives with whose lives she could barter, we would probably all have bolted – and all been rounded up and executed. But happily neither we nor our guards knew any of it. More astonishingly, no one in the world knew any of it, except those in Tokyo immediately concerned. Though the War Ministry was convulsed, though the national polity was about to be assailed by those whose duty it was to defend it, neither a hundred million of the Emperor's subjects nor any of his thousands of millions of enemies suspected that anything was amiss.

Yet the consensus in Tokyo had been shattered, and harmony had become cacophony. Probably no other race could have endured such tumult so privately. As often before (and since) the Japanese government was confronting the outside world with an apparently obtuse and maddening lack of urgency. Ever the victim of rivalries, Japan had long since learned to harness her incompatible passions until an acceptable policy emerged; but this time the policy was unacceptable, and consensus apparently unattainable. The situation was not, however, unprecedented.

For more than a decade before 7 December, 1941, the Army had been in a state of conflict with the diplomats, the Navy with the Army, the Strike North Faction of the Army with the Strike South Faction of the Army, the Army and Navy with the industrialists of the Zaibatsu, the generals with their junior officers, and the disciples of twentieth century bushido with the practitioners of *realpolitik*.

By so being, of course, they merely anticipated a society that today thinks in Japanese but writes in Chinese; dresses in Western clothes at work and Japanese clothes at home; makes its office buildings of concrete and glass but its homes of wood and paper; adopts cheap Western fads, yet cherishes its own ancient theatre; paints with delicacy but idolises wrestlers who are obese; makes gardens that are magical, but revels in anecdotes of samurai warriors whose exploits are bloody; clings tenaciously to the traditional yet is as instantly adaptable to radical change as a chameleon is to changing colours.

From 7 December 1941, to 10 August 1945, however, this same society had become a monolith waging war with single-minded passion. But then, from 10 August to 15 August, it had reverted to its pattern of double standards in a frenzy that was almost schizophrenic.

*　　*　　*

At long last the mutineers approached General Mori to solicit his support. They told him that the Palace was in their hands and General Umezu on their side; that their coup could not fail.

'Whatever truth there may be in your words,' he replied, 'the fact remains that the Emperor has spoken his decision. As Commander of the Imperial Guards, I must obey that decision, and I must insist that my men obey it too.' When two more conspirators came to see him, he presumably said the same thing, because one of them promptly shot him and the other hacked his arm off at the shoulder.

'There was no time to argue,' whispered the first, 'so I killed him. What else could I have done?'

Unlikely though it was that General Tanaka, to whose Eastern Command one of the late General Mori's Guards Divisions was attached, would now even condone, still less participate in the coup, the mutineers were too committed to call off their attack. Instead, they rampaged through the Palace gardens and offices, frantically searching for recordings of the Rescript. If they could not find and destroy them, the broadcast scheduled for the following noon would bring their war to an ignominious end.

By this time Anami had returned to his official residence – a simple one-storeyed Japanese house. After a bath and his daily

119

injection of vitamin, he dressed in a kimono, poured himself a drink and sat down to brush his final testament on to the sheets of thick paper he had asked his adjutant to find him.

Already he had apologized to Suzuki for having been so difficult over the past five days, and thanked him for having allowed the Foreign Office to send yet another note to Washington suggesting that the Army be permitted to disarm itself. And after his departure, Suzuki had told his Cabinet Secretary 'I think that the War Minister came to say goodbye.'

Now, however, he was about to say goodbye to the Army, to his Emperor and to life itself; but not in unseemly haste. His brother-in-law joined him, and they drank sake. 'As you probably know,' Anami said, 'I decided to commit seppuku some time ago. I shall do it tonight.'

His brother-in-law replied that he had realized that this was his intention, and that he would not attempt to dissuade him.

They talked on, and drank a great deal. Anami asked that, should his suicide attempt fail, his brother-in-law would kill him; but added wryly that he thought he was capable of taking his own life.

Another officer joined them; and later an Air Force officer dropped in to confess to Mori's murder. 'One more thing for which to apologize,' Anami sighed.

The sound of shots reached them from the Palace. 'For that also I will offer my life,' he said. And, to ease his companions' anxiety that he was getting too drunk, explained that the sake would dilate his veins: the blood would flow more freely. 'There's nothing to worry about,' he insisted.

Taking up his brush once again, he added a postcript to the back of his final testament.

Though he had said of the Emperor's broadcast, 'I could not bear to hear it,' he now donned a white shirt that had been a gift to him from the Emperor, and wound a white sash round his belly. Because it would have been dishonourable to commit seppuku with his sword, he examined two ancient daggers, said, 'This is the one I shall use,' and handed the second to his brother-in-law. 'Keep this in memory of me,' he said.

Pinning all his decorations to his dress uniform, which he then carefully folded, he asked his companions to drape his body with it when he was dead. He placed a photograph of his second son (who had been killed in China) on top of his folded uniform. The Commander of the Kempeitai arrived, and left a message that General

120

Tanaka had gone to the Palace to order the Imperial Guards back to their barracks. Anami dismissed his companions: it was time to die.

Rejecting both the garden and his inner room as the site for his suicide (the former because to have killed himself there would have implied too great a crime; and the latter because its bloodstained mats would have implied that he was blameless) he knelt in the corridor, removed the dagger from its scabbard and cut open first his belly, and then his throat.

His brother-in-law entered the corridor and knelt before him. Though the blood gushed, Anami remained upright. 'Shall I help you?' his brother-in-law asked.

'No,' choked Anami, 'leave me.'

*   *   *

But not even so cruel and scrupulous a seppuku could atone for the Army's latest crimes. Already city papers had printed its pronouncement that it was in revolt against a cowardly government. Already the Palace Police had been disarmed, and every telephone line with the outside world severed. Already dozens of Palace doors had been kicked in, dozens of desks and cupboards ransacked, dozens of court officials threatened. 'But what fools they are,' Kido lamented from his hiding place. 'It's too late to achieve anything now.'

A chamberlain was waylaid. 'We're looking for the Emperor's recording,' he was told by a bellowing second lieutenant. 'You know where it is. And you know where Kido is, don't you?'

'How *would* I know?' the chamberlain parried.

'Kill him,' shouted one of the lieutenant's squad.

'And what will you gain by that?' the chamberlain demanded. So they beat him up instead.

Suzuki's official residence had been attacked, as had Kido's home; and the NHK building had been cordoned off by angry guardsmen. But then one of the principal conspirators had come to the Palace and told the mutineers that they had no chance of success: that if they occupied the Palace any longer they would find themselves under attack from General Tanaka's Eastern Army.

As the man primarily responsible for the Emperor's safety in Tokyo, Tanaka had wanted to kill himself as long ago as 1944, when the Palace had been partially destroyed during an air raid he could not conceivably have prevented: now he was determined to put an end to this much worse insult to His Majesty. Later, nothing would

121

deter him from suicide; but first he must ensure that the Emperor's orders were obeyed, and that the Emperor himself was safe.

Unaware of which, Hirohito, who had just been awakened and given details of the coup, said, 'I will go outside myself. Gather the troops together in the garden and I will speak to them. I will explain my decision to the Imperial Guards myself.'

Remote in his personal quarters from the official buildings through which the mutineers had rampaged, he had slept undisturbed; but it clearly did not occur to him to remain remote, though no one knew better than he, who had personally quelled the mutiny of 1936, how dangerous the Army could be when it decided to reject the rule of government.

It was General Tanaka, however, who spoke to the mutineers in the Palace grounds, and convinced them that their cause was futile. And as suddenly as it had begun, it was over. The ringleaders withdrew and killed themselves on the lawn in front of the Palace; Tojo's son-in-law followed their example; the Imperial Guards stomped back to their barracks; and the siege of the NHK building was raised.

'Everything is all right now,' Tanaka advised one of the Emperor's chamberlains. 'I deeply regret that so much inconvenience has been caused.' Only a Japanese would have referred to a mutiny as 'so much inconvenience'; and only a Japanese would have interpreted the words to mean that a disaster had just been averted. The long night was over.

But not for Anami, who had knelt in an hour long agony. Finally his brother-in-law took up the discarded dagger, plunged it into the general's neck, watched him topple forward and draped his corpse with his bemedalled uniform.

Having received from
His Imperial Majesty
many great favours
I have no final statement
to make to posterity,

his testament read. But then came his post-script:

In the conviction that our sacred land will never perish, I offer my life to the Emperor as an apology for the great crime.

Loyal to the last, Anami had not merely taken his life; in his postscript he had echoed the sentiments he knew to be the main burden of a Rescript he had chosen not to hear broadcast – that

Japan must live on, its people dedicating themselves to the nation's reconstruction.

*　　　*　　　*

15 August was a broiling day, and all over the country Hirohito's subjects were wondering what they would hear when their Emperor spoke to them.

At 11.30 a.m. the recording for which the conspirators had searched half the previous night was delivered to Studio 8 of the NHK building. Just before noon, Hirohito sat down by a radio to listen to his own voice. General Tojo and his wife knelt before their radio. In every street people knelt beneath loudspeakers attached to lamp posts. At every factory and back street workshop, in every house and office and barrack, all work stopped and all traffic halted as the people of Japan knelt and waited.

'A broadcast of the greatest importance is about to commence,' radios and loudspeakers warned them. 'All listeners will please rise.'

Of the whole nation, apart from the sick and disabled, only Hirohito remained seated.

'His Majesty the Emperor will now read the Imperial Rescript to the people of Japan,' said the announcer. 'We respectfully transmit his voice.'

'To Our good and loyal subjects,' it said. 'After pondering deeply the general trends of the world and the conditions actually obtaining in our Empire today, we have decided to effect a settlement of the present situation by resorting to an extraordinary measure.

'We have ordered Our Government to communicate to the Governments of the United States, Great Britain, China and the Soviet Union that Our Empire accepts the provisions of their joint Declaration.'

Which meant nothing especially ominous to the people of Japan who had been told nothing of the Potsdam Declaration and none of the details of the Notes cabled between Tokyo and Washington over the past six days.

'To strive for the common prosperity and happiness of all nations, as well as the security and well being of Our subjects, is the solemn duty which has been handed down by Our Imperial Ancestors and which lies close to Our heart.'

Whatever followed, it was now understood, was not merely for the well-being of Japan, but of all nations.

123

'Indeed, We declared war on America and Britain out of Our sincere desire to ensure Japan's self-preservation and the stabilization of East Asia, it being far from Our thoughts either to infringe upon the sovereignty of other nations or to embark upon territorial aggrandizement.'

Which may well have been true of Hirohito himself, but was a bare-faced lie by those who had written the Rescript for him.

'But now,' the thin, deliberately high-pitched voice went on, 'the war has lasted for nearly four years, and despite the best that has been done by everyone – the gallant fighting of the military and naval forces, the diligence and assiduity of Our Servants of the State and the devoted service of Our hundred million people – the war situation has developed not necessarily to our advantage, while the general trends of the world have all turned against Our Empire's interests.

'Moreover, the enemy has begun to employ a new and most cruel bomb, the power of which to do damage is indeed incalculable as it takes its toll of so many innocent lives. Should we continue to fight, not only would that lead to the ultimate collapse and obliteration of the Japanese nation, but it would also lead to the extinction of human civilization.'

For the second time it was being made clear that it was not of the Japanese alone that the Emperor was thinking, but of all mankind; not even Hirohito can have believed that.

'Such being the case,' the voice proceeded inexorably, 'how are We to save the millions of Our subjects or to atone Ourselves before the hallowed spirits of Our Imperial Ancestors? It is to that end that We have ordered the acceptance of the provisions of the joint Declaration of the Allied Powers.

'We cannot but express the deepest sense of regret to Our allied nations of East Asia, who have consistently co-operated with the Empire to secure the emancipation of East Asia,' the Imperial voice asserted.

Comparatively few of those listening to it appreciated that Japan's allied nations had never been willing allies and were all now rejoicing in her defeat; but that was not the real import of Hirohito's words – which were an oblique invitation to the colonies of East Asia to seek emancipation from their masters, Britain, France and Holland.

Hirohito had doubtless felt more sincere, and no one can doubt his sincerity, as he recorded the words that followed.

'The thought of those officers and men, as well as others, who have fallen on the battlefield, of those who died at their posts of duty, or of those who met with untimely death, and of all their bereaved families, pains Our heart night and day.

'The welfare of the wounded and the war sufferers, and of those who have lost their homes and livelihood, are the objects of Our profound solicitude.'

Then came the crunch, and the exhortation.

'The hardships and sufferings to which Our nation is to be subjected hereafter will certainly be great. We are keenly aware of the innermost feelings of you all. However, it is in accordance with the dictates of time and fate that We have resolved to pave the way for a grand peace for all the generations to come by enduring the unendurable and suffering what is insufferable.

'Having been able to safeguard and maintain the structure of the Imperial State' – a generous lie aimed at averting any opposition to the coming occupation – 'We are always with you, Our good and loyal subjects, and We are relying upon your sincerity and integrity.

'Beware most strictly any outbursts of emotion which may cause needless complications, or any fraternal contention and strife which may create confusion and lead you astray and cause you to lose the confidence of the outside world.

'Let the entire nation continue as one family from generation to generation, ever firm in its faith in the imperishability of its sacred land, and ever mindful of its heavy responsibilities and of the long road ahead.

'Unite your total strength and devote it to rebuilding for your future. Cultivate the ways of rectitude; foster nobility of spirit; and work with resolution so that you may enhance the innate glory of the Imperial State and keep pace with the progress of the rest of the world.'

As he sat in his Palace, head bowed, and listened to his own words, Hirohito must have known that he alone of the Heads of State of the three defeated Axis powers had spoken to his people as a leader should; that he had touched the heart of every one of his subjects; that he had given them hope even as he prepared them for the worst; and, above all, that he had never once mentioned the word surrender. In short, that he had laid down the guide lines for their spectacular future.

CHAPTER THIRTEEN

>>>>>>><<<<<<<

'All you Men have
Bright Futures'

SWITCHING OFF HIS RADIO, Tojo turned to his wife and said, 'Well, up till now it's been our life for our country. Now things have changed, and reconstruction may be more difficult than giving our lives. But, if that is the Emperor's will, we must do everything we can to bring it about as long as we live.'

At that moment the telephone rang and Tojo was told of his son-in-law's suicide. He warned his daughter that her husband's body was being brought home. Completely composed, his daughter observed that in death her husband would remain forever a major.

All over Japan, but particularly in Tokyo, there were suicides; and outside the Palace people were kneeling, foreheads touching the ground, murmuring, 'Forgive us, oh Emperor, our efforts were not enough.'

Doubtless, Hirohito's generals overseas heard his broadcast, but if one is to judge by the reaction of those who guarded us in Johore, the rank and file of the Imperial Japanese Army did not. While their comrades in Japan wept, mutinied and killed themselves, they behaved as they always had done.

The likelihood is that they were also told nothing of Anami's last order cabled to all Headquarters under his name the day before the Imperial Broadcast. *The Emperor has made his decision*, it began. *The Army expects you to obey that decision and make no unauthorized moves that would disgrace the glorious traditions of the Imperial Army and its many distinguished achievements. You must so behave as never to incur the judgement of posterity. It is expected of you that your conduct will enhance the honour and glory of the Imperial Japanese Forces in the eyes of the world.*

Yet mere hours after the war had been terminated, those American fliers who had survived Fukuoda's first and second mass-acres were taken down the same road to the same field outside

126

Aburayama, stripped, driven into the nearby woods and cut to ribbons in a carnival of swordsmanship.

*   *   *

Knowing none of this in Malaya, we nevertheless knew our Imperial Japanese Army; and when our guards ordered us out to work as usual, we behaved as usual, carefully concealing from them the fact that they had lost the war; until someone came and disarmed them, none of us was safe.

For those Japanese in detention in Australia, the situation was very different. 'Gentlemen,' their Australian commandant told them, 'the war is over – and with it the life you have had to endure as prisoners of war. No doubt you will be able to return home within a few months.'

They were appalled. In his broadcast the Emperor had specifically exonerated everyone except those who had allowed themselves to become prisoners of the enemy. They found the prospect of going home frightening.

For the moment, though, it was we who should have been frightened, because Itagaki, now standing in as Commander in Chief in South East Asia for Field Marshal Terauchi, who was ill, was on the point of disobeying Hirohito. Speaking of and to his hitherto undefeated forces, he broadcast from Singapore that they had 'an unchallenged dignity' and were eager to 'crush the foe'. Although the ashes of war were two days old, its embers still glowed wickedly in the Philippines, Indo-China, Thailand, Burma and Malaya.

*   *   *

Japan's press and radio were already taking up the Emperor's plea of mitigation. The war had been lost, they insisted, because of the Allies' 'scientific offensive'. Defeat was only temporary. The sooner the Allies were convinced that the Japanese had submitted to their terms – by accepting occupation, the prosecution of war criminals and a change of government – the sooner they would be gone.

Nor was General Tanaka prepared to fail his Emperor a third time. When a group of students threatened further rebellion, he told them, 'All you men have bright futures. It is you who must lead Japan from now on. The atom bomb has changed the state of the war completely. It is the will of god that we abandon the long history of the Japanese Army. New generations will come. Please concentrate on the construction of a new nation.' On the ninth day of Japan's defeat, he shot himself.

But we were as yet enjoying only the third day of a decidedly muted victory, working in our tunnel and suddenly examining every green pit prop with acute mistrust. There was no news, because our enterprising thief, upon hearing the whispered *Red Light*, had thrown his radio down a thirty foot borehole from which, since boreholes were used as latrines, no one had felt inclined to retrieve it.

It was either that morning or the next that we were called out of our tunnel to be confronted by a Japanese colonel. His jack-boots were glossy, his sword too long, and his face wreathed in a strangely avuncular smile. He saluted us and bowed. Warily we bowed back.

'War finish,' he said. 'All men go home' – and bowed again. We remained vertical.

*   *   *

'If you insist upon this form of surrender,' Slim's advisers assured him in the days of Itagaki's sullen procrastination, 'all the Japanese senior officers will commit hara kiri.'

'Offer them every facility,' Slim had retorted – and it was Itagaki who had compromised. But he and the rest of the Imperial Japanese Army had elected to live not because Slim had made it obvious that he was quite happy for them to die, but because Suzuki had recorded a message (which was broadcast on the hour every hour, from 6 p.m. till midnight) saying, 'So far as the preservation of our national structure is concerned, I have a positive plan. You must all behave with the utmost calm, maintaining a dispassionate attitude.'

And dispassionate they were; and almost relaxed – because at that time they believed that the Emperor had 'terminated the war', not surrendered. It was ten years, in fact, before the Japanese admitted that their armies had surrendered rather than stopped fighting. *Shusen* was the word they used until 1955; but then they changed it to *haisen*.

In Changi we ignored the Imperial Japanese Army, lay in the sun, ate regular meals (of rice, which suddenly was available in abundance) and waited for someone to take us home.

Eventually, Mountbatten's fleet and soldiers arrived – so big and fit we were unable to believe that we had ever been their equals – and looked fierce when they saw what the Japanese had done to us. Lord Mountbatten (whom we had dubbed Linger Longer Louis when he failed to release us in 1944) arrived the following day. Standing on a wooden box in our gaol courtyard he told us that he knew what we had called him, and said, 'So now I'll tell you why I lingered so long!' The delay had been caused by the people planning the invasion of Normandy and southern France. 'Every time I was ready to invade Malaya,' he said 'they pinched my landing craft.' We forgave him instantly. And when he said that he had come to Singapore to accept Itagaki's surrender, we roared our enthusiasm. We had waited a long time to witness the Imperial Japanese Army's surrender.

But our senior Australian officer indulged himself in one last officious fling and ordered us *not* to go into the city. I suppose he thought we might get lost. A number of us ignored him. Watching Itagaki hand his sword to Mountbatten was a perfect way of celebrating the war's end – and a marvellous moment of theatre.

*   *   *

Great theatrical experiences suspend all disbelief in their audiences, and we who watched Itagaki submit to Mountbatten were no exception. There were huge gaps in the drama we had witnessed, yet it never occurred to us even to ask how the intransigent Imperial Japanese Army, in a matter only of days, had been transformed from fanaticism to compliance. Satiated with the drama we had merely *seen*, we were incurious about the Japanese, and asked no questions. We just waited for ships to come and take us home, serenely uninterested in the details of Japan's formal surrender to MacArthur on the decks of the *Missouri* in Tokyo Bay, and completely unenthused by the prospect of the promised War Trials. Not because we disapproved of them: simply because we had won the war and thought nothing Japanese any longer mattered.

The day of departure – and of partings – came abruptly. As I walked toward the convoy of jeeps that would transport us to the docks, I passed one of the Imperial Japanese Army's few English-speaking officers who was being escorted into the gaol. In a spirit half of elation and half of spite, I turned and shouted, 'This war last one hundred years?'

'Ninety-six years to go,' he called back; and neither of us bothered to bow.

129

CHAPTER FOURTEEN

>>>>>>><<<<<<<

'Torches Don't Dance'

WE SAILED HOME and, unbeknownst to us, the Imperial Japanese Army went into captivity. Had we known it I think we would have disapproved: the Japanese had been cruel to everyone, including themselves, but they had not been perverse, like the Nazis. We wanted no more to do with them, not even as vicarious captors, still less as vicarious executioners.

The vessel on which we travelled was battered and inelegant, and the food as primitive as our accommodation, which was on the open deck; but none of the voyages I have taken since, on liners that were shamelessly luxurious, has matched that one on the *Arawa*. Thumping her way through glassy seas, she bore us unhurriedly toward Australia.

It was an idyllic voyage – until the morning we were due to dock at Darwin. Then, at the instigation of whom I shall never know, we were ordered to queue up and examine a photograph of a half-naked, bearded, blindfolded young man kneeling by the feet of a Japanese officer who was about to cut off his head. It was not suggested that any of us might know the victim, or be able to identify his executioner; nor was any other reason given for submitting us to so distasteful an exercise. The idyll was spoiled.

A week later, however, our voyage ended and all such images were expunged from our dazed minds by the extravagance of our welcome. Driven in open cars between huge crowds, we were cheered, kissed, patted and handed bunches of flowers. Had we been Lindbergh returning to New York after his trans-Atlantic flight to France, or the Beatles en route to Liverpool in the sixties, we could not have been received with more abandon. All we had done was surrender of course, so it was more than we deserved; but nice. Briefly, we even thought that nothing had changed during our absence.

But it had, all over the world, for ever. And nowhere more cruelly than in Japan, about whose fate I thought not at all, and about whose defeated armies we spoke not much more, because no one was very interested – until an invitation came to attend at Victoria Barracks there to meet a legal officer.

He sat behind a table on which rested a pile of dossiers, a virgin pad of lined paper and his folded hands. Had I, he wanted to know, witnessed any atrocities?

I said that was not what I wanted to talk about. He asked what I wanted to talk about. I said Japan's hundred year war and the communist insurrection about to erupt in Korea. He allowed me to expatiate on these two themes for all of a minute, then changed the subject back to atrocities. He wanted dates, places and names.

I told him that I was unable to remember the date of the murders I had *heard* being committed, was unsure of the place where they had *been* committed and had not had the privilege of being introduced to any of the murderers.

Scrabbling his way through a dossier, he gave me the date and place of the murders of those taken for questioning from the copra shed by the side of the road that ran west to Ayer Hitham. All he needed from me, he said, was a description of the murderers. I began to suspect that it was he who had made us look at the photograph on the ship outside Darwin. I have never met a man so obsessed with atrocities.

The better to escape him, I told him that each victim had been selected by the arbitrary beam of a torch. The torch had come to the entrance of the copra shed, danced up and down, flashed from one figure to the next, and eventually settled on a face.

'Torches don't dance,' he corrected.

'Synecdoche,' I told him. He looked blank. 'The use of a part for the whole,' I defined.

'Describe the whole,' he demanded.

The whole having been no more than a silhouette in the night-light, I was unable to oblige. 'But it was a big torch,' I told him helpfully.

He handed me a batch of photographs of Japanese soldiers and asked did I recognize any of them. They were the sort of photographs normally seen on passports and could have been likenesses of almost anyone in the Imperial Japanese Army except General Tojo. I told him so.

He dismissed me with the instruction that I was to go back to my college and write a full report of the events of that night. I made a last

131

effort to convince him about Korea's imminent insurrection and Japan's continuing war. His pen went nowhere near his pad of lined paper. I returned to college and wrote a graphic account of the dancing torch and the sound of half a dozen men being done to death. I did not hear from him again.

Nor, to be honest, did I pursue the matters of a possible conflict in Korea and a resurgent Japan winning her war against the West some time in the next 96 years. The Australian public had been warned that we would all be a little mad. Now that we were home no one thought it wise to let us talk about our experiences; so I played a lot of tennis and left the safety of the world to saner minds than mine.

But then, in 1950, came the Korean War; and one insane suspicion having been confirmed, my second returned.

I read the text of the Imperial Rescript of 15 August 1945, and my fears grew. I read Toshikasu Kase's *Eclipse of the Rising Sun*, which asserted the logic of Japan and China becoming sister nations, and was alarmed by the prospect of such an alliance. I watched the protective arm of Holland, France and Britain being shrugged off the shoulders of South East Asia, and was dismayed. And I greeted the United Nations' inability to do better than draw their war in Korea with a despair exceeded only by my terror when America started a war in Vietnam that I was certain she would lose. The Imperial Japanese Army had educated me: I would have been half-witted had I thought otherwise.

In 1965 I wrote a book postulating America's defeat in Vietnam by 1972, thus leaving the whole of Asia and Australasia defenceless before the mighty sisterhood of China and a remilitarised Japan; but it was 1968 before I began to realize that I had completely misread Hirohito's Rescript – that the second stage of her Hundred Year War was to be fought not on battlefields but on the factory floor.

The question then became, could she beat the West at its own industrial game? And if she could, with how great a victory would she be satisfied? Or would she demand, as the West had demanded of her, nothing less than unconditional surrender?

Today only the last two questions remain unanswered; and the third question poses two more. First, has she acquired the self-control (which she lacked in 1942) to demand less than unconditional surrender. Second, if no less a victory than global economic domination will satisfy her, how will the rest of the world react? To answer

132

those two questions, we must first learn to understand the Japanese a great deal better than we do. To do that, we must revert to the day of their defeat, and to the man who made it possible for them to surrender.

CHAPTER FIFTEEN

>>>>>>><<<<<<<<

'I am not concerned
with what may happen to me'

Accustomed though Japan had been, since time immemorial, to the shock of earthquakes and the fury of typhoons, she had never known so catastrophic a day as 15 August 1945. In her long history she had seen cities destroyed and the innocent slaughtered, war lords toppled and millions of workers made unemployed; but never before had she faced defeat, occupation and the wrath of the outside world. She contemplated the retribution to come with terror and shame, and has forgotten neither.

As he broadcast to them, Hirohito had had no need to tell his subjects that this day would see the obliteration of everything that the Meiji and Showa Restorations had meant to them. The mere fact that they were being allowed to hear his voice proved that. And elliptic though his language had been about the causes of the war, and the reasons for terminating it, he had left them in no doubt that the Japan they knew was dead, that they had no choice but to build a new one.

Peace had come strangely enough even in Europe, who had known war for only six years, and to America, who had known it only three and a half; but to Japan, who had known it for almost fifteen, it came like a massive stroke that left her almost paralyzed and witless.

She had waged her long war with frenzied xenophobia; but it had brought her only desolation. It had brought that to Germany too: but Germany's was a brief history in which defeat, being not unknown, had held fewer terrors. Japan's was long and hitherto inviolable, and her terror was compounded by her dislike of everything unexpected.

Certain things she could anticipate, and either forestall or prepare to endure. Thus she sent as many of her daughters as possible to the country and dressed the others unbecomingly to avert the expected epidemic of rape. She left it to her militarists to find their own escape from prosecution as war criminals by seppuku; and awaited the long-promised gouging out of eyes and cutting off of noses with stoic disbelief.

It was the imponderables of defeat that the Japanese dreaded most, however. For how long would the shame of occupation endure? How profoundly would their war-time sincerity be doubted? How could they reconstruct Japan?

The humiliating surrender ceremony conducted on the deck of the *USS Missouri* in no way reduced their anxiety. Shigemitsu had been accorded none of the courtesy due to an old man. The defeated generals Wainwright and Percival had attended and gloated. And MacArthur had been unchivalrously curt. 'Let us pray that peace be now restored to the world and that God will preserve it always,' he had said – as if only Japan was to blame for the war. 'These proceedings are closed.'

*   *   *

If the second half of August was a time of anguish for the people of Japan, it was a time of degradation for 50,000 of the Imperial Japanese Army in the Philippines, who had still not come out of the jungle to surrender, and for Kimura's few thousand survivors in Burma who were still fighting.

'We had lost all dignity and wandered like a pack of wild dogs,' one of Yamashita's soldiers was to write about his last months in the Philippines. 'To survive, we dug yams and caught crabs and rats and snakes from the swamp.' But most of all they had to elude the Filipinos, of whom they had killed more than 100,000, and who now offered them no quarter.

'We were expected to suffer, suffer and then to die,' wrote a veteran of Burma. 'Grass and pieces of wood were our food.' Of the 1400 who originally had made up his unit, only 48 had survived to go into captivity. Slim's men had been killing them at the rate of 100 for each of their own men killed. But, scorning all of XIV Army's efforts to induce them to surrender, Kimura's men had fought on.

'Soon it will be the dread mosquito season,' leaflets had warned them. 'Men bitten by these insects lose their sexual potency: they become half men. Come over to us. We will give you good, warm food.'

But sexual impotence was no deterrent to men convinced that

135

they could never go home; and good, warm food was no inducement to men convinced that any fate was preferable to surrender.

'The strength of the Japanese Army lay in the spirit of the individual Japanese soldier,' wrote Field Marshal Slim. 'He fought and marched till he died. If 500 Japanese were ordered to hold a position, we had to kill 495 before it was ours – and then the last 5 killed themselves.'

But at least those who were tricked into laying down their arms by the ambivalence of their Emperor's Rescript, and Tokyo's subsequent orders, were to prove themselves almost human once they had been put behind barbed wire. 'We found ourselves living in huts like pig sties,' snarls Yuji Aida of the accommodation provided for them by the British – quite disregarding the fact that those same huts had hitherto been the accommodation provided by his Army for us.

That said, however, it cannot be denied that his description of the society to which eventually he was repatriated in 1947 is strikingly succinct. 'In Japan,' he wrote, 'times were very bad.'

Even worse was the invisible havoc that had been wrought by the war at sea. As well as her entire navy, Japan had lost 8,600,000 tons of merchant vessels. Indeed, Aida and his comrades had spent up to two years in captivity simply because there were no Japanese vessels on which to repatriate them whilst the first priority of Allied vessels was to feed Europe and repatriate Allied armies.

All too long, then, 500,000 Japanese soldiers had languished in captivity. Yet time after time, as they caught their first glimpse of the sacred homeland from the decks of ships belatedly repatriating them, they had killed themselves rather than inflict on their families the shame of their 'surrender'.

These, then, were the subjects, civilian as well as military, to whom Hirohito would direct his words a second time when he addressed their Diet a few days after the surrender.

'It is our desire,' he declared, 'that Our People will surmount the manifold hardships and trials attending the termination of the war and, making manifest the innate glory of Japan's national polity, win the confidence of the world and contribute to the progress of mankind.'

If Churchill was the architect of the Allies' victory in World War II, Hirohito must be said to have been the architect of Japan's industrial counter-offensive against its former conquerors; but no one in Japan ever says so.

*   *   *

At the war's end, however, his ex-enemies had been much less reticent. The governments of Holland and Australia had wanted him deposed at least, as had a lobby of Republicans in Washington who considered monarchies no less reprehensible than empires. There were even those in MacArthur's entourage who presumed to suggest to him that Hirohito be tried as a war criminal – or at least summoned to the general's headquarters like a common criminal.

But MacArthur had declined. Thanks to the discipline of the Japanese, and the easy-going generosity of the American forces under his command, the occupation had been achieved without incident. True to their traditions, the Japanese had almost unthinkingly transferred their allegiance to the dominant power in their land, which was now an army of occupation comprised almost entirely of Americans.

Who, far from gouging out Japanese eyes and cutting off Japanese noses, seemed anxious only to spend large sums of money, share their gum and get themselves laid. Finding them infinitely more congenial than their own militarists had ever been, the Japanese unlocked their daughters, set up a chain of brothels, provided anybody who wanted one with a charming mistress, and forgot their terror. Life would remain 'very hard', but at least there were no longer any Thought Police to monitor their every word, no Kempeitai to torture them, and no generals to demand that they die for their Emperor.

It was MacArthur, in fact, who now ruled Japan; and he ruled it as not even the great Shoguns of the Toshugawa family had thought to rule it. Half amused, half incredulous, his subordinates said that he was often to be observed walking on the waters of the palace moat, and called him Our Father Which Art in Tokyo. The Japanese called him the Blue-eyed Shogun. Nevertheless, he frequently displayed an understanding of his subjects that no foreign statesman has since matched. Thus, far from summoning Hirohito to his presence (which, as he said, 'would be to outrage the feelings of the Japanese people and make a martyr of the Emperor'), he waited for Hirohito to solicit an interview with him. And quite soon the appointment was made, and Hirohito, small, bespectacled and nervous arrived. 'I come to you, General MacArthur,' said the man who only weeks before had been deemed a god by all in his land, 'to offer myself to the judgment of the Powers you represent as the one to bear sole responsibility for every political and military decision made. and action taken, by my people in the conduct of the war.'

Before the surrender, he had told those assembled in his palace bomb shelter, 'I am not concerned with what may happen to me: I want to preserve the lives of my people.' Now he had come to MacArthur to prove that he had been indulging in no mere rhetoric.

It has been argued, of course, that the sole responsibility *was* his. But the truth is something that only he knows; and he, with monumental impassivity, declined until 1971 ever to elaborate on those few words he spoke to General MacArthur.

In 1971, however, on a State Visit to Britain, where an unforgiving public virtually ignored him, he broke his silence at a banquet at Buckingham Palace. 'We cannot pretend,' he said, 'that the relations between our two peoples have always been peaceful and friendly.' But added, 'It is precisely this experience which should make us all determined never to let it happen again.'

Unmoved, the British continued to ignore him; and, when he went to Holland, the Dutch responded with overt hostility. Noting that everywhere on his tour the speeches of welcome were 'perfunctory', the Japanese press began to carp that the tour was 'ill advised'. Undeterred, Hirohito plodded on. His task was to re-establish his nation's credentials in the eyes of a still contemptuous world: he was 'not concerned' with what might happen to him.

Worse, though, was to come when David Bergamini's massively researched book, *Japan's Imperial Conspiracy*, charged him with personal responsibility for starting and conducting the Pacific War, and for condoning all the atrocities perpetrated by his forces during it. In November 1971, he submitted himself to his first press conference and, denying Bergamini's accusations, insisted that he had acted throughout the years of Japan's aggression only 'as a constitutional monarch'.

If, in fact, he was guilty, his refusal in 1945 to stay silent until the likes of General Tojo could cover up for him, as they planned to do at their trials, was the act of a man whose integrity should not be denied. If, however, he was innocent, his 1945 attempt to offer himself to MacArthur's judgement, thereby to expiate thousands of crimes, to save the lives of thousands of war criminals, and to exculpate an entire nation, was a huge sacrifice for so small a man.

*   *   *

Beyond doubt, the crimes of which some would still accuse him sprang originally from the militarist adventures upon which his army embarked in 1931. In March of that year the Army assassinated its most prominent opponents in Tokyo. The only excuse it gave was that it was 'purging' Hirohito of those influences that made him unsympathetic to the Army's intentions. He could hardly have been a party to the militarist's plot if he was at the same time so unsympathetic to it that he needed 'purging'.

The Army had next faked an 'incident' in Manchuria, to justify its occupation of much of that province. 'We are now in a constitutional crisis.' Kido confided to his dairy as one incident followed another in China.

By 1936 the government was totally at odds with its generals, who were themselves being intimidated by their junior officers; but if the government had had its way, a policy of good neighbourliness with China would shortly have been initiated. The Army, therefore, embarked upon yet another voyage of assassination.

This, the then Minister of War explained to a furious Emperor, was simply another 'incident' aimed at removing 'bad influences'. To which Hirohito brusquely retorted that it was not an incident but a mutiny; and tartly enjoined, 'Whatever their excuses, I am displeased with this "incident" that has brought disgrace on our national character.' He then made his Imperial wishes uncompromisingly clear. 'I want this rebellion ended. And I want its instigators punished. See that it is done.'

As Tokyo thereupon ground to a halt, and an armed uprising seemed inevitable, a young officer burst into Hirohito's presence, bearing a statement of the rebels' demands. His orders were that he was to kill the Emperor should His Majesty decline to ratify the statement. Confronted by this fanatic, Hirohito leaped from his seat and snarled, 'How dare you come in here? Do you not know that I am your Emperor?'

At which the would-be assassin knelt before him, his forehead touching the floor, then, bowing repeatedly, withdrew abjectly. Upon his return to his fellow mutineers, he apologized for his insult to the Emperor and killed himself.

The Emperor's fury was swiftly known to all; but, convinced of the rightness of their cause, the ringleaders demanded a public trial at which they could expatiate upon the government's disloyalty.

Hirohito expressly forbade it. 'It is not to be forgiven,' he said. Nor would he allow the fifteen ringleaders to commit hara kiri before one of his chamberlains, who then could report to him their act of apology. Nor, once they had been sentenced to death, would he allow them the privilege (invariably accorded officers facing execution) of a silk screen between them and the firing squad. And least of all would he allow their ashes to be sent to their families.

Seven statesmen – among them two admirals, one of whom was the premier – had been assassinated, all of them devoted to the cause of peace. Fifteen officers had been executed, and eighty more either jailed or dismissed the service, all of them devoted to the cause of war. Tragically for the Emperor, however, the man chosen to root out the remaining hotheads from the Kwangtung Army was General Tojo, whose progress to the premiership began with that assignment. By 1937 Hirohito knew no more about the China Incident than the Army cared to disclose – and it certainly did not wish to disclose the details of the rape of Nanking to an Emperor whose Rescript for his soldiers at the time warned: 'If you neglect valour, and act violently, the world will come to detest you, and look upon you as a wild beast.'

With Hirohito's approval, Koki Hirota, a commoner, was made premier in an effort to reduce international tensions; but the Army refused to nominate a Minister for his War Cabinet unless it also approved his Minister for the Navy. Either could then resign at any time and no replacement be nominated. Then there would be no government. A precedent had been established. The last obstacle to a military dictatorship had been removed. But Hirohito had played no part in that. By punishing the Army in 1936, he had merely precipitated it.

With Hirota hamstrung in his attempts to restore peace with China, the Kwangtung Army planned fresh adventures. In 1938 it attacked the Soviet Union's border forces. The Russians gave it a bloody nose and Hirohito gave it a tongue-lashing, forbidding any further such enterprises. His instructions were disregarded at Nomonham, and his armed forces took another hiding. Clearly, Asia was a softer option. The march toward war became a gallop; but the reins of power were never in Hirohito's hands.

In 1940 it was one Toson Shimazaki, not Hirohito, who wrote the Battlefield Commandment; and it was not Hirohito who had it promulgated in January, 1941, but the then Minister of War, General Tojo. With that little book in their breast pocket, Hirohito's devoted soldiers had marched to war.

In which, all too soon, Japan had been destined for defeat. Nevertheless, Tojo was still expressing his confidence as to the outcome as late as June 1943, and Hirohito was the only man ever to challenge him. 'You keep saying the Imperial Army is indomitable,' he protested, 'but whenever the enemy lands, you lose the battle. You have never been able to repulse an enemy landing. If we do not find somewhere to stop them, where, I ask you, is this war going to end?'

But then had come the destruction of Hiroshima; and Hirohito had declared, 'This tragedy must not be repeated.' At his meeting with the Supreme Council on 10 August, he not only repeated the harsh words he had once said to Tojo, he also laced them with sarcasm. He was tired, he made it plain, of bombastic plans, 'final battles' and broken Army promises.

When the War Ministry sought to pre-empt the Foreign Office's conditional acceptance of the Allied demands on 11 August, it was he who summoned Anami to his presence and so fiercely rebuked him that the War Minister thereafter devoted all of his efforts to ensuring that the Imperial decision was obeyed.

When the Army and Navy Chiefs of Staff sought to change that decision, he remained adamant. When Suzuki requested his decision a second time, he gave it in the most explicit language. And never once did he seek to justify his conduct as Emperor. It must therefore be assumed either that he had nothing to justify, or that he was guilty and being guilty would commit seppuku.

Yet he had not done so, even though such an omission in a man who was guilty of planning the war and condoning the way it was conducted would have indicated a lack of sincerity – or courage.

But no one has ever charged him with lacking courage. Nor, since it was he who lamented of Konoye's suicide that it was 'such a shoddy way to die', can he convincingly be accused of lacking sincerity. And even were he both cowardly and insincere, the fact remains that without him the Japanese war would have ended in a holocaust.

Japan today is the poorer for the fact that Hirohito's new role as a democratic monarch has deprived her of his logical mind and his lucid command of her complex language. Either she must find a statesman like him, or the West must speak to her as he did. Failing that, 'the world situation will develop not necessarily to our advantage'.

CHAPTER SIXTEEN

>>>>>>>><<<<<<<

The Tomb of the
Seven Martyrs

BECAUSE HE REALIZED that Hirohito was for the moment the lynch-pin of the edifice over which he presided, and perhaps because he found him guiltless anyway, MacArthur refused to take action against the Emperor. For the moment he merely offered him a cigarette – at which the Emperor, a non-smoker, puffed nervously but politely before the general packed him off home to his palace.

To others MacArthur was less generous; and, about one of them, less discerning. General Yamashita was arrested as a war criminal in the Philippines, convicted and executed, although his record in the Malayan campaign had been exemplary, the rapists and looters of Penang having been summarily punished at his insistence and the atrocities at Alexandra Hospital having been Tsuji's doing, not his. The atrocities perpetrated against the citizens of Manila in the last days of the war were likewise not his responsibility. They were committed by a naval contingent whose participation in the campaign he had expressly forbidden.

Like Yamashita, thousands more were arrested, many of them in Japan, to face trial as war criminals – among them Tojo, who sought to kill himself when American military policemen arrived at his home to take him to jail; Hirota, the commoner and liberal who had been made Premier in the hope that he could reverse the militarist trends in China; Itagaki, who had crowned an unsuccessful career in China with unfulfilled boasts of continued resistance in Malaya after the surrender; Shigemitsu who, as Foreign Minister, had alleviated the plight of Allied prisoners of war and internees not at all; and 24 others.

All these 28 had been charged either because they had been close to Hirohito, or because they had been involved in the prosecution of the war. Their show trial in Tokyo was not a distinguished example of jurisprudence. There are few who do not now regret it.

Hirota refused to defend himself at all, and was condemned to death largely because his adolescent passion for martial sports was used, in his old age, to brand him a militarist. His case could have been convincing; but it was not helped by Kido, who had always despised his lack of breeding. Kido's diary, much quoted in support of many of the accused, had deliberately excluded all references to Hirota that might have enhanced his reputation in the eyes of posterity (or, as it turned out, of an Allied court of law).

Tojo was a clever witness who seized the opportunity both to exonerate Hirohito and to reassure the Japanese people that the war they had fought had been forced upon them and been purely defensive.

The Japanese press reported him faithfully, *'War of Defence forced on us'*, one headline ran. *'Emperor not responsible'*, proclaimed another. And the rest followed suit. For the first time in his life Tojo commanded the nation's sympathy. Almost, but not quite, it forgave him for having failed to kill himself at the same time as Anami.

Six others of the accused, including Itagaki and Hirota, were condemned to death, and were hanged with Tojo in 1948. Though the people of Japan considered their sentences harsh, they accepted them as a symbolic punishment for the crimes committed by their Imperial forces – of which crimes the trials had given them their first inkling.

MacArthur, for his part, wielded the axe of democratic reform with the zeal of a nineteenth century missionary confronted by a tribe of naked – but docile – heathens. He abolished the Zaibatsu – that body of cartels that had financed both Japan's rearmament and her war. He purged the nation of most of its leading industrialists, bankers, government officials, Army and Navy officers, editors and patriotic activists – for it was they, he was afraid, who would seek to undermine his authority.

He imposed upon an Oriental people a peculiarly Western constitution – in which he insisted upon the inclusion of Article 9, whereby Japan foreswore war and even the right to rearm. He changed the system of education (which had made the Japanese the most literate race in the world) so that it resembled America's (and, as Kenichi Yoshida ruefully, if not altogether accurately, observes, made of Japanese children a breed as wilful as those in the United States). And when he left them, to run the war in Korea, he was, like many another, convinced that they were transformed, and that their nation would forever be America's grateful protégé.

About that, though, Tojo had had the last word. Just before the victors hanged him, he wrote his final testament; and warned that a third world war was inevitable. It would be between the United States and the Soviet Union; and it would be fought in Asia.

Thus forewarned, when the United States sprang to the defence of South Korea, the Japanese elected to stand on the side-lines of the conflict between *their* patron and Russia's clients. If a third world war was about to erupt, they intended being no part of it.

John Foster Dulles, as Secretary of State, told Premier Yoshida then, 'You *must* rearm.' The Japanese people, Yoshida responded, were, 'sincerely attached to Article 9'; and anyway, rearming 'was incompatible with a healthy economy'! He did, however, allow his hungry industrialists to supply the United Nations forces in Korea with material worth £567 million; and he did allow himself to be bullied into the creation of a Reserve Police Force – which has since become a compact and respected (but comparatively cheap) Defence Force – just in case Japan should ever desire to become a military power again. The nucleus is now there; and 'defence' has never meant to Japan what it means to others. Back in 1950, however, the Japanese had lost all taste for military adventures.

Nor were they to be any more inclined to participate in America's later defence of the South Vietnamese against Russia's clients, the Vietminh and the Vietcong. Not only might Tojo's promised world war still have ensued, but the Americans had only just been able to force a draw in Korea. And anyway, China, their sister nation, their largest potential market, would never have agreed to end its state of war with *them* if *they* had gone to war in support of America – which Peking now loathed just as much as it loathed Russia, its erstwhile friend.

World politics and doctrinaire wars were to exert no charm at all upon America's enigmatic protégé in 1965; she had, by then, another and much less dangerous strategy in mind. She may even have had it in mind as early as the end of 1942; and it had certainly been mooted at Tojo's Liaison Conference in 1941. It was to eat stones and sleep on logs for twenty years until Japan was America's industrial equal.

*　　*　　*

The Occupation ended shortly after the outbreak of the Korean War. Declining to rearm, as America suggested, the Japanese never-theless saw no reason to deny themselves the rich profits that would accrue from helping the American war effort. It was the Americans who had insisted that they foreswore war, in return for which they would be protected against any future enemy. With not a little complacency, *they* kept *their* word – and made sure that America kept hers. Spared the need to spend on armaments the capital they needed for reconstruction, they set about revitalizing their moribund economy.

*   *   *

But these are familiar facts. What matters is the manner in which they are interpreted, the context within which they are quoted and the background against which they are viewed. Given that Japan is waging a Hundred Year War which began in 1941 – or, as now seems more apposite, with the Triple Intervention in 1895 – even the most hackneyed aspects of her recent history lend themselves to reappraisal.

This is by no means to allege that Japan's present industrial offensive is either unethical or unfair. She is playing the capitalist game exactly as she was taught it; but now that she is winning, her principal rivals want to change the rules; France and Italy are cheating; and most of the lesser nations think it pointless even to enter the arena.

Australia, for example, has made almost no attempt to become an industrially competitive nation, and has settled complacently for a life of ease based on the sale – largely to Japan – of her agricultural and mining products. Yet eating the one, and reprocessing the other, Japan has become an industrial colossus. Had Australia been populated this last quarter century by thirty million Japanese, it would by now have become the world's richest nation. It is a lack of Japaneseness in its national character, rather than the lack of opportunity (or investment capital) that has held it back.

Yet, of all Westerners, it was the Australians of the first half of the twentieth century who, in retrospect, seem to have had most in common with the Japanese. Admittedly, any shared attitudes lay in the darker recesses of their respective souls, and became evident only in the unnatural glare of war, but the two races were by no means as dissimilar as each would have liked to think.

Like the Japanese, the Australian infantryman was unconcerned with smartness, swiftly modifying his neat uniform to the demands of the environment in which he fought. Just as the Japanese squad was

145

bound by the spirit of Ka, so was the Australian platoon bound by the spirit of what it called mateship. Like the Japanese, the Australians fought most effectively at close quarters or in the jungle. Like the Japanese, they evinced the prowling wolf-pack's instinct to surround and destroy its prey. And like the Japanese, it has been alleged that, on at least one occasion, they were murderous captors.

In his 1971 book, *Japan's Imperial Conspiracy*, David Bergamini claims that Australian commanders ordered 6000 surrendering Japanese soldiers to stack their arms at Pensiangan, in British North Borneo, and march 150 miles to the coast for internment; then encouraged vengeful local tribesmen to massacre them en route, so that only a few hundred survived.

Bergamini's source, it would seem, was K. G. Tregonning's 1967 book, *A History of Modern Sabah*, which tells the same story but makes no mention of Australian complicity.

And Tregonning's source is apparently I. H. N. Evans 1953 book, *The Religion of the Tempasuk Dasuns of North Borneo*, which mentions the display in a *few* villages of *several* shrunken Japanese heads. In every case the head came from a straggler behind the main group marching defenceless into captivity.

No primary sources support Tregonning's claim of almost 6000 victims, or Bergamini's of Australians both provoking and condoning their massacre; but there is evidence that the Australian victor took his responsibility to protect those who had surrendered to him less than seriously. And Bergamini's story does persist. Is even corroborated, some vaguely remember, by the subsequent confessions of a couple of the Australians involved. What emerges quite incontrovertibly from every effort to uncover the truth, however, is that for at least ten years after the war almost no one in Australia would have cared if 6000, or indeed 60,000 Japanese soldiers *had* died on the march into captivity because, in Australia's view, Japan had been punished far too lightly for its war-time barbarities.

Likewise (according to Japanese journalists) the benevolent reputation of the Allied Occupation Force was marred by only one instance of the sort of gang rape that disgraced Japan when her troops ran amok in Nanking. That rape was perpetrated by twenty Australians upon one Japanese girl in Hiroshima.

If the rape charge is as true of those twenty Australians in the Occupation Force as it certainly is of the Imperial Japanese Army in Nanking, it is perhaps relevant to reflect that all the guilty men represented admirable but emotionally repressed races both of which have emerged from a harsh background, both of which have long memories about the smallest slights, both of which have suffered from a sense of inferiority, and that gang rape, though still prevalent in Australia, is nowadays sublimated, so far as the Japanese are concerned, in sex tours where the participants descend as a group upon foreign bordellos.

They did so on one of Sydney's better known brothels one winter's night in 1981. Business was slow and the girls were watching television. When the group's leader rang the door bell, the proprietress answered it reluctantly, took one look at her prospective clients and slammed the door in their collective face – because she and her girls had been watching that episode in *A Town Like Alice* wherein an Australian prisoner of war was crucified.

It is not uninteresting to recall that, apart from these girls (whose profession was the marketing of sex) Australians in general evinced no hostility toward the many Japanese who visited the Commonwealth during the months when *A Town Like Alice* was being screened; and that, of all foreigners, it is with Australians that the Japanese most easily make friends.

It is likewise interesting to reflect that those other notorious rapists of World War II, the Russians, also represented a repressed society whose history is harsh, whose inferiority complex has been evident since the days of Peter the Great and whose ability to harbour grudges seems limitless.

However, even were it agreed that Japanese and Australian soldiers have in common military virtues and psychological flaws, the fact remains that today's Australians, who are rich in raw materials, would starve if their economic well-being depended upon the export of *manufactured* goods, while the Japanese, who lack almost all the necessary raw materials, have become an affluent exporting society. If the failure of the one, and the success of the other, is to be explained, it becomes necessary to pin-point those Japanese qualities which are *not* shared with Australians, and which, in fact, are lacking in Westerners in general.

It is not a difficult task; but the answer comes best from the Japanese – who describe themselves as patriotic, pragmatic, frugal, hard-working, loyal, highly educated, socially unenvious, energetic, prepared to take risks, adaptable and dedicated to the bushido principle of striking first.

They are not being boastful when they so describe themselves, each of these attributes being, in their eyes, less a virtue than an

147

obligation. As a visitor to their country, one is constantly confronted with examples of their eagerness to accept the most daunting challenges.

I asked my hotel waiter whether his job was full-time. 'Part time,' he said. 'I am also a student.'

'Of what?'

'European history.'

'Which period?'

'Period?'

'Mediaeval, modern, pre-World War II?'

'Ah so! Which period? All of it, sir!'

Herbert von Karajan tells the story of auditions held one July to find a new viola player for the Berlin Philharmonic Orchestra. Only one player, and he uninvited, was not deplorable; and he was superb. But he was a Japanese who spoke no language but his own, so he could not be hired. In September he returned, speaking German.

Dame Joan Sutherland, whose brother was a prisoner of war in Japanese hands, recalls her performances in Tokyo. 'All those little men in the orchestra pit,' she murmured, *'hurling* themselves into Mozart! They're incredible, aren't they? Mind you, I could have done without a few of those meals sitting on the floor. I haven't got the build for it.'

Mozart, a foreign language, the entire history of the whole of Europe, a railway through Thailand, it's all the same to them. Challenges have never daunted them. But the challenge they faced when the Occupation ended, and they were left to their own devices, was a daunting one indeed.

They could only live by exporting, they could only export in ships, they could only build ships with steel, they could only make steel by importing ore, they could only import in ships.

And even had they had the ships, they had no investment capital with which to rebuild their factories. Had they had investment capital, they had no fuel with which to power them. And had they had a sufficiency of oil, coal and therefore electricity, what were they to manufacture that the rest of the world would want to buy?

Not silk: the world craved only America's nylon. Not ships: Britain was the world's great builder of ships. Not steel: America made an abundance of that. Not cameras or optical lenses: the Germans made those. Not television sets: the British had invented them, and there seemed no future in them anyway. Not motor cars, nor motor-cycles: Japan had never really gone in for making them, and the rest of the world had been making them for years.

The Korean War helped, by providing them with American contracts; but still they lacked technology. So they began to buy it: to buy other nations' patents by the thousand, borrowing the money to do it.

'You're not exporting enough,' they were advised, 'because your prices are too high. And your prices are too high because you're not exporting enough.' It was 1955, and their problems seemed as insuperable as they were circular.

By 1960, though, they would know where they were going. They would even feel confident enough to erect a monument to Tojo and his six fellow war criminals who had been hanged in 1948 on which was inscribed simply, *The Tomb of the Seven Martyrs*. Perhaps it is true then, as Mr Tajitsu suggested, that Japan was applying to industry the principles of Bushido. It is certainly true that, on the 1982 anniversary of Japan's defeat in World War II, Tojo was one of those whom Premier Suzuki and most of his cabinet honoured when they visited the Yasukuni Shrine and that Suzuki's successor, Yasuhiro Nakasone, took his countrymen into 1983 with the hawkish warning that thus far Japan's military programme had been 'inadequate' – that they should be prepared to defend their country on their own.

CHAPTER SEVENTEEN

>>>>>>>><<<<<<<<

Bushido and Industry

I ASKED MANY JAPANESE how they thought the code of Bushido could be applied to the management of, or harmonization of relationships within, industry. Of the numerous examples they gave, I quote only those in which I could perceive some glimmer of relevance – and for which (substituting employee for warrior, and employer for master) I could find some form of corroboration in Yamamoto Tsumetomo's *Hagakure*.

What was most fascinating about them was the fact that so many of them were complementary. Thus, 'A man of spirit may hope to do anything his master can do;' but, 'A warrior aspires to serve his master as if his body were already dead;' because, 'in death he becomes one with his master.'

'A warrior's duty is to think always of his master;' but, 'A master who deserves a rebuke from an inferior should receive that rebuke from an equal;' and, 'In peaceful times, words demonstrate bravery.'

On the other hand, 'To be argumentative, unsociable or contrary is to be petty and stupid;' whilst, 'To be extravagant or over-proud in times of prosperity is dangerous;' and, 'At any time, a man without a daily sense of purpose deserves to be penalised.'

So much for the rights and duties of the employee, or trade unionist, vis à vis management: for management itself the admonitions were less oblique.

'At all times,' said the first precept, 'one word should be enough. A man should think before he speaks!'

He should also be paternal. 'If a master shares his profits, and feeds his inferiors, he will enjoy their loyalty.' Or, more grandly, 'If a ruler thinks of his subjects as his children, they will think of him as their parent, and their relationship will be one of harmony.'

Both employer and employee, however, would need to be Japanese to respond to the dictum that, 'Not to endure suffering is to achieve nothing good.' Perhaps my mentor was referring to the

Occupation; but his next example seemed valid. 'What matters is one's sense of purpose at any given moment, because life is merely a succession of moments.'

Next came the subject of Japan's willingness to take entrepreneurial risks, and the West's reluctance to follow her example. 'Anything can be done if one sets one's mind to it,' may sound trite; but, 'The mind of a man who chooses only to do what is most agreeable to him has already grown old,' is decidedly challenging.

The challenge was repeated. 'Be the first into battle; and if you are killed, die facing the enemy,' because, 'It is even better to die for a cause than to kill one of the enemy.'

I could hear Mr. Tajitsu saying that to his colleagues; but it lacked conviction when I imagined it coming from any of the great bankers or industrialists of the West. Much more likely that *they* would quote, 'Always be conscious of the fact that you never know what will happen next,' which sounds admirably cautious. The corollary, 'When confronted with a problem, don't hesitate,' they would doubtless omit, seeking solace instead in, 'Impatience is harmful and makes great achievement impossible.'

Each succeeding precept, however, became more alien. 'A warrior knows nothing more honourable than death,' for example; or 'When in doubt, don't hesitate – choose death.'

More akin to the spirit of Japanese industry was, 'Don't waste time thinking – attack first and kill or be killed, even if you face a thousand enemies,' because, 'By dying one avoids shame, unless one has allowed oneself to die without having at least tried to achieve one's objective.'

The Japanese general who summoned Laurens van der Post to his presence in 1945, to tell him the war had ended, assured him, 'We Japanese have decided to switch: and when we Japanese switch, we switch sincerely.' But sincerity, according to the devotees of classical bushido, is, 'becoming as a dead man in one's daily living.'

Because they switched sincerely, the Japanese have today become what they call *Japan Incorporated*: but, being sincere, they have also become as dead men at their daily post on the factory floor, or behind their desk. Which to us – who see them as people who are vibrant, excited and alive – is absurd. Therefore, 'to become a dead man' must mean something to them the true purport of which eludes the comprehension of the likes of us, and we are tempted to retreat into a less metaphysical – albeit even more alien-zone of bushido's esoteric philosophy.

'Once discretion appears on the battlefield it cannot be dismissed,' seems as apposite to risk-taking in industry as it is to valour in war; and so does, 'Win first, by preparing for victory; fight later.' But the precepts which follow disturb the Western reader's equanimity, both because they were so often put into practice by the Imperial Japanese Army, and because they derive from the original code of bushido, as written in 1716, rather than the distorted code of the Battlefield Commandment which was published in 1941.

As a fifteen-year-old, *Hagakure* tells us, Lord Katsushuge was told to practise his swordsmanship on some men condemned to death. He was offered ten victims, who stood in an unprotesting line. One after another the boy decapitated them, until only the last – a strong young man – survived. Appreciating this man's splendid physique and rude health, Katsushuge said, 'I am tired' – and allowed him to live.

'Today even lower-class children perform no executions,' lamented a contemporary of Lord Katsushuge. 'This is extreme negligence.'

A less negligent upper-class child of those long ago times went to the Execution Ground and decapitated his quota of criminals. It gave him, he confessed, 'an exteremely good feeling'. To be unnerved by the experience, he insisted 'indicated cowardice'.

And more than anything else, a samurai despised cowardice. 'If your sword be broken,' every samurai was adjured, 'strike with your hands. If your hands be severed, attack with your shoulders. If your shoulders be severed, tear open a dozen or so throats with your teeth. That is courage.'

Finally, the fate of a robber sentenced to death by torture: first, his body was singed hairless. Next, each of his fingernails was torn out. After that, each of his tendons was severed. Then he was drilled full of holes. And so it went on – until, having sliced open his back and boiled him in soy sauce, his noble executioners folded his body back in two, until the nape of his neck rested on his heels, and he died.

It comes as a shock to Westerners to realise that the field to which the captured American fliers were taken from Fukuoda, to be put to death, was just such an Execution Ground as that upon which the adolescent Katsushuge practised his swordsmanship. It is even more shocking to realise that both the manner of their execution and the techniques employed by the Kempeitai, were pre-ordained by the code of the eighteenth century samurai, not by some Japanese disciple of the Gestapo.

It is necessary, of course, to remember that all the Allied victims of the Imperial Japanese Army were, in *its* eyes, criminals sentenced to death – the American fliers being guilty of the capital offence of bombing Japan; and every Allied prisoner of war being guilty of mortal cowardice.

Deserving no more than Katsushuge's victims, or even than the robber sentenced to be tortured to death, Allied prisoners were taken to Japanese Execution Grounds and accorded no less. Confronted by criminals who were also cowards, Japanese captors were required by a code of conduct more than two hundred years old to kill no less pitilessly than the warriors of bushido's golden era had killed, and performed their duty with equal zest.

It is even possible that the squad who captured my small group of stragglers, having chosen their Execution Ground, decided to spare us as abruptly as Katsushuge decided to spare his tenth victim because (our sergeant apart, whom they later killed) we were strong and healthy.

What is impossible to decide is to what extent today's Japanese – whose television soap operas glorify the eighteenth century samurai; who buy, read and quote from copies of *Hagakure* – continue sincerely to accept precepts relating to the treatment of 'criminals' which the Western world ostensibly rejected long ago.

Undeniably the West was no less barbarous than Japan in its treatment of criminals in the sixteenth and seventeenth centuries, almost as barbarous in the eighteenth and not much less barbarous in the nineteenth – when witches may no longer have been burnt at the stake, and torture may have become a comparative rarity, but capital punishment was both public and commonplace.

Even in the twentieth century we have executed soldiers deemed guilty of cowardice, killed non-combatant civilians by the million, practised tortures much more refined than those of the samurai, and developed genocidal techniques compared to which the rape of Nanking was a momentary aberration. But we exalted none of these cruelties, exulted in none of them, and were eventually to proscribe all of them. Most of them remain in *Hagakure*.

That, though, might be of no more significance than the West's exaltation of violence on the screen or the printed page. The Japanese are more literate than Westerners. Their best selling books and most widely read newspapers are more serious than ours. And, being more pragmatic than we are, they may simply have accepted that mankind – however unctuous his protestations to the contrary – is innately vicious. Having accepted that, they may also have elected to translate that innate viciousness into a military virtue by codifying its diverse applications to war.

There remains one startling anomaly in this chronicle of cruelty. Addicted though they are to television soap operas that extol the fearsome samurai, intellectually stimulated and morally challenged though they are by bushido's catalogue of selfless carnage, today's Japanese are a singularly charming people, full of generosity and good humour, bursting with modestly suppressed pride and conspicuously in control of the viciousness which lately has shamed almost every other society.

Every large company employs receptionists whose sole aim in life is to make the visitor feel important. Apparently unaware of the fact that they are exquisite, they bow and smile and bow again, as fresh as flowers and unselfconscious as kittens. On each office floor, another is stationed, neat, glossy and smiling. To see one is a joy: to be greeted by one is briefly to recapture one's youth and innocence.

To enter a Japanese garden, however, is to recapture one's childhood, because those who created them never forgot what all children know: that it is only where water trills and rocks slumber and leafy trees close out the crassness of our adult world that enchantment is still to be found.

No less enchanted is Fujiama, even as one hurtles past it in The Bullet, en route from hideously vibrant Tokyo to cunningly exploited Hiroshima. Fujiama is a fantasy mountain designed by some primeval Disney and colour-printed by Hiroshige. And none but the Japanese would have the courage to leave an asymmetrical bump on its peak – or the pride, once every year, to remove from its dramatic, snow-streaked flanks about half a million empty beer cans.

Their houses – though crammed with the devices produced by Mr Matsushita's *Electric Company* and Mr Ibuka's *Sony* – are tiny, like houses made of playing cards, so flimsy that they must, it seems, tumble at the first tremor of the mildest earthquake. But their occupants refuse to worry.

'Is this building earthquake proof?' I asked an executive of a major company as we marched down its long corridors past a series of bobbing, bowing and smiling receptionists.

'No,' he said cheerfully. 'If earthquake happens, this building all fall down.'

154

They love word-play, and their timing is superb, so that in conversation they are constantly laughing – which suprised me who had thought that mostly they laughed at someone who fell and broke both his legs.

'Tea, sir?' suggested a waiter.

'Do you have English tea?'

'*English* tea?'

'Yes.'

'No, sir. We have Japanese tea, Chinese tea, Indian tea, Saylon tea . . .'

'That's it.'

'Saylon tea is *English* tea?'

'Yep.'

'The English call it English tea because they, ah, *consume* so much of it?'

'That's right.'

'You are English?'

'Australian.'

'Ah so. English tea. I must tell Mrs Bandaranaike.'

I did not have the heart to tell him that Mrs Bandaranaike had been out of office for some years. Obviously his study of the whole of *Asian* history had covered the period from the year dot only to 1976.

Asked how confident he felt about Japan's future, a university student (whose favourite sport was Rugby football) said, 'Not very.'

'Why?'

'I'm a pessimist.'

'When your country is doing so well?'

'I've always been a pessimist. But I quite enjoy it. Pessimism is an art.'

Professor Inohara of Sophia University took the student's point. 'All of us Japanese are pessimistic in a way,' he acknowledged. 'We constantly await the next earthquake or typhoon.'

If pessimism be an art (and who am I to contradict that premise when I have not yet really understood it?) so is irony: and the art of irony lies in conveying one's meaning by expressing the opposite. Japanese life is rich in irony.

Most of its younger women go to work each day smartly dressed, coiffeured and made-up in the Western fashion; but when they laugh they cover the mouth with a demure hand, and when they go home they submit to the authority of a permanently resident mother-in-law, and at all times they cope contentedly with their menfolk, whose

155

attitude toward them lies somewhere between those of the lugubrious Osamu Dazai, who wrote, in *No Longer Human*, 'I never could think of prostitutes as human,' on the one hand, and, on the other, 'When a woman suddenly bursts into hysterics, the best way to restore her spirits is to give her something sweet.'

Though Japanese receptionists are marvels of human sweetness, their younger sisters, immaculate in white tracksuits, are aggressively athletic. They gallop out on to their school tennis courts where they play every stroke with the grace of a Rosewall and strike every ball with a violence that would startle a McEnroe; and straight from this ferocious pursuit of elegant individualism they flock together to submit to the demands of a Physical Training Instructor at whose behest they work with a zeal reminiscent of the Imperial Japanese Army at its most suicidal. Little wonder that five of these girls went on to a volley-ball court in November 1981, and demolished five giantesses from the Soviet Union.

Yet these same aggressively self-confident and accomplished girls are represented on television by equally delightful girls whose role it is to say nothing but 'Hai'. Standing beside a male colleague, who talks interminably, they say, 'Hai'. Not once but hundreds of times: and are unbelievably boring.

Though ostensibly pacifist, the Japanese love uniforms. Receptionists wear them and office girls wear them. Schoolboys looking like cadets wear them. Schoolgirls looking like nannies wear them. Dustmen, policemen, foremen, train guards, ticket collectors and taxi-rank controllers wear them – all of them looking like officers from the Imperial Japanese Army. Millions who wear no uniform compensate by wearing at least one of the Imperial Japanese Army's accessories – gauze masks, white gloves or web-toed canvas boots. Pedestrians and motor cyclists wear masks. Labourers wear web-toed boots. Taxi drivers and joggers wear gloves.

But these are mere accoutrements: what one notices most, when one mingles with the Japanese, is their vitality, courtesy and good humour.

To one who knew it rather well, they are reminiscent, in fact, of nothing so much as an Imperial Army that has decided to switch from severity to laughter, conquest to productivity, and death to life – and, having decided to switch, has 'switched sincerely'.

*   *   *

156

Sincerity, however, was not enough in 1945. Japan also needed new blood, a sense of personal freedom, the latest technology, a common purpose – and daring. Happily for her, MacArthur gave the Japanese the first and second by purging business and industry of their hundreds of elderly aristocratic presidents (whose jobs then became available to younger men – even to commoners) and by abolishing the Thought Police; the third was on sale to them from any Western industrialist who had it; loss of face and their highly developed sense of vengefulness provided the common purpose; and daring was as natural to them as inertia is to the sloth.

Soichiyo Honda is the supremely successful example of the thousands of Japanese who have benefited from MacArthur's pro-scription of the traditional, aristocratic, zaibatsu boss. Far from being an aristocrat, he is an exuberantly shameless commoner given to wearing pink mohair suits, jewelry and pointed shoes. The mere sight of him must make his fellow tycoons in Tokyo feel faint. But before the war he was a rural mechanic; and at the war's end he was 39 and penniless. Today he has factories making motor cycles and automobiles in 32 countries because Japan lost the war. He said so himself. 'I'm no hero,' he said, 'but had I not had to live through a period of starvation and turmoil, I'd probably still be an auto repairer some place out in the country. And if MacArthur had not purged all those aristocratic old men, who would ever have taken any notice of me? But things change. As a child at school, I always got bad marks. Today my marks are quite good!'

Others whose marks have become quite good since the war are Matsuda of *Mazda*, Oshida of *Toyota*, Shoriki the one-time policeman who became a press baron and television tycoon, and Ibuka of *Sony*.

'You must not assume, though,' Honda warned, 'that because things are going well today, they'll go on going well forever. A century is a very short time in history, and much changes in a century; yet few of us live to be 100.'

He shrugged philosophically; and even had so many others in his position not said the same thing, one would have known that he meant what he said. Life had been so harsh until he was 39, and so cruelly hard from his fortieth year till his fiftieth, that the prospect of renewed adversity held no terrors for him – nor for a dozen other Japanese magnates like him.

Edmond Onishi, an adviser in External Relations to Matsushita's colossal *Electric Industrial Company*, spoke with equal candour of the abolition of the Thought Police. 'Even in 1938, when I was only 23, mind-control was very strong,' he said. 'It had been strong for ten years. Since 1945, even though I'm a commoner, I have been free.'

At the time of speaking he was 67, well placed in the Matsushita organization, well dressed, well paid and secure; but it was clear that the freedom to think what he liked was just as important to him as his professional success. And even after 36 years, the novelty of it had not worn off.

Though defeat brought long years of physical hardship, it also brought psychological amelioration. The Japanese were suddenly relieved of the burden of being a race of divine descent superior to all other races and constantly required to prove it. If they so wished, they were at liberty to complain about their misfortune, berate the militarists locked up in the Allies' jails, abandon their traditions of hysterical fanatacism, suicidal violence and horrid bloodshed, and become whatever different a sort of people they chose.

In point of fact, they elected to remain much as they had always been; but free. And being much as they had always been, were able to identify strongly with Yuji Aida when he told them how much more insufferable it had been for the Japanese, as prisoners, to be treated with indifference by 'cool' British soldiers than ever it was for the British to be treated brutally by Japanese soldiers 'aflame with hatred'. Even though Japan knew all the details of the brutalities inflicted on its prisoners by the Imperial Japanese Army, it somehow could not refrain from agreeing with Aida. 'He who insults a man deserves to be killed,' a bushi believes. Japan believed that Aida and his comrades had been gratuitously insulted by the British. His book became a best seller.

For some years the Japanese even held true to the samurai's code that death is preferable to capture. The survivors of the Cowra mutiny crept home – and were greeted more often than not with dismay. 'You were alive after all,' one father reproached his son – who knelt, placed his hands on the ground, bowed low and offered his apologies 'to Heaven, Earth and the Gods'.

The villagers were not told that he had been a prisoner of war. He subsequently married, but has never talked to his wife about what happened to him during the war because he knew how strongly his kind was despised by all those who had fought the war from Japan. Though this attitude was eventually to soften, he remained fearful. 'There is no guarantee that such thinking will never again be revived,' he reminded himself.

That those Japanese soldiers who survived their frightful war in New Guinea and Burma should have been denied a rapturous home-coming seems cruel – until one is reminded that even today school children punish themselves by committing suicide. No less than 856 of them did so as long ago as 1978 – because they had failed their exams. As the competition for University places gets more intense than ever, the figure will probably be higher.

Shame is no less intolerable to today's Japanese than it was to the Imperial Army; and the sources of shame are innumerable. To be unusual, to do the unexpected, to fail to conform, to do less than one should – each of these is shameful, not least because others are aware of the culprit's offence.

One Allied prisoner of war caught stealing was punished by having to wear a placard proclaiming, 'I AM A THIEF'. To the surprise of his Japanese guards, he endured this ordeal with complete equanimity. It was with a sense almost of self-disgust, on the other hand, that Yuji Aida admitted to stealing from his British guards; and when I asked the interpreter to ask Shichihei Yamamoto whether *he* had ever stolen from the Americans, she was most reluctant to do so. Perfectly at home with Westerners, she nevertheless recoiled from asking so insultingly Western a question of so distinguished a compatriot.

But he, who reads English easily, and understands the spoken word rather better than he pretends, insisted that she translate the question. In answer to which – clapping his hands with glee – he shouted, 'YES!' It must be remembered, however, that Yamamoto is a philosopher. The prisoner's need to defy would very soon have become apparent to him – even though, as he admitted, 'The Americans were kinder to us than we would have been to them.'

He is also a man who has spent more than a decade liberating his mind from those concepts of bushido which seem meretricious. It was as a philosopher and prisoner of war that he responded to my question so gleefully, not as a Japanese.

'Do you feel a sense of guilt that you once believed in the Imperial Way, or a sense of resentment that you were ever conditioned to believe in it?' I asked.

'Both.'

'Should there be another war, would your rather kill yourself than surrender?'

'I would not kill myself.'

'What are your feelings about the war?'

'When I think of those last months – I have no words.'
'Is there any hatred left?'
'I have no words.'
'How many of your men were killed?'
'Nine out of every ten.'
'Will you ever write a novel about it?'
'No.'

He gazed at the books behind and to both sides of him, books that seemed to begrudge him even a space for his desk – over which they had already sprawled, as if to make it their own; as if they knew that they and the cubby hole that housed them were his only refuge from 'those last months'.

They being all that we had in common – apart from our need to explain the spirit that underlay them – I was tactful enough to take my leave of him.

*　　*　　*

Masanobu Tsuji, had he not allegedly been killed by the Vietcong, would inspire in me no such delicacy of feeling. When he wrote *Singapore*, in 1960, he seemed to have lost none of his lust for conquest and, unlike Yamamoto, to have seen no need to expunge the evils of the militarist philosophy.

He made no apology to his Emperor for the failure of the war he extolled, nor once paid lip service to Hirohito's concept of a nation dedicated to peaceful but scientific reconstruction.

Instead, he wrote: 'The young people of today must, for the sake of the nation, develop the same spirit of altruism, self-sacrifice and purity of motive as actuated the young of Japan on the battlefields of Malaya. I cling fast to the bright hopes for the future of our people and our nation.'

The young to whom he addressed his words have indeed responded to the nation's cause with all that spirit of altruism, self-sacrifice and purity of motive that triumphed on the battlefields of Malaya; but have they responded in the way that Tsuji intended? Or was he summoning them to rearm – and die in yet another war?

'Certainly not,' say those who know nothing of the Japanese. Yet who, in 1930, would have predicted that so polite and industrious a people would (in the words of Yoshio Kodama) have been waging 'a war without a Rescript' in 1937 which was 'a mad carnival of debauchery carried out by gangs of ignorant bullies'?

'*Nations at Peace*' is the credo of the Japanese cartels of today; but should the rules of the game they are winning be changed, who can assert that they will not follow the example of the Zaibatsu in the 1930s, and finance a hugely expanded Self Defence Force?

In 1941, Roosevelt's embargo made it impossible for Japan *not* to go to war. Should the industrial nations of the Western world gang up on *Japan Incorporated* in the coming decades, who can swear that they will not make it impossible for the Japanese to stay at peace?

More than any other race, the Japanese are capable, like a flock of birds in flight, of instant and unpremeditated changes of course. Even their swarming pedestrians respond to some unseen and inaudible drill instructor at whose command they dart left or right with all the precision of a school of fish below the branches of a coral reef.

In their time they have switched from aboriginal illiteracy to the complexity of China's literate culture, from divisive feudalism to a united shogunate, from the sword to the gun, from the gun (for two centuries) back to the sword, from medieval isolation to modernized competition, from Divine Empire to unholy dictatorship and, most recently, from vanquished subservience to industrial supremacy. They could switch again at any moment – to total automation, or uncompromising economic warfare, or massive rearmament. They could even turn their back on industry, as once they turned it on the gun, revert to the exquisite life-style of eleventh century Kyoto, and withdraw entirely from the world into which Perry so recently dragged them.

Or they can continue as they are; but to do that, they must learn to understand the foreign mind, and foreigners must at least attempt to understand theirs, and bushido must never again mean to them what it was made to mean between 1941 and 1945.

CHAPTER EIGHTEEN
>>>>>>><<<<<<<

'With Diligence
and a Strong Spirit'

EVEN BEFORE DULLES had pounded the table as he told Yoshida, 'You *must* rearm,' America's almost immediate post-war antagonism to Russia had offered the ostensibly powerless Japanese a lever. They used it skilfully: Washington began to envisage Japan as a cold-war ally as early as 1949.

American dollars were therefore made readily available, and advice and technology. Japan availed herself of all of them, spending not a cent or a moment on her own comfort, devoting herself as single-mindedly to reconstruction as she had to war. She was used to discomfort: she did not intend to become accustomed to dependence.

Playing upon American anxieties no less cunningly than she had evaded any direct involvement in the Korean War, she allowed herself to become a tactical base for that war, and was rewarded in 1951 with a Security Pact whereby – at no expense to herself, apart from the miniscule cost of her Police Service – she was guaranteed American protection while she would be at her most vulnerable. The long trek back to the pre-eminence of early 1942 had begun.

Accepting the impossible logistics of their economic situation – no exports, no food; no steel, no ships; no ships, no exports – the Japanese had first borrowed the necessary money from America and then reconstructed their shipyards and steel mills.

Acknowledging that iron ore for steel reached Japan in ships, and that ships were made of steel, they had built their shipyards close to their steelworks, and their steelworks on the foreshores of deep water harbours. Ore was unloaded from ships almost into the maws of blast furnaces, from which it poured to be processed into steel plate that slid almost directly on to keels laid ready and waiting in the dockyards.

The Japanese had always made good steel. In the sixteenth

century, they made, and exported, the best and cheapest in the world. Sixteenth century Japanese swords can still chop through any other sword ever made. They can still (and there is film to prove it) with one blow, cut clean through the barrel of a twentieth century machine gun. Using the latest techniques, Hirohito's hungry subjects were determined to make the best and cheapest steel in the world once again.

By 1954 they were producing almost seven and a half million metric tons of it a year; but Germany was producing almost ten million tons more, Britain eleven million more and America seventy five million more. Undeterred, the Japanese increased their production year after year, improved their techniques and, by 1960, were producing twenty-three million tons to Britain's twenty-four and a half, Germany's thirty-five and America's ninety.

By 1965 they had left Britain and Germany far behind, producing forty million tons and planning to raise that total to fifty million by 1968. In fact, they produced almost sixty-seven million tons in 1968, compared with America's one hundred and nineteen and Russia's one hundred and six.

By 1979, at almost a hundred and twelve million tons, they were breathing down America's neck; and in 1980 overtook her. Russia, by virtue of her enormous armaments industry, still led by a short head; but Japan no more envied the Soviet Union its profitless output than she desired armaments – on which she spent only a tiny proportion of her annual Gross National Product.

At shipbuilding she had been even more successful in even less time than she had required to become the world's leading manufacturer and exporter of steel, the steady growth of the former hugely assisting the growth of the latter. But her triumph was by no means a foregone conclusion.

In 1954, for example, she launched only 573,871 tons deadweight of shipping compared with Britain's 2,147,057. Over the next ten years, however, she was steadily to overtake her greatest rival – mainly by building ships in about a third of the time the British needed. She even began launching the first of the world's mammoth tankers. The rest of the world would not attempt to follow her example until Nasser had closed the Suez Canal and huge tankers became a necessity, but by that time Japan had mastered techniques of which the others knew nothing, and could produce the vessels at a price they could not match. In 1961, Japan overtook Britain by 1,490,877 tons to 1,292,146.

163

Thereafter, as the world switched from electricity stations powered by coal to stations powered mainly by oil, and industry's demand for power increased, Britain fell farther and farther behind. By 1965 Japan was producing three and a half million tons of shipping a year (which included the first 150,000 ton tanker) and had cornered 31% of the world's shipbuilding orders.

In 1966 her output was almost seventeen million tons (including tankers of 209,000 tons). She had raised her share of the world's total orders to 40% (including six vessels of 276,000) and could afford to gaze complacently back at Britain, Sweden and Germany, who had produced only three million tons among them.

From 1967 (when she cut the time she needed to build a 100,000 ton tanker from seven months to less than five) she consistently built 40% or more of the ships launched throughout the world in any one year. At various times new rivals, like Sweden or Brazil, would emerge; but only briefly. In 1971, she collected orders for no less than 1061 vessels – mainly tankers, containers and bulk carriers – and her rivals were left gasping. By 1978 her lead over Russia, Britain and Brazil, both in output and orders, was massive. It remains unassailable; and her rivals are bankrupt.

In the motor industry her success has been more phenomenal both because she entered the race late and because she challenged not only America but Britain and Europe as well. In 1962 she was not even listed as one of the world's eight leading producers of automobiles. Significantly, however, she was already seventh among the world's *exporters* of cars and commercial vehicles – with 16,000 of the former and 33,000 of the latter.

But as a manufacturer of motor cycles, Honda (the nattily dressed commoner who believes he owes everything to Japan's defeat and MacArthur's purge of the Zaibatsu) startled the world by producing more than a million motor cycles in 1962, and increasing his exports by 117% over 1961. Supported by his Japanese rivals in the industry, he had made his country the world's largest producer of two-wheeled vehicles.

It was in the field of four-wheeled vehicles that their real ambition lay, however; and one after the other Japanese firms began to manufacture them, each confident that it could outsell the other in a suddenly car-conscious and more affluent domestic market.

Able to pick and choose, the Japanese consumer imposed upon these rival manufacturers much higher standards than would otherwise have been provided; and when the domestic market became

164

saturated, these same rivals had either to export their surplus production or go bankrupt. For the rest of the world's car makers the effect of this was to be deadly. Most of *them* went bankrupt.

In 1963, Japan produced a mere 407,000 motor cars and 875,000 commercial vehicles, and exported about 10% of each. Britain exported about ten times as many of both, and America manufactured about fifteen times as many.

The story of the succeeding eighteen years is more succinctly told by combining and approximating the total output of both cars and commercial vehicles. It makes sombre reading – unless one is Japanese.

From two million vehicles in 1968 (which exceeded Britain's output, but was a million less than Germany's, and seven million less than America's) Japan's production leaped to six and a half million in 1974 (which was exceeded only by America's ten million).

By 1979 Japan was producing almost ten million automobiles a year (not to mention six million motor cycles) and America, now less than two million in the lead, and her sales falling, had become anxious.

'Workers will find true happiness through work, for work will always be the basis of society,' says a slogan pasted on a Toyota factory wall.

'Work together to serve the company and the state with diligence and a strong spirit,' is the motto of Yamaha. Japanese production and sales, unlike America's, increased in the ensuing twelve months.

In November of 1981, as the Japanese produced more than eleven million vehicles, and the United States output had declined even further, the Americans sullenly admitted defeat. Despite the fact that Japan had voluntarily curbed her exports to all her foreign competitors (especially America), that France and Italy were refusing to move her cars from their docks to the sale rooms, that Britain was exhorting its people to 'Buy British', not one of them had escaped a mauling. But at the very moment when all of them were finding it impossible to sell sufficient of their products to their own people, the Japanese were opening up factories, or launching joint projects, in one enemy camp after the other, and succeeding.

As Sir Michael Edwardes was to put it in 1982, British Leyland – then seeking a further large injection of government aid, and hoping for profitability no earlier than 1985 – aimed at matching European productivity levels but could never hope to compete with the Japanese. Furthermore, should the Japanese abandon their policy of

165

voluntary curbs on their exports to the EEC and America, they 'would take over the world motor industry'.

The brutal truth was that the Japanese were making better cars than their rivals, and selling them more effectively. As they had done in Japan, so now they were offering their customers overseas everything that they had ever wanted in a motor car. When British Leyland produced its *Acclaim*, in collaboration with Honda, the general comment was that it was years ahead of any Western model, but why had Britain had to wait so long for its like?

The answer is that in no other country than Japan had domestic manufacturers competed with one another to the death for their domestic market. Everywhere else they had merged and, hugely monolithic, had required their customers to like what they gave them, or lump it. Unfortunately for all of them, the Japanese were to offer their customers a more attractive option, and only the larger and more luxurious products of the non-Japanese automobile industry have survived unscathed.

In almost every sphere of industrial competition the story is the same. Apparently unassailable as manufacturers of the world's best cameras and electrical products, the Germans – though they lack nothing in expertise and zeal – were long ago supplanted as to the first and are now being hotly challenged as to the second. Meantime, watches, radios, television sets, bicycles, video recorders, pharmaceuticals, pianos, sporting goods, computer hard-ware, machine tools, optical lenses, domestic appliances and a thousand other unlikely but impeccably designed products have poured from Japan – to the dismay of those who had always regarded it as *their* prerogative to make them.

Nor is it any longer possible for the West to comfort itself by saying that Japan owes everything to foreign technology – not that Japan has at any time been impressed by that argument. One could as well ascribe Einstein's Theory of Relativity to Sir Isaac Newton, or atomic weapons to Ludwig Boltzmann, they point out. Or America's exploration of space to the Germans who invented the rocket bomb. Technology, they remind one, has always travelled. Today it merely travels faster than it used to, because it can be purchased in the form of patents.

Of these they have bought hundreds of thousands since 1945, and they admit that they have improved upon almost all of them that they chose to exploit. The day has now arrived, however, when they too have become technologically inventive, and soon they will be in a

166

position, should they wish (which is far from certain) to sell as much technology as they will doubtless continue to buy.

At the moment, though, the Japanese industrial innovation that the West would most like to buy is what they themselves call QC – or Quality Control. QC is what makes a Japanese product more attractive to the consumer than its Western equivalent because it looks better, offers more, works more efficiently, costs less and lasts longer. It is not, however, a technique that can be purchased, it is a spirit (shared by all concerned in the manufacture of any given product) that is peculiarly Japanese.

It is the willingness to make suggestions, offer criticism, be criticised, do more than one job, read the relevant literature, be part of a group, work loyally and believe in the importance of what one is doing, however menial that may be.

It is the willingness of small firms, sub-contracting to supply components to the giant companies, to fend for themselves in times of recession.

It is the willingness of women to work for three fifths of a man's wage, and of all factory workers to accept a fatal industrial accident rate six times greater than in the West.

It is the determination of every school child to pass his exams and, if possible, get a university degree. It is the willingness of his parents to *buy* him the best possible education. It is the readiness of management to share a uniform, the factory floor, cafeterias and washrooms with its workforce.

It is the acceptance, by all concerned, of paternalism in industry, which demands life-long service from the workforce, and imposes upon the employer a responsibility to keep his employees on the pay-roll through bad times as well as good.

It is patriotism, assiduity and pride: pride in the product, pride in the company, pride in *Japan Incorporated*, and pride in Japan's recovery from defeat. And it is the knowledge that almost every factory has been strategically sited close to a deep water port, often on land reclaimed from the sea, and that the plant installed in each factory is the best available.

Significantly, the three nations who have made the greatest industrial progress since the war are the three Axis powers who were defeated (partial acknowledgement of which was made on St George's Day 1981 at the London School of Economics, when a lecture was given entitled 'Why has Britain failed?' The lecture was sponsored by Suntory and Toyota, the chairman was Professor Michio

167

Morishima and the speaker was Professor Ralf Dahrendorf). Equally significantly, the only nation to match Japan in patriotism, assiduity and pride is West Germany. But not even the West Germans have all those other traits which have made the Japanese the unique exponents of that invaluable industrial attribute, QC.

If the ailing West is ever to compete successfully with today's surging Japan, it must either embark upon another industrial revolution or acquire those qualities of 'altruism, self-sacrifice and purity of motive' which Tsuji so admired on the battlefields of Malaya.

Far from being mere imitators of other people's skills, the Japanese of today are displaying a spirit of innovation ranging from the device that plays music to any telephone caller asked to hold the line, to the machine in subway stations that accepts bank notes, swallows them up and spits out an equivalent amount of change, to motorized roller skates that propel the wearer at 25 miles an hour, to optical fibres so sophisticated that America can compete with them only by reneging on the tender system and buying a more costly product of her own. Looking ahead, Toshihiko Yamishita, who is President of Matsushita's colossus, promised, 'In the latter half of the eighties I will be able to talk to you through an electronic translating machine – a little computer that will translate whatever *you* say into Japanese, then I can answer you right away, and just by pressing a button you'll be able to get translations of my reply in English. And in German and French as well,' – which somewhat gave the lie to the assertion of Yasuo Kato, of Nippon Electric, that the Japanese 'are not so creative because the creative mind is peculiar and we Japanese don't like anything peculiar. We believe that everyone should be the same.' Unless, or course, Mr Kato was warning the rest of the world that so many Japanese are now electronically literate that it is not in the least peculiar for them to envisage telephone exhanges that translate from one language to another as one speaks, super computers perhaps a thousand times stronger than any now marketed, unmanned factories worked twenty-four hours a day by robots, superminiaturization, optical fibres, and the marriage of lasers with micro chips.

The West's answer to all this ingenuity and gadgetry – for which the Japanese have a passion – seems to be only an eight foot high, four-legged monster whose head emits an unearthly shriek and blinding flashes of light. Japanese farmers are queuing up to buy it. It is a British-manufactured scarecrow.

All this said, the hugeness of Japan's leap from poverty in the

1950s to affluence in the 1980s is still not adequately described. Regrettably, more statistics are necessary. Be comforted by the fact that they are staggering.

Japan's population in her shrunken Empire had only reached 88 million by 1957, but by 1967 – precisely when a large domestic market was required to sustain its sudden industrial expansion – it was a hundred million. Since then, its increase has been sensibly but voluntarily controlled.

Japan began exporting again in 1947, but her trade figures were negligible. Nevertheless, they increased year by year until, in 1956, her trade gap was only $103 million and her total exports were valued at $2½ billion.

By 1960, her total exports to the world earned her $4 billion – of which a quarter came from America, with whom she had an adverse trading account of $240 million. The value of her exports to Britain was $120 million (a profit of $50 million) and to the EEC $174 million (a profit of $44 million).

By 1973, however, her total exports to the world were worth $28·6 billion, her total imports cost her only $23·47 billion, and the rest of the world (except West Germany, which was also flourishing) had begun to complain that such a surplus threatened its future economic stability.

America being amongst the more vehement of her critics, Japan switched some of her attention from there to Europe – where, in a single year, her exports leaped by 35%. It was a tactic she would frequently repeat. As soon as one country became unduly agitated, she would allow it a brief respite while she concentrated on another. Meantime, year upon year – undeterred by oil shocks, Nixon shocks, inflation, recessions or depressions – she increased her exports by five or six per cent a year until, by 1978, she had a trading surplus over the rest of the world of $20 billion.

By the end of 1981, her annual trading surplus with the United States alone was $15 billion (with the EEC it was $9·5 billion), and Tokyo found itself playing host to a flurry of extremely agitated statesmen from Washington, Bonn, Paris, Brussels and London, all of them, with varying degrees of tactlessness, demanding that she curb her exports of those things that she made better and cheaper than they, and import more things she neither wanted nor needed from them.

The sad truth of the matter, of course, is that (apart from raw materials and a short list of manufactured goods), Japan needs to import only what she eats, drinks, wears or wants to show off. Advised of Mr Tajitsu's *bon mot* that Britain and America might solve *their* vast trade imbalances with Japan by sending her whisky and chocolate respectively, Mr Wataru Hiraizumi was able to cap it, adding, 'And France could send us silk ties! Taiwan makes excellent silk ties, I know; but that Dior label is so much more impressive.' Sometimes, as the Japanese discuss the West's dilemma with such sympathy, it is almost easy to doubt their sincerity!

However tactlessly the West's supplicant statesmen may have expressed their case in Tokyo at the end of 1981, they became little short of strident once they returned home. 'If European industry cannot count on Japan,' rapped Viscomte Étienne Davignon on behalf of the EEC, 'then Japan cannot count on the European market.' And thereby obliquely reminded his recent hosts that Japanese cars off-loaded on to French docks often stay there for the lack of proper authorization to move them. Day after day, and week after week, French dock officials simply omit to sign the required documents.

In effect, explained France's special envoy to Japan, those officials are only doing to her what her officials do to France. 'We are showing the Japanese just how annoying non-tariff bureaucratic barriers can be. Everybody has to play the same rules, or nobody plays.'

'The problem is a pervasive attitude that Japanese companies should only buy *domestic* products,' Malcolm Baldridge complained as America's Secretary of Commerce in November 1981. Admitting that this attitude was slowly changing, he nevertheless demanded, 'The change must accelerate.'

The Japanese dislike such imperatives. They dislike intemperate language even more. And they detest slurs upon their integrity. In an interview with the *Los Angeles Times*, a few days later, Mr Baldridge went too far. 'The Japanese,' he said, 'must open up their damn markets to us,' or accept the risk of 'serious repercussions'. They were 'great at talking about free trade', but, '*We're* free trading, they're not!'

Japan having only a few weeks earlier voluntarily foregone the privilege of complete free trade with the United States, as far as the export of her motor vehicles to America was concerned, her Premier, Mr Suzuki, was not pleased. Pressure from Congress to compel Japan to increase her defence expenditure (and thereby reduce her investment capital) pleased him even less.

'This kind of action against another country is hard to understand,' he rebuked Japan's critics – and went on to assert that Japan was 'by no means getting a free ride from the United States' as far as her own security was concerned.

But the criticisms and demands from foreign countries continued unabated, and even the normally bland Masaya Miyoshi of the Keidanren was for once provoked. 'Criticisms are harsher than we expected,' he said in a television interview for the BBC at the beginning of 1982. In Japan, language that is harsh, severe or loud is impolite, and is received with repugnance.

Better 'long-term international co-operation' than 'a short-term trade war', Miyoshi warned, because a short-term trade war would put 'an end to the prospect of co-operation'.

Here, though, he exhibited once again that national tendency to regard anything Japan wants as her inalienable right. The Japanese may not have been myopic as soldiers, but they suffer from tunnel vision as statesmen. Upon behalf of whom a spokesman from their Finance Ministry, appearing in the same television programme as Miyoshi, declared, 'The government is now at the stage of trying to gather together the various views and establish a policy' – by which he meant a consensus. A consensus being more than improbable, when 'the various views' were so patently irreconcilable, what he was really saying was that, for the moment, the government intended doing nothing.

Let no one believe, however, that the Japanese have been blameless. They have exploited every loophole in every agreement and have taken ruthless advantage of America's ingenuous, if not disinterested, post-war generosity.

When Premier Kishi conferred with President Eisenhower in Washington, in 1957, he successfully negotiated a free trade agreement between the two countries. To the Americans, that agreement doubtless seemed a promise of almost exclusive rights to export to 88 million people who had nothing, could make nothing and needed everything. From the very beginning, though, the Japanese blocked America's expansionist urge to establish companies of her own in their country, and argued convincingly that they could only feed themselves by protecting their new industries until they had at least survived infancy. In no Western country, consequently, are there so few multi-national corporations as in Japan; and in no other country do industries seem to pass so imperceptibly from infancy's vulnerability to full-blooded manhood. By the time America realized

171

that her helpless beneficiary had been transformed overnight into a muscular rival, it was too late.

And when she then insisted that Japan was in a position to abide by all the precepts of free trade, Japan either retorted, 'Then make us something we want at a price we are willing to pay,' or resorted to the use of such delaying tactics as would have delighted the heart of Fabius Cunctator himself. The transformation continued apace; and the muscular man became a giant. The extent of that transformation deserves a précis at least.

In 1946 Japan's industrial output was only a third of her output in 1937; expectation of life was less than forty years; she had no overseas factories; no social services; no ships and an appalling transport system; she was liable for reparations to all those East Asian countries unfortunate enough to have been 'liberated' by her during the war; and she had millions of ex-servicemen looking for work.

Today, her industrial output so exceeds that of 1937 as almost to defy measurement; expectation of life is about seventy; she has overseas factories by the thousand; she claims that her social services compare favourably with Britain's; her road and transport system is excellent; she has the largest merchant navy of any nation except those that fly a flag of convenience; she has not only paid off her reparations and all the debts she incurred to America between 1945 and 1962, she also makes adequate annual contributions, in the form of foreign aid, to most of East Asia and the Third World; her percentage of unemployed (like her rate of inflation) is lower than that of any other industrialized nation; the duty free shops in the airports of the world look like Japanese trade fairs; South East Asia has virtually become a Japanese satellite; Australia's economy would crash overnight were Japan, exasperated beyond all endurance by that Commonwealth's feckless propensity for strikes, to find another supplier of minerals and coal; and although she represents only 3% of the world's landspace, she was producing 10% of the world's manufactured goods by 1981 – and was confidently planning to produce more.

The extent of the problem this represents to the rest of the industrialized world can be even more briefly defined.

Should the West defend itself with tariffs, Japan will simply concentrate her exporting offensive on the Third World and displace Western exports therefrom as ruthlessly as she has already displaced them from South East Asia – where, as a trade official in Kuala

Lumpur recently put it, 'We get up in the morning to a Sony alarm, listen to the news on a National Panasonic radio, brew a cup of coffee on a Sanyo percolator, drive to work in a Toyota, curse the swarms of motor cyclists on Hondas and check the time on a Seiko.' Should the West refrain from imposing tariffs, however, its few remaining bastions of industrial success will probably be toppled.

Japan Incorporated's Achilles heel is not her total dependence on the oil, coal and raw materials of others (she can always buy them from non-industrial nations only too happy to sell them to anyone) but her latest 'disease' – which is government borrowing.

Until 1971 she avoided this sickness by denying herself those post-war luxuries (like roads, parks, comfortable schools, modern hospitals, sewage and drainage, pollution control and rehousing) in which the vote-conscious governments of every other industrial nation had indulged so extravagantly; but by 1971 her frugal constituents were beginning to demand some of them at least.

With cars available to them, and savings to buy them, they wanted roads on which to drive them. With industry clamouring for graduates, they demanded adequate schools in which their earnest children could work to pass the necessary exams, and more universities from which they could obtain their essential degrees. With the advent of television, they caught a glimpse of an outside world in which ordinary people like themselves had houses such as they had never dreamed of; and even if they were too modest to demand such houses for themselves (they still do not have them) they certainly wanted better drains and sewage, more parks, air to breathe that was less than noxious, and industrial effluents that were less than lethal. They had seen what could be done when Tokyo city was degutted and refurbished, and the railway and road systems modernized, for the Olympic Games of 1964: now they wanted more of the same. So the government began to borrow money.

The Japanese being great savers, that was not difficult; but just as the Japanese Disease of 1942 led to a fatally over-extended line of communications for the Imperial Japanese Army, so has the Japanese Disease of the seventies and eighties led to an over-extended national deficit today.

Faced with the repayment of, or interest due on, loans both to frugal savers and to dutiful industrialists and bankers, the government simply borrowed again. And again and again and again. Until suddenly, in 1982, it became difficult to pay civil servants their salaries, and the old and sick their pensions; and the only way to find

173

the money seemed to be by increasing taxes (which would not only reduce purchasing power but also cost votes) stinging the rich (which would infuriate the Keidanren) or reducing public expenditure (which would cause hardship to half the population).

Impossible for the government though this dilemma might seem to be, three other factors must be taken into consideration. First, the Japanese people are as proud of *Japan Incorporated* as they were of their Imperial Army and Navy: second, if they can be convinced of the need for it, they will submit as eagerly to whatever spartan disciplines are necessary to save *Japan Incorporated* as they did to uphold the Imperial Way: and third, if spartan discipline alone will not save it, they may just as readily subscribe to more drastic remedies in the future as they did to keep their conquests in China and Indo China in 1941.

The diminution of *Japan Incorporated* tomorrow would be no less a loss of face to them than the loss of Korea in 1895. The unemployment caused by such a diminution would be no less dangerous in the 1980s than the unemployment caused by the Depression which swelled the ranks of the Imperial Japanese Army in the 1930s. To avoid that diminution, to cure the latest Japanese Disease, to persuade Japan (in its own interests) to import something other than whisky, chocolate and silk ties – these are the tasks confronting any Japanese government today. To solve any one of them would require no less resolute leadership than Hirohito displayed in August 1945. But Hirohito has been stripped of the divinity which made it possible for him to lead; and for anyone less than an Emperor to lead would be completely un-Japanese.

Unless, of course, like Tojo, he first became a dictator.

CHAPTER NINETEEN

>>>>>>><<<<<<<

'Japan's international voice has been too small'

THE SKILL with which successive post-war Japanese governments played upon America's determination to be both more magnanimous and more powerful than any other nation in history is almost as impressive as the skill with which post-war Japanese industry has steered its way from defeat through successive economic crises to victory.

From 1945 to 1950, of course, Japanese governments simply did what MacArthur told them; but the cunning with which Yoshida outwitted John Foster Dulles was a portent of things to come.

When Premier Kishi visited President Eisenhower in Washington, in 1954, it was agreed that Japan should enjoy all the advantages of free trade with America, which was already her main market, and her main supplier of raw materials and technology. Over the next three years, she exported more and more to the United States.

In 1960 – ignoring all domestic protests from students, and even external pressure from the Russians – her government signed a pact with the United States whereby her security was guaranteed until 1970. Relieved of the obligation to defend herself, she invested almost all of her national income in industrial redevelopment. The extent of that investment can be judged from the fact that Washington felt it necessary to grant her only $69 million of Foreign Aid in 1960 (compared with $206 million to Korea, $141 million to Italy and $100 million to Turkey) and that the government had the confidence to promise that Japan's national income would be doubled by 1970.

1961 saw a marked increase in Japan's imports of raw materials (for reprocessing and export) and a vote of confidence from the International Monetary Fund in the form of a substantial loan.

In 1962 the government agreed to repay all the debts Japan had

175

incurred to the United States since 1945. Repayment was to be made over a period of fifteen years, and interest was fixed at 2½% per annum.

Meantime student indignation mounted at the continued presence in Japan of American servicemen and visits to Japan of nuclear submarines; industry's resentment of American-imposed restraint on trade with China grew more bitter; and Russian threats about Japan's unfriendly attitude (as evidenced by her friendly attitude to the United States) became more strident.

The government not only coped with them all but even gained confidence in itself to such an extent that, in 1964, Premier Sato was able to declare, 'It is now time for Japan to assert a voice in international affairs commensurate with the country's status as one of the world's leading economic powers.' Then, lest anyone doubted that his people had long since recovered from defeat and ignominy, he declared, 'Japan's international voice has been too small.'

She lost no time in speaking more loudly. Branding her existing constitution as 'one forced upon' her, she proceeded to revise it. The Emperor would remain her Head of State: her 'self-defence force' was legitimized: and industry was encouraged to invest in the latest technology and plant. That year wages increased by 10% and productivity by 9·8%.

Further to assist 'a voice in international affairs commensurate with her status as one of the world's leading economic powers', and ignoring Washington's displeasure, Japan not only signed an eight year credit contract with Russia to build the Soviets a urea fertilizer plant but openly solicited China's 'friendship'. Furthermore, her Premier asserted, the entire Asian Pacific Zone was to be transformed as swiftly as possible into 'a zone of Japanese economic privilege'.

Thus recklessly supported, Japanese manufacturers would never again hesitate to install the latest plant. They were even to do so before the plant already installed had earned its keep. The result was that by 1980, when 69% of America's machine tools were more than 10 years old, 60% of Japan's were less than 10 years old.

In 1966, with a world recession threatening, Japan forged ahead, increasing her annual total exports to other industralized countries, especially America, by no less than 31% – and Sato bluntly told Washington that Japan could no longer 'stand idly by, leaving our countrymen in Okinawa at the mercy of an aggressor' – the implication being that (Article 9 of the Constitution notwithstanding) the Self-Defence Force would be sent to American occupied Okinawa

176

should anyone ever threaten it.

In 1969 the Japanese Finance Minister promised the nation that by 1989 its per capita income would be the highest in the world; and no subsequent Finance Minister has seen fit to qualify that prediction. That same year (while America's war in Vietnam was patently failing) Premier Sato, on a visit to Washington, bluntly asserted that the Japanese, as 'the guardians of Asia', would have to 'shoulder new and expanded responsibilities not only for their own defence but for the security of Asia'.

Between 1967 and 1971 Japan's exports increased by 20% or more per annum: her imports declined just as dramatically. She no longer needed most of what the rest of the world was making. While America recorded its first trade deficit since 1935, Japan (in common only with the EEC) had so large a surplus that she had to revalue the yen; and while industrial production in every other country declined, Japan's increased by 4½%. Though she defined this as 'a recession', America's industrial leaders, when they met with her industrial leaders at a conference in Washington, formally demanded both that she become a less aggressive export promoter and that she import more.

The Japanese contingent could have replied that the industrialists it represented had spent no less than $413 million on patent royalties that very year, but did not. Nor did it confess to a massive investment in research and technology, which would only have alarmed the Americans even more.

With 1972 came the shock of President Nixon's visit to Peking and the likelihood of detente with China – with which Japan had still not made her peace. Premier Tanaka – determined to prevent America from snatching what Japan had always considered to be *her* potential market – promptly followed Nixon's example. At the conclusion of his visit, a communiqué was issued which said, in part, 'The Japanese side is keenly aware of Japan's responsibility for having caused the Chinese people enormous damage through war, and deeply reproaches itself.' In return, China renounced all her demands for reparations and agreed that relations between the two countries should return to normal.

In 1973 came the first of the oil shocks. As the world's second largest consumer of oil (after America) Japan was particularly affected by the Arabs' rationing of oil to 'unfriendly' countries, and panic ensued as the entire population began buying up everything from food to toilet paper. Convinced that their days of prosperity

177

were over, they began hoarding: ignoring the government's announcement that there were massive stocks of every household commodity, they prepared for a seige.

For the West this reaction was a reminder of the swiftness with which the mood of the Japanese can change and threaten even their national stability. Though the West omitted even to notice it, the Japanese government responded with alacrity. Once again disregarding Washington's policy, it quickly adopted a pro-Arab stance, was just as quickly re-classified by the Arabs as a 'friendly country', and was allowed to purchase all the oil it wanted.

In the same year, as a reward for Tanaka's abject apology in Peking in 1972, Japan's trade with China increased by 62% to the value of $871·5 million. In 1974 her total exports to the world were worth $60 billion. In 1975 and 1976 her best customers, in order of precedence, were the United States, Saudi Arabia, Iran, Australia and Indonesia; but, like everyone else in the industrialized world, she suffered adverse balances of payments – $700 million and $2·9 billion. She more than compensated for that in 1977 and 1978, however, with surpluses of $11 billion and $20 billion. Meantime, only West Germany had succeeded in keeping inflation and unemployment as low as it was in Japan, and the American dollar was declining.

More than ever alarmed, American industry began to lobby Washington for tariff protection against the Japanese; and although a truce in their long-running trade dispute was soon declared, Robert Strauss warned the Japanese that, 'The drive toward protectionism will probably not abate.'

Premier Fukuda thereupon promised that his government would seek to re-establish trade equilibrium, and the Bank of Japan loyally bought hundreds of millions of dollars to prevent that currency's further decline. At the same time, however, Fukuda set Japan a target of 7% growth – which could only worsen the plight of her competitors and was hardly likely to 're-establish trade equilibrium'.

At a subsequent seven nation meeting in Bonn, six nations begged the seventh to halve its surplus of that year so that they might the more easily survive. As ever, Japan was polite; but was to relax her export drive not at all.

The West Germans followed up this conference with unilateral discussions in Tokyo in the course of which they urged Japan to import more from the EEC and export less to it.

Likewise the Australian Prime Minister, and India's Foreign Minister, made visits – the object of which was to ensure that they be allowed to remain on, or leap aboard, the Japanese bandwagon.

178

Even Russia suggested a treaty of co-operation – and was coolly rebuffed for her pains. And China proposed that her representative visit Tokyo in 1979. Not since 1938, when Hitler was ensconced in his eyrie at Berchtesgarten, had so many sought such urgent favours from one nation. In the economic world, it was now Japan who was the power broker.

And so, in 1979, Premier Ohiru was at last able to declare that Japan had entered a new 'age of culture', and promise that his government would begin Japan's transformation into 'a just welfare society'. More than most, she could afford the transformation. Her gold and foreign exchange reserves totalled $33·1 billion and her trade surplus with the United States that year was $11·5 billion – 40% of America's total trading deficit.

Many of her most powerful industrialists now doubt whether, in the long term, she will be able to afford the welfare structure she has since created. Her rivals, they point out, have not been able to do so. But certainly she is doing her best to ensure that the task will not defeat her as it has defeated (or seems certain soon to defeat) so many others. Though she makes concessions here and concessions there, now to this country, next to that, the flood of her exports continues, more and more Japanese factories spring up in more and more countries, and her rivals grow ever more desperate.

As long ago as 1971 the Japanese Government planned that its industrial output would exceed that of the United States by the year 2000. None of her post-war economic plans has failed to meet its target by the appointed date, and America has good cause to fear this planned offensive.

But no more cause than she had to fear the military offensive she knew she must face in 1942. Now, as then, she has allies. Now, as then, their situation is even more desperate than hers. Now, as then, Japan's succession of victories has been the result of a unique spirit combined with novel tactics. Now, just as the US Navy had by the time of Midway, America has realized that she must employ the same novel tactics. But now, as it could not from 1942 to 1945, spirit can prevail: Japan's technology is fuelled by it no less than it is by oil and coal.

*   *   *

Should the West, though lacking Japan's industrial spirit, nevertheless decide to resort to a war of brutish technology and retrograde protectionism, it will find that its enemy also has allies – and powerful allies too.

The Arab oil states are well disposed to her, and she has a tanker

179

fleet more than capable of supplying her needs. Australia, which she failed to capture during World War II, has not only become her economic satellite but has been so totally alienated by the exclusivist policies of the EEC and Britain that she has no sympathy for them at all. Compared with the EEC, the Australians allege, the Japanese are passionate and selfless disciples of free trade! Meanwhile they have provided Japan with a huge proportion of the coal and minerals, and a substantial proportion of the food, she has needed since 1965, and hope to continue providing them forever.

Canada is likewise Japan's willing and important supplier, her strategic dependence upon the United States for too long taken by Washington as grounds enough for Ottowa's unfailing compliance. In a United States shooting war against Russia, Canada might well fight with the Americans: in a United States economic war against Japan, her sympathies would probably lie with the Keidanren.

China, whose honeymoon with America ended in 1981, whose vast population is still the world's most tempting market, and whose perennial hatred of the Soviet Union is equalled only by that of the Japanese for Russians in general, needs Japan's expertise and manufactured products no less than Japan needs China's goodwill and custom.

From Thailand to Asia Minor the Japanese are king of the exports castle, and dominant in the field of industrial co-operation. The Indonesians may still not like them, but they could hardly do without them. The Malaysians and Singaporeans, who had every cause to loathe them, have long since forgotten the Imperial Japanese Army's excesses and (building on Britain's bequest of independence both from communism and colonialism) have become an immensely rich people who buy everything they need from Japan.

From Fiji to New Zealand – with the exception of French Tahiti – the Pacific islands are part of Japan's exporting domain, New Zealand especially depending upon Japan's millions to buy the meat and butter she used to export to Britain before Britain joined the EEC.

When it buys an imported product – be it anything from a camera to a motor car, a ship to a grand piano, a pocket calculator to a video recorder – about half the world's population buys Japanese: of the other half (if one omits those who live behind the Iron Curtain and are unable to buy any foreign consumer goods) only a minority have nothing in their homes that was *Made in Japan*. Not even in the days of their unchallenged industrial supremacy were the British and Americans able to claim the same.

CHAPTER TWENTY

>>>>>>>>>><<<<<<<<<

Semantics

IF JAPAN CONTINUES to export so successfully that every other industrial nation suffers, the day will arrive when those other nations will
be unable to import from her, and Japan, her industrial supremacy
notwithstanding, will grow not richer but poorer. A dialogue
between her government and the government of each of her rivals is
plainly vital.

A dialogue presupposes a lingua franca as comprehensible to the
one as it is to the other, however; and no such language seems to
exist. Not only does Japanese not lend itself to precise translation
into any other language, but the semantics of every other language
apparently defeat those whose task it is to translate them into precise
Japanese.

An eloquent race, the Japanese communicate with each other in
a language that, to a foreigner, is elusive, elliptic and even obscure.
Hirohito's surrender Rescript has been translated into English a
score of times, and varies so greatly from one version to the next that
it is only by a kind of synthesis that one can reproduce in English
what was probably said in Japanese.

Even more confusing is the fact that some foreign words which
translate exactly into a Japanese synonym do not convey to the
Japanese mind what they convey to the foreigner who spoke them.

The rhythms, cadences, nuances and even the mechanics of
Western languages are alien to the mind of a Japanese. To him,
English lacks gradations of 'politeness' and diplomacy; and the
principles of lucidity and logic upon which its use is based are the
antithesis of those principles of allusion and unassertiveness upon
which Japanese is based. English speakers like to get to the point: the
Japanese like to spiral round it. As a consequence, they are both
more flowery and less conceptual in their use of language than
Westerners.

'I hope you will take good care of your health,' Hirohito told
Prime Minister Lloyd George when he visited England as Crown

Prince in 1921. Doubtless Lloyd George was flattered; but 22 years later our Japanese commandant in Thailand was saying almost the same thing to us as we built his tiresome railway from Bam Pong to Rangoon. On both occasions, in effect, the words were platitudinous to the point of being meaningless.

'The Navy was a past master of the art of equivocation,' Toshikasu Kase complains. But so are most Japanese, who use words to save face, mislead, bluff or blur; and they can switch with amazing speed from the explicit to the euphemistic.

The West coined words like 'pigs' and 'fuzz' for policemen only in the 1960s: the Japanese were just as explicitly calling them 'dogs' in the 1930s; but the Army more euphemistically described its assassinations in 1931 as 'deeds of negative daring'; and the Japanese people always referred to their war in China as 'the pacification of our brother'.

To us, cynical lies: to them, a package of facts wrapped in aspiration wrapped in metaphor. 'Negative daring' means counter-productive assassination wrapped in militarist ideals wrapped in the language of heroism. The 'pacification of our brother' means aggression wrapped in gratitude (for China's gift of culture) wrapped in the language of adventurism. We understand what is said: the Japanese understand what is left unsaid.

It is in their rhetoric, though, that Westerners perceive the widest gulf between the Japanese articulation of ideas and their own. Explaining his country's war against China to the American Foreign Policy Association in New York, in 1937, a Japanese spokesman said: 'Hitting someone on the head for his own good is not so illogical as many of you are prone to think.' His English was perfect; his language was evocative; but the effect produced on his audience was the opposite of what he intended.

When Premier Konoye addressed the Japanese in 1938, he invited them, 'to unite monolithically' behind the Emperor in an 'unselfish effort' as they fought 'a holy war' to achieve 'liberation for all Asian peoples'. To Japanese ears it was nothing less than Chur-chillian: to us, Goebbels-like propaganda.

Konoye's successor in 1939 used metaphors so contradictory that he would have been lampooned by every political correspon-dent in the land had he been British, or American, or European. Not even Hitler would have dared announce, as he did, plans to mobilize 'the defence state' for a 'total war' in which Japan was to be the aggressor.

But Konoye was very conscious of the fact that Japan had been a signatory to the 1928 Paris Convention that outlawed wars of aggression. Therefore any war that Japan might decide to wage had, by definition, to be a defensive war. So her state was overnight transformed into a 'defence state' and the Supreme Council was able to take the self-contradictory decision to complete Japan's preparations for 'defensive aggression' by late October, and incongruously to resolve, 'as a matter of national preservation, not to avoid war with the United States'.

When French Indo-China was invaded in 1941, its tiny garrison resisted bitterly for 72 hours: the occupation was reported in Japan to have been completed 'peacefully'.

Naturally the Americans were upset. They terminated the United States-Japanese Trade Agreement, froze Japanese assets and imposed their embargo. The Japanese ambassador thereupon warned the State Department that such a policy would render future relations between the two countries, 'unpredictable'.

Since anything 'unexpected' in relationships is distasteful to the Japanese, 'unpredictable' was one of those words (like loud, harsh, severe, difficult and rude) which are veritable storm warnings when uttered by them. Just one month later, however, Admiral Yamamoto would abandon such diplomatic niceties and refer to America's embargo as the 'final outrage of breaking off economic relations with us'. And only days before Pearl Harbour, the Emperor, in an exquisite example of Japanese understatement, would put it just as menacingly. 'The times have become very difficult, haven't they?' he sighed.

At almost the same time Admiral Nomura, as Ambassador to the United States, was frantically negotiating with Cordell Hull in accordance with a brief handed to him by Foreign Minister Matsuoka just before his departure to Washington. It contained ten paragraphs, almost any one of which would have boggled the mind of a Western diplomat. The fourth began, 'The United States must be prevented from waging war on Japan . . . in the cause of humanity'; but infinitely more tortuously, and less logically, the sixth admitted, 'It may be that some of Japan's actions in China have seemed irregular, unjust or aggressive, but that is a passing phase. Our country will always ensure peace and reciprocity between China and Japan. The day will come when the great ideal – the world under one roof – will become a living reality.'

Unfortunately for those foreigners who seek to understand them completely, the Japanese can also be frighteningly literal in their interpretation of single words.

As Foreign Minister, Togo was anxious to start the war respectably. 'Naturally,' he instructed the Navy, 'we should give notice of the commencement of hostilities.'

'But we are going to make a *surprise* attack,' protested the Navy's Chief of Staff.

The American Pacific Fleet's battleships and cruisers having been destroyed in Pearl Harbour, the Japanese sought out Britain's *Prince of Wales* and *Repulse* off the east coast of Malaya. By the time the two battleships had been sunk, the 24 surviving Japanese bombers had no ammunition left. Making a chivalrous virtue out of necessity, the pilot of one of them dropped a message to a British destroyer busily plucking sailors out of the sea. 'We have completed our task,' it read. 'Carry on.'

The Imperial Japanese Army's less than enchanted prisoners of war were subsequently and constantly required to read official pronouncements, the style of all of them pre-ordained by Yamashita's letter to Percival of February 1941.

In a spirit of chivalry, he wrote, *we have the honour of advising your surrender. Your army, founded on the traditional spirit of Great Britain, is defending Singapore, which is completely isolated, and raising the fame of Great Britain by the utmost exertions and heroic fighting. I disclose my respect from my inmost feelings.*

So Percival acceded to Yamashita's polite request, and we went to Thailand. Eden sent Shigemitsu a strong note about our condition and treatment there. The Japanese reply read: 'The Imperial Government, by exercising great vigilance as to health and hygiene of prisoners of war, takes added measure such as a monthly medical examination of each camp to enable sickness to be treated in the first stage.'

This last was true. Once a month, from that time onward, we were lined up naked outside one of our huts and a Japanese soldier wearing a gauze mask and white cotton gloves would insert a pencil-thick glass rod into one's rectum. As one straightened up, a Japanese NCO would instruct one, 'Put spirit in you! Look after your health!' That was our treatment. Lloyd George had had a dose of it from Hirohito.

The glass rod was inserted to obtain a smear, but there were neither pathologists nor laboratories in Thailand. When all the rods had been used, they were used a second time, and a third and a fourth and a fifth.

'I am pleased to find that you are in general keeping discipline and working diligently,' Colonel Nakamura congratulated us. 'At the same time regret to find seriousness in health matter . . . due mainly to the fact for absence of such firm belief as, "Japanese health follows will", and "Cease only when enemy annihilated".'

In Burma, shortly thereafter, it was the Imperial Japanese Army that was being annihilated. It therefore began to 'tenshin' – which means 'to advance elsewhere'. Or, in English, retreat.

Suzuki was made Premier. 'The art of government,' he used to say, 'lies in non-government' – by which he meant consensus. The same art is practised today, to the frustration and fury of those other governments who continue to delude themselves that a Japanese cabinet will one day do something to end the exports war.

Even when it had at last been impressed upon Admiral Suzuki's cabinet that 'unconditional surrender' meant 'surrender without conditions', the 1945 peace negotiations very nearly foundered because Anami would not accept the sentence in the proposed Rescript which read, 'The war situation has daily deteriorated.'

Even when that difficulty was resolved, and a note despatched to Washington advising that the Emperor would broadcast to his people the following day, the Foreign Office was unable to resist the temptation to cable yet again suggesting the condition that Japanese officers (contrary to the terms just accepted) be allowed to disarm the Army. Since 'unconditional surrender' was anathema to them, Suzuki and his colleagues simply could not believe that that really was what was being required of them.

As noted, when Hirohito's Rescript was broadcast, the word *shusen* was used, not *haisen,* so that Japan believed herself simply to have stopped fighting, not to have surrendered. None of the Allied interpreters monitoring the broadcast noticed the difference. But the Japanese language is one of almost habitual euphemism, and none knew it better than we who were their prisoners. 'Very sorry,' they would say, when we asked for medicines or food, or when they saw us beaten up. 'Very sorry' means anything from 'Certainly not' to 'Tough cheese': it never means sorry.

'That is very difficult,' they would say when we asked for medicines or food. 'That is very difficult' means, 'Sorry, but no, although we could easily do it.'

'That is a difficult question,' on the other hand, means, 'I know the answer but I don't intend giving it to you because it would embarrass me/you.' If it is accompanied by the pressing of all the finger tips (like a closed tulip) to a small area of the forehead just above the nose, it means, 'I am very sorry but I'm not allowed to answer that question, much as I would like to.'

And if it is said with a smile, it means, 'No comment.'

We sailed home and the Occupation Force marched into Japan; but the Japanese called it a 'Coming-in-Force' – thereby saving themselves a considerable loss of face and leaving themselves free to treat it at first with disciplined courtesy and finally almost with warmth.

* * *

Little wonder, then, that the young minister plenipotentiary about whom Kenichi Yoshida wrote should have suggested that the Japanese abandon their language and use English instead; but how amazing that so few Western statesmen have realised that, when they and the Japanese use the same words, the Japanese frequently mean, or have understood, something quite different.

'Japanese is simply *not* a language of logic,' a Japanese professor assured me.

'Japanese is the most logical language in the world,' a British civil servant in the Department of Trade crossly contradicted, quite unaware of the fact that he was disputing something the professor had never said. It would have been as logical to contradict the assertion, 'English is simply not the language of love,' by retorting, 'English is the loveliest language in the world.' Yet it was one of the responsibilities of the said linguist to advise on trade relations with Japan.

Though Westerners are just as often misunderstood by the Japanese with whom they are in conversation as Japanese are mis-understood by Westerners, the Japanese are at least aware of the dangers, and distressed when they succumb to them. Responding to a petition that the United States permit Japanese citizens to visit graves on Ogasawara, Defence Secretary McNamara replied, 'I'll consider it.' Translated literally into its Japanese equivalent, this answer was taken by McNamara's dismayed petitioners to mean, 'Request denied.'

'Our misunderstanding of the Defence Secretary's reply was a disgrace,' a Japanese academic apologized: yet all that the 'dis-graced' petitioners had done was to treat McNamara's words as if they had been spoken in Japanese. Western diplomats constantly

186

misunderstand Japanese statements (and just as disgracefully) without even realizing, still less apologizing for, what they have done.

An even greater barrier between dialogue and comprehension is the attitude of Westerners to those Japanese with whom they are negotiating, and to whom they are supposed to be listening.

In October 1981, Mr Watanabe, Deputy President of the Bank of Tokyo, addressed a group of British businessmen in the Committee Room of the Royal Automobile Club in London. His audience arrived looking unenthusiastic and shop-worn, and left the afternoon tea table, to take its seats, reluctantly. The public address system, which was British, hummed, to the irritation of the Japanese delegates; but Mr Watanabe applied himself to the task in hand with a mixture of Japanese courtesy and determination. His theme was, *'Industrial co-operation as the key to economic revitalization'*.

'We Japanese are now taking the problem of Europe's trade imbalances with us very seriously,' he said. An Englishman sitting ten feet away from him turned sideways in his chair and began to read a paperback.

Mr Watanabe expatiated on Europe's trade imbalances with Japan, and the measures that might be taken by each side to reduce them. A gentleman in the front row went to sleep.

'We take a long time to make decisions,' Mr Watanabe confessed. 'However, once the decision *is* made, our execution of it is rapid and single-minded.'

Undeterred (indeed unmoved) by that ominous 'single-minded', a younger, keener-looking type of Englishman than the rest furtively extracted his pink edition of the *Financial Times* from his overcoat pocket and even more furtively opened it. The entire audience (apart from the man who slept) was thereby fascinated.

'The way ahead,' Mr Watanabe suggested, valiantly attempting to recapture his audience's attention, 'is one of free trade and expansion rather than controls and contraction.' He further suggested the interchange of investment, the exchange of technological information, and collaboration in such things as design; but even as he explained the virtues of these three aspects of industrial co-operation it was obvious that half his audience was no longer listening. British male audiences (who know everything already) seldom do, of course; but Mr Watanabe was a distinguished guest from whom there was much that it could have learned, and from whose country it was doubtless hoping to extract concessions.

'Develop technology jointly,' Mr Watanabe concluded his

187

address. 'Better still, export jointly through joint international suppliers.'

There was muted applause. His chairman asked for questions, and there was a long silence. Eventually a representative of the Confederation of British Industry asked him what sectors Mr Watanabe could suggest as suitable for international investment in *Japan*.

Mr Watanabe pressed the finger tips of his right hand tulip-like against the centre of his forehead, paused and then replied, 'That is a difficult question.'

Omitting to answer it, he spoke instead about 'the severity of the situation that faces us in the eighties'. No one pressed him on the discrepancy between his enthusiasm for joint ventures in Europe and his lack of enthusiasm for joint ventures in Japan. It is precisely that discrepancy that has most exacerbated trade relations between the West and Japan.

Instead, a journalist asked a complicated question about Japanese exports in relation to the value of the yen. Only he and Mr Watanabe understood it. Mr Watanabe answered learnedly. The journalist wrote down every word. Then came the punch line. 'But now,' Mr Watanabe warned, 'our eyes are beginning to focus on Europe.' And his audience reacted with even less alarm than we had, forty years earlier, when it became evident that their eyes were beginning to focus on South East Asia. Despite all the evidence to the contrary, Mr Watanabe was just another myopic little man from Japan. The following day he went to the Foreign Office to discuss Britain's trading problems with Lord Carrington.

In 1936 Toto Ishimaru wrote a book entitled *Japan Must Fight Britain*. The battle, he said, would be for Singapore. No one in Britain took any notice of Mr Ishimaru. Japan did fight Britain; the battle was for Singapore; and Britain lost.

In 1965, Premier Miki warned that Japan intended converting South East Asia into 'a privileged economic zone'. No one took any notice: it is now an almost exclusive Japanese economic zone.

In 1981, Mr Watanabe declared that Japan's eyes were 'beginning to focus on Europe'. Though his audience at the RAC responded not at all, it is not known whether Lord Carrington responded with alarm or disdain. In any event, he resigned in April 1982, whereupon Anglo-Japanese relations became the responsibility of Mr Francis Pym, whose effusions on the subject of foreign policy rarely made sense even to the British.

By July, however, it was the Japanese whose effusions were confounding world opinion. Having once again succumbed to their propensity for euphemism, and their insensitivity to the feelings of foreigners, they issued a high school history book in which both their long and ruthless occupation of Korea and their brutal war of aggression against China had been so 'prettified' as to make them sound respectable.

China protested promptly and angrily – and was just as promptly assured that Japan 'took humble note of her serious concern'. But the damage had been done. From Seoul to Singapore, Rangoon to Manila, bitter memories were revived and distrust rekindled. Semantics remained the greatest barrier between Japan and her desire to endear herself to the rest of the world.

CHAPTER TWENTY-ONE

>>>>>>>>><<<<<<<<

Ethics and Morality

IN THE MIDDLE of January 1982, the newspapers of America, Europe
and Britain ran a story headlined JAPAN'S TRADE PACT WITH WEST. At
last, apparently, the semantic block had been broken. Indeed, President Reagan's trade representative even spoke of 'an enormous
commitment' by the Japanese to abstain from protectionism. 'The
proof of the pudding will come in the next several months,' he
warned, 'but I think we have made a good beginning.'

The Conference of EEC, American, Canadian and Japanese
trade officials had lasted two days, but Mr Shintaro Abe had finally
responded to allegations that Japan maintained an unfair system of
indirect restrictions on imports even though she had removed almost
all *direct* restrictions. Despite the fact that her trade surplus for the
year was forecast at $34 billion, she imposed over-strict health con-
trols and superfluous safety standards, for example, and took
months (even years) to carry out the various tests to satisfy those
controls and standards. And if that failed to block the goods in
question, she used her complex system of distribution to ensure that
they reached their destination too late and in too small quantities.
'But,' promised Mr Abe, 'Japan will take drastic action before the
end of the month' – in fact it was by mid June – 'to *reduce*' – not
abolish – 'these non-tariff barriers.'

A sceptical British official responded wearily on behalf of the
Common Market countries, 'The Japanese have made such promises before. If all they do is cut tariffs on biscuits from 35 to 32%,
that's not going to solve our problems' – and thus not only predicted
one concession with total accuracy but also publicized yet another
obstacle in the path of those who seek to negotiate an armistice in the
export war of the eighties. When it comes to agreements or treaties,
the West instinctively asks itself (in the words of a London *Daily
Telegraph* headline of 3 March 1981) 'CAN EUROPE TRUST THE
JAPANESE?'

With a fine disregard for such of its own breaches of faith as America's insistence in 1951 that Japan flout Article 9 of her constitution, or Germany's invasion of neutral Belgium in 1914, or Britain's invasion of Egypt in 1956, or Italy's of Abyssinia in 1935, or France's present flouting of any free trade rule she finds inconvenient, or the betrayal of Poland by Roosevelt at Yalta in 1945, or a thousand other acts of expediency, the West is suspicious of Japan: Roosevelt's 'Day of Infamy' lingers on.

In this respect, not only does the West apply to Japan standards of ethics and integrity from which it habitually excuses itself, it also omits to judge Japan by her own standards.

'In our country,' wrote the philosopher Arai Hakusaki three hundred years ago, 'those who have won are invariably right, and those who have been defeated are wrong.' Were he alive today, he would alter not a word – for which no one should have been more grateful than General Douglas MacArthur in 1945.

When he entered Japan at the head of his Occupation Force, he and it were hopelessly outnumbered by more than two and a half million fully armed Japanese who could easily have murdered him and wiped out most of his small army before an invasion could be mounted to suppress them. They refrained from doing so not only because their Emperor had told them, 'Beware most strictly any outbursts of emotion,' but also because the practice of defecting to the victor was enshrined in their long history of internecine wars.

The Japanese social contract, in feudal times, imposed an obligation upon every man – soldier or civilian – to obey his Lord; and he who conquered his Lord had always become his new master.

Ethics entered into the new relationship not at all: it was, and remains, a de facto acknowledgement that, 'those who have won are always right'. Any who were unwilling so to transfer their loyalties simply killed themselves.

'Morals were invented by the Chinese because they were an immoral people,' wrote the Shintoist philosopher Motoori two centuries ago. 'In Japan there was no need for any moral code,' because, to live a moral life, a man needed, 'only to consult his heart'.

His heart, however, was governed by his innumerable obligations – to his Emperor, his Lord, his master, his village, his group, his parents, his family – and to fail in any one of them was to offend so unpardonably that only death could exonerate him. Trapped in a web of a thousand silken threads of obligation, he scrupulously

191

declined to add to them either the chains of morality or the bonds of outside relationships.

Stirred to pity by the suffering of a prisoner of war, he simply said, 'Very sorry.' To have done more would have implied a moral judgement upon those who had maltreated the object of his compassion. Worse, it would have introduced yet another obligation into his life to the man he had rescued. And every obligation, of which he had too many already, was assumed for life. Confronted by so many barbarian enemies to whom he owed no sort of obligation, it was, in fact, almost irresistibly tempting to regard every one of them as 'his father's murderer', and to release upon any one of them who crossed his path the pent-up fury of a life-time's servitude.

'A man away from home need feel no shame,' a Japanese proverb excuses: the Imperial Japanese Army felt no shame. Whether the peace-loving generations that have succeeded it regard their foreign rivals in the trade war as people to whom they now have any kind of obligation, or whether they still regard them as 'barbarians' to whom no obligations are owed, only they know – and they have not chosen to tell us. If, however, the truth of the matter is that they feel no obligation to us, because they are once again victors, and therefore right, trade negotiations with their official representatives will be as meaningless as Ambassador Nomura's were in 1941 with Secretary of State Cordell Hull.

*   *   *

Diplomacy in international affairs is the art of presenting self-interest in the guise of the common good, and war in the guise of self-preservation cloaked in idealism: it is an art that the Japanese have never mastered.

Hampered by pragmatism on the one hand, and a regard for truth on the other, they felt justified in embarking on each of their twentieth century adventures, but always lacked the ability to lie about them convincingly.

Westminster, in the great days of the Empire, and Washington while it alone possessed the Bomb, both lied so convincingly that they convinced all but their near impotent rivals that they had brought the world a Pax Britannica and a Pax Americana respectively; but Tokyo (like Moscow, Berlin, Pretoria and OPEC) has never managed to disguise its aspirations so flatteringly.

When it ordered the invasion of Korea in 1894 it was unnecessary

192

to lie because every sovereign state at that time enjoyed the right to wage aggressive war; but any confidence Japan may have had in the integrity of her fellow sovereign states was promptly extinguished by the intervention of Russia, Germany and France.

Likewise any confidence she may have had in the consistency of her fellow sovereign states was dissipated by the tacit approval of Britain and America of her sneak attack on Port Arthur in 1904.

Yet those same two powers were to intervene most forcefully when Japan took advantage of World War I to invade China in 1915. Having condoned her occupation of Germany's island possessions in the Pacific, and the German concession of Tsingtao on the Chinese mainland in 1914, they insisted that she surrender her third conquest. Until 1945, she was never again to trust anyone; and since 1949 she can have seen nothing in the consistently cynical policies of the West to cause her to start trusting it.

Nevertheless, she did, in 1928, allow herself to become one of the 63 signatories to the Pact of Paris which outlawed war except in self-defence; and a mere three years later, as she began her fourteen years of aggression, was regretting it.

Aware that she had blundered, perhaps, she declined to ratify the Geneva Convention of 1929 which required all its signatories to treat their future prisoners of war humanely. To sign the Convention, the Japanese objected, would be to license an enemy to send bombers over their cities from double the normal range. Having done their worst, their crews would simply parachute from aircraft that had run out of fuel and spend the rest of the war in the safety of a prison camp.

As the thirties began, it was the British, says Aida, whom Japan saw as her enemies, 'or rather,' he somewhat ominously amends, 'as our rivals'. Desperate to avert war, Britain began to negotiate. In a position of power for the first time, the Japanese proved obdurate. Even as *potential* winners, they knew that they were in the right.

'Co-operation of the kind which would be welcome to Japan,' the British government was warned by one of its experts, 'would mean supporting her in a perfectly unscrupulous pursuit of exhorbitant claims. Japan certainly cares nothing about her moral position in the eyes of the world.' Why should she have cared? She had consulted her heart, and her heart had told her to do what was most profitable for Japan.

While every other nation cared intensely about its moral position in the eyes of the world, Japan's only concession to the morality of the Paris Pact was to describe her war against China as an

193

'Incident'; and she circumvented the morality of the Geneva Convention (even though she had refused to ratify it) by taking no prisoners.

In 1939 she was disconcerted to realize that not even the admirable Nazis were reliable: Hitler had negotiated a Neutrality Pact with Russia in flat contravention of the Anti-Comintern Pact he had so recently signed with Japan.

'However we consider the Anti-Comintern Pact and its attached secret protocols,' Kido lamented, 'we are startled that there has been this breach of faith.' Yet the secret protocols he mentioned required Japan to attack Russia should Germany do so, and Japan had already decided *not* to attack Russia should Germany do so until she was *certain* that Germany would win.

Equally, however, the protocols required Germany to attack Russia should Japan do so. Quite unaware of any inconsistency in her two attitudes, and determined to test *Hitler's* loyalty, the Japanese launched an attack against Nomonhan, a Soviet outpost on the border between Manchuria and Siberia. To their chagrin and shame, Hitler refrained from attacking Russia, and the Russians, led by General Zhukov, routed their Kwangtung Army.

Nomonhan, Hitler's failure to come to their assistance and the Navy's desire to participate in the war, combined to convince the Japanese that they should drive southwards not northwards. They ceased focussing their attention on Russia, signed a Tripartite Pact with Germany and Italy and then (the better to protect their Siberian flank) sought a six year neutrality pact of their own with the Soviet Union.

When it was done, as David Bergamini relates in his book *Japan's Imperial Conspiracy*, Foreign Minister Matsuoka raised his glass to Molotov and said, 'The treaty is made. I do not lie. If I lie, my head shall be yours. If you lie, rest assured that I will come for your head.'

In less than a month, however, Hitler had dishonoured his Non-aggression Pact with Stalin and invaded Russia, and Matsuoka was insisting that Japan fulfil her obligation to the Fuhrer by invading Siberia. In this he was supported by the leader of the Privy Council, who argued, 'The Soviet Union is notorious for her acts of betrayal. Were we to attack the Soviet Union, no one would regard it as treachery.'

Matsuoka's plea was rejected not because it could have been regarded as treacherous but because Nomonhan had finally convinced Japan's militarists that it was upon America and Britain that Japan should focus its attention.

Reeling under Hitler's onslaught, the Soviet Union was anxious to learn whether Japan would abide by the terms of the Anti-Comintern Pact, or of the Neutrality Pact Matsuoka had signed with Molotov. Enjoying her new-found sense of power, and hoping to persuade Hitler to disengage from Russia and concentrate all his strength against Britain – to facilitate her own conquest of Singapore – Japan was slow to give Molotov a favourable answer.

For the moment, though, Hitler had persuaded his puppet Vichy government in France to agree to the occupation of Indo-China by his ally Tojo, and Cordell Hull had persuaded his President, Roosevelt, to treat the Japanese uncompromisingly. They were to withdraw from the Tripartite Pact as well as from Indo-China, they were told.

'It was impossible for us to abrogate the Axis alliance . . . without reassuring ourselves as to the true intentions of the United States,' commented Toshikasu Kase. 'Moreover, we could not come to terms with the United States except by abandoning our policy of expansion on the continent.'

Hoist on her own petard, Japan was unable to withdraw from what, in fact, was a war as easily as she could have done from what she had always described as an Incident: so she attacked Pearl Harbour. Still seeking respectability, however, she adhered to the spirit of the 1928 Paris Pact by calling what was incontrovertibly an aggressive war, 'a war of defence'.

Just as untruthfully – but with vastly more effect – Roosevelt described 7 December 1941, as 'the day that will live in infamy'. It was infamous because the raid took place before Japan formally declared war. Roosevelt did not reveal that he had known that the Japanese were about to launch an attack. Still less did he confess that he had expected the target to be Singapore. Instead, he deployed lies, half-truths and irresistible rhetoric to convince the United States and the world that the war against Japan (and Germany) was a selfless one.

Now it was Japan's turn to seek reassurances from Moscow about their Neutrality Pact. Hard pressed by Hitler's armies to the west, and determined to avoid a Japanese onslaught from the east, Moscow insisted that the Pact was binding. But, commented Shigemitsu, 'We could not rely too much on the assurances of Mol-

195

otov' – entirely disregarding the fact that Russia, had she but known it, could have relied on the assurances of Matsuoka not at all.

The more easily to attack Malaya, the Japanese now invaded Thailand – with whom they had previously signed a treaty of friendship. 'Although it seemed a breach of international good faith,' commented Tsuji, 'we had to disregard it for the sake of the conquest of Singapore.'

Singapore fell, then the Dutch East Indies and Burma, and finally the Americans found themselves in a hopeless position at Bataan.

'The Japanese commander demanded my unconditional surrender,' General King relates. 'I attempted to secure from him an assurance that my men would be treated as prisoners of war. He accused me of declining to surrender unconditionally and trying to make a condition.' Three years later, when the Allies demanded Japan's unconditional surrender, her militarists saw no inconsistency in their attempt to impose four conditions.

The Wehrmacht's defeat at Stalingrad convinced Japan that Germany's efforts were being wasted in Russia. As her own war faltered, Shigemitsu suggested that Japan attempt to persuade Russia to renege on the Allies and negotiate a separate peace with Germany. Stalin – for whom a continued war now offered rich pickings in Central and Eastern Europe – would have none of it.

Japan's argument against ratification of the Hague Convention had been that enemy fliers could take advantage of it, but it is still impossible to defend her subsequent execution of captured air crews simply by stating that she was not a signatory to the Convention. Both seem to be entirely and logically the consequence of the indoctrination of the Imperial Japanese Army and the orders laid down for it in *The Battlefield Commandment*.

Be that as it may, the war was irredeemably lost by 1945, and on 5 April the Soviet government denounced its Neutrality Pact with Japan – which, said Shigemitsu, 'was a bolt from the blue, shattering all our illusions'. Again and again, in their statements about the attitude of others toward them, one is made aware of the fact that the Japanese have never learned that what is good for the goose is good for the gander, that what they hope to receive is not what *must* be given to them, that what they should give is not necessarily only as much as they choose to spare.

'The Emperor should have no immunity from responsibility for Japan's acts of aggression,' Canberra cabled to Washington in an attempt to influence President Truman's decision about the future of Hirohito. 'The Japanese will remain unchanged, and a recrudescence of aggression in the Pacific will only be postponed to a later generation,' should the Imperial system not be demolished.

Truman left the decision to MacArthur; he and his Occupation Force were so obviously the winners that, to the minds of the occupied, they had to be right; the GIs wanted sex, so a recent munitions factory was transformed into a vast brothel in which 250 girls processed 15 GIs apiece a day; and Premier Higashakuni blithely declared, 'Japan has already tried her war criminals – and it may be taken for granted that their punishment has already taken place!' Pressed for details, he advised that no less than two officers had been sent to prison for brutality to those who worked on the Thailand Railway!

Unconvinced, MacArthur's investigators arrested some 7000 others and punished many of them rather more severely. MacArthur himself, meanwhile, was busy turning the Japanese into ersatz Americans.

At the time of their surrender, it had been stipulated that they build no ships of more than 5000 tons or capable of a speed of more than eleven knots. In 1949 this inhibition was cancelled: for the first time MacArthur's administration had admitted that the victor could sometimes be wrong. In the years that followed, more admissions would be made, and the Japanese would slowly regain their national pride. Ostensibly under the thumb of Washington, they began to assert their independence.

In 1953, while Mussadeq sought unilaterally to nationalize Britain's vastly profitable Anglo-Iranian Oil Company, it was a Japanese who took advantage of the dispute to ingratiate himself with the Iranian government, buy Iranian oil cheaply and establish himself as his country's first oil-tanker tycoon.

Though Japan's publicly declared foreign policy was 'to have no foreign policy', she could more accurately have defined it as one of cautious opportunism akin to that of France – and little different from that of any other country.

Thus, in 1973, she would again deny her supposed allies the better to endear herself to the Arab oil states. And in 1980, during the 444-day American hostage crises in Teheran, she would attempt to breach President Carter's embargo on the purchase of oil from Iran by offering to buy the previous United States allocation for herself. This action was deemed doubly reprehensible by President Carter in view of the fact that Premier Ohira had only recently agreed that 'gas-guzzling' Japan would keep her 1980 oil consumption at the level of the previous year.

Nor was Prime Minister Margaret Thatcher to be any more pleased with Japan's refusal to adopt an anti-Argentinian stance during the Falklands Crisis of 1982.

Until 1981, however, Japan gave no foreign government cause for outspoken complaint except by trading too successfully, about which they all complained. Zenko Suzuki, the new Premier, responded to these recurring waves of criticism by announcing, 'Transcending our passive posture of the past, our aim will be to fulfill on our own initiative our international responsibilities to reinforce and consolidate peace in our increasingly vulnerable world community.' Japan, he declared, was preparing for a 'third, fresh start' – the first having been her entry into world affairs at the behest of the United States government and Commodore Perry; and the second her days of reconstruction after her defeat in World War II. 'From passive beneficiary to active creator: this may be Japan's third start,' he concluded.

It was a typically obscure Japanese speech, densely rhetorical and disturbingly ambiguous – particularly in its failure to say, 'active *benefactor*' (which would have been the logical rhetorical antithesis to 'passive beneficiary') rather than 'active *creator*'.

It was no less disturbing in its vagueness about the three 'starts'. All too soon after the first, Japan had embarked on her first war against China; and only six years after that, in 1900, General Katsuro Taro, whilst Governor General of Taiwan, had drawn up the first plans for Japan's occupation of Malaya, the Dutch East Indies and the Philippines. Admittedly they were shelved; but in 1942 they came to pass, and were even extended to cover everything west of Malaya as far as (and including some of) the Middle East, and everything east of the Philippines including South America, half of Mexico, part of Peru and Chile, parts of Canada and the USA and all the Pacific islands including Australasia. And it was these plans that had finally made defeat, and Start Two, inevitable.

But that had been signalled by the propaganda from 1943 to 1945 about the Hundred Year War. And Suzuki's Start Three, in 1981, had been forecast in the final passages of Hirohito's Imperial Rescript of 15 August 1945. So what exactly did the Premier promise when he declared that Japan would switch from passive beneficiary to active creator?

But then Admiral Elmo Zumwalt, late of the US Navy, visited Canberra and told a startled Federal Government that Australia could no longer rely on effective American support in the event of a full scale attack on the Commonwealth. 'The situation that I think most naval men see coming to pass is an incompetence on the part of the free world to defend its merchant marine,' he said. Australia and Japan were mutually dependent on the Japanese merchant marine. Since Japan's small, though professional, Navy was incapable of defending that shipping – nor was the US Navy able to do so – Admiral Zumwalt's advice was unhappily received.

Almost immediately General Goro Takeda (who had just retired from the post of Chairman to the Joint Chiefs of Staff of the Japanese Self-Defence Forces) declared that Japan could not defend herself alone. The Navy had only 58 ships (any one of which could be destroyed by Russia's accurate missiles from ranges of thirty to sixty miles), her Army had only 300 tanks (although it required a minimum of 1100) and she spent only 0·9% of her gross national product on defence when a minimum of 3% was essential if Japan was effectively to resist an anticipated (but unspecified) attack in the mid 1980s. She must re-arm, he suggested, so that she could at least hold out until America came to her help.

He was not without allies in this cause. Some demanded the re-introduction of conscription; others demanded that Article 9 of the Constitution be scrapped; over 30% of the high school students in Tokyo, Osaka and Sapporo declared themselves in favour of Japan acquiring nuclear weapons and transforming herself into 'a fortress of peace'; and a few months later 37% of 3000 adults polled nationwide declared that they entertained 'only slight hopes or none at all, for Japan's material welfare in the twenty-first century'.

While the Japanese of 1981 were happily indulging in the 'art of pessimism', Europe and America were as obsessed by their trade imbalances with Japan as they had been by Hitler in 1939. Ignoring the fact that the Japanese might well seek an even greater revenge than their existing trade surpluses to compensate for the war-time loss of 2500 merchant ships, 50,000 aeroplanes and 5,000,000 casualties, the West thought of nothing but deficits and how Japan might help reduce them.

No less foolish was the EEC's conviction that Japan would not feel threatened by its policy of exclusivity. On the contrary, from its inception she had been as provoked and alarmed as Australia; and had responded with the sort of single-minded vigour that is peculiarly hers – so that by the mid seventies the EEC had begun to accuse *her* of exclusivity.

'There's no principle in GATT which will support the EEC argument that Japanese efficiency is unfair,' rapped a highly placed Australian government official. 'There will always be Japanese restrictions of some kind or another on imports, but the EEC is far *more* restrictive than Japan – *or* than the United States, Canada and Australia – especially since the EEC *dumps* its agricultural surpluses, to Canada's disadvantage *and* ours.

'And as to manufactured goods, the EEC offers a degree of aperture for imports that is miniscule! There should be some room at least for imports into *every* country: it's a fundamental principle of international trade. The EEC complains about Japan's trading surplus of $10 billion last year. There are about 200 million Europeans: but the EEC has a trading surplus of $2 billion with only 15 million of us Australians, and will make none of the trading concessions to us that it's presently insisting Japan should make to it. What the EEC – and, for that matter, the United States – have to learn is that one must never attempt trickery with the Japanese. They don't like it, and they never forgive it.'

In January 1982, ignoring this advice, Britain's Minister of Trade declared that there were only two options open to the West and Japan: either Japan would liberate her domestic market, whilst reducing her exports, or the West would retaliate with protectionism. Japan's response was to release her projected trading figures for the year: both America's deficit with her and the EEC's would rise by 50%! At that rate (which had been constant for the past four years) America's deficit with Japan would be $75 billion by 1985, and the EEC's $40 billion.

'If Japan were to behave again as she behaved in the past,' Shigemitsu warned his compatriots in 1960, 'her victory will turn to ashes once more.' Obviously he regarded that victory as inevitable; and patently Japan has achieved it without inflicting economic atrocities on her rivals. Instead, she has perpetuated her Security Pact with the United States (as much in response to Washington's needs as her own – and despite the threats of the Soviet Union) and has played the exports game exactly as her rivals play it. Unfortunately for them, she has played it too successfully. Only diplomacy or a Western technological and spiritual revolution can reverse the trend.

Just as Japan opened up a world-wide network of spies in 1934 (to prepare for military conquest) so – since 1960 – has a network of salesmen, trading companies and tourists provided her with a ceaseless flow of world-wide up-to-date data for her economic conquests.

Expert as she was, during World War II, at infiltration, she has contrived both to prevent foreigners from infiltrating her present industrial base and to seize industrial beach-heads in almost any foreign market she chose, so desperate has been each host nation's need to find jobs for its millions of unemployed.

The Japanese themselves are under no illusions about any of these matters. Speaking of America's ruinously expensive demand for Japanese products, Yoshizo Ikeda, Chairman of Mitsui, said flatly, 'These imports of high quality, low priced goods are *beneficial* to the United States economy; but unfortunately they sometimes cause political problems when the trade imbalance reaches a high level.

'In response to these *political* problems, various measures have been taken in recent years to control Japanese exports to the United States. These include Japanese self-restraint in the export of textiles . . . steel . . . colour television sets . . . and automobiles.

'This self-restraint of exports is an *emergency* measure to prevent the initiation of protectionism, and to maintain the free-trade system; but it should be resorted to *most* sparingly, and be *limited* in its scope.

'What I must emphasize is that such measures can only be temporary: they cannot solve the fundamental structural problems of the industry which is affected by import competition.'

The last thing America desired, however, was that Japan's self-restraint should be 'resorted to most sparingly and be limited in its scope'. It wanted self-restraint exercised extravangantly, and its scope to cover the entire gamut of America's manufacturing industry.

The Keidanren, said Yoshihiro Inayama, its Chairman, would persuade its members to co-operate in a wider policy of self-restraint provided *the government* decided that such steps must be taken to avert friction with the United States and the Western European nations.

That the government thereupon made no such decision is not surprising: its main party was financed by the Keidanren, and the Keidanren had made it abundantly clear to that party that 'it was divided on the wisdom of taking measures to enforce export restraints'. The ambivalence and dualism of the 1930s had surfaced

201

once again. Then it was government and Army: now it is government and Industry.

'Japan today feels that she is becoming great again,' admitted Katsuhiko Sakiyama, a publisher. 'And not all are sure that they want greatness again.' Since all are employed by *Japan Incorporated*, it is unlikely, however, that they will be asked.

'We have been motivated since the war by our memories of poverty,' a Japanese diplomat told me.

'When will those memories fade?'

'When we are as secure as the Americans.'

'And how much more damage must you inflict before you feel secure?'

'That is the question,' he said, and looked gloomy.

By November 1982 it was the West that was feeling insecure. 'What do we want our kids to do,' demanded former Vice President Mondale as the first step in his bid for the 1984 Democratic Presidential nomination, 'sweep up round Japanese computers?' And having issued his challenge, proceeded forthrightly to elaborate on it. 'We've been running up the white flag when we should be running up the American flag . . . We've got to get tough, and I mean really tough, with nations that use our markets but deny us their markets.'

'Step up your export efforts,' retorted Japan's Foreign Ministry.

'We have no intention of working out what is called the third market-opening package,' Prime Minister Nakasone assured his agricultural constituents at Toyama, as unmoved by Mondale's challenge as, a few days later, he would be by Mrs Thatcher's rasping demand for concessions and the EEC's bureaucratic threat of a panel of arbitration.

'New nationalism casts shadows on Land of the Rising Sun,' commented the *Christian Science Monitor*.

'Japan wants stronger ties with Asian nations,' said Bangkok's *The Nation*.

In short, by 1983 the crisis that had erupted in November 1981 had not only *not* been resolved but, exacerbated by the Depression, had worsened.

CHAPTER TWENTY-TWO

>>>>>>><<<<<<<<

American Ineptitude: Japanese Illogic

SINCE WOODROW WILSON enunciated his Fourteen Points in 1918 it has been a cherished American delusion that US Presidents could (and indeed, if they wanted to be re-elected, should) transform the world.

Wilson gave the world the League of Nations to rid mankind of war; but in 1919 his Senate rejected his proposed peace-treaty, and the new-born League of Nations had to make do without the co-operation of its sire, the United States, which thereafter devoted all its energies to becoming richer, and circumventing Prohibition's anti-social sobriety.

Then came the Depression, which ruined Japan no less than it did the rest of the world. Desperate to cut their defence costs, America and Britain began to preach disarmament. Fearful that Japan might seize this opportunity to build a navy able to challenge either of theirs, they forced Japan to sign the London Naval Treaty of 1930. The Japanese felt demeaned: their army invaded China.

China, in the opinion of Secretary of State Stimson, was America's protégé; but neither he nor President Hoover was inclined to protect her. Not by force of arms, anyway, nor by economic sanctions. Moral pressure was the weapon the State Department deployed against the Japanese Government; but the Japanese proved immune to American morality.

Meantime, Britain's Chancellor of the Exchequer refused to allocate more funds for the building of battleships and cruisers, and the First Sea Lord pointed out that, unless he did, Britain might well lose her Empire.

President Roosevelt was no more sympathetic to the plight of the Royal Navy than the Chancellor of the Exchequer, and no more interested in Britain's theoretical need to defend herself and her

Empire than he was in the arrival upon the European scene of Adolf Hitler and Benito Mussolini. The only thing about Britain that concerned Roosevelt was that she might improve her relations with Japan. Should she even attempt to do so, he let it be known, he would seek to persuade New Zealand and Australia that their future safety lay with the United States of America.

Fearful of Japan's intention to switch her main attack from China to Hong Kong, Malaya and Singapore, Chamberlain sought the co-operation of the US Navy in a show of force in Far Eastern waters. Washington suspected Whitehall of attempting to use the American Navy to defend the British Empire – of which Roosevelt disapproved. As Japan rampaged through China, his Defence Secretary would do no more than moor America's fleet in Pearl Harbour. Despite every British plea, he refused to join in any attempt – military or economic – to dissuade the Japanese from waging war. Economic retaliation, Washington declared in 1938, was altogether too risky: it would look to the Japanese like collusion with the British. It was decided to send aid to Chiang Kai-shek instead. Despite this aid, Japan's war prospered.

Late in 1941 – some eight years too late – Roosevelt accepted that Japan was determined to go to war with Britain and America. He allowed Cordell Hull to send the Japanese Government a rude note; and the Japanese attacked Pearl Harbour.

President for the fourth time, Roosevelt had still learned nothing about foreigners. First, he imposed the doctrine of unconditional surrender; next – convinced that he had earned Stalin's undying devotion – he gave the Soviet Union as much of Europe as it could conquer; and finally, on the advice of General Marshall, he persuaded Stalin to join in the war against Japan once Germany had been defeated.

The war won, the Americans decided to reform the world a second time. With great generosity they financed the reconstruction of that part of Europe that Roosevelt had not bequeathed to Russia, and showed occupied Japan how to become a decent, if impoverished, democratic nation. When MacArthur abdicated as Shogun, to become Commander in Chief in Korea, he modestly declared that his Occupation Force had probably achieved the greatest reformation and revolution of all time.

'They could not rearm themselves for war within a hundred years,' he said. Starting today, they could do it in ten.

'The new Japanese Constitution is the most democratic in the world,' he said. More, it was 'the Magna Carta of Asia'. They have re-written it.

'The Japanese have got the spirit of the Sermon on the Mount,' he said. Which is about as true as his other celebrated dictum: 'The average Japanese man has the mentality of a twelve-year-old child.'

Between 1945 and 1950 the Japanese were allowed to do only those things of which MacArthur approved. In 1949, nevertheless, Joseph M. Dodge berated them for doing so little. 'It is time,' he said, 'the Japanese began to face up to the unalterable facts of their own life.' With MacArthur's approval, he abolished export subsidies (so that only the most efficient companies survived) and insisted that Japanese manufactured goods be sold abroad rather than at home. 'Wealth must be created before it can be divided,' he preached. His captive audience was delighted to take him at his word.

On 8 September 1951, a peace treaty was signed by representatives of those forty-eight countries who, earlier or later, had declared war on Japan. It did not include the clauses Britain had requested limiting Japan's future freedom to trade. The British would have preferred Japan's future outlets to be found in Mao Tse Tung's Communist China. America was prepared neither to allow her new protégé to be contaminated by the false creed of her old protégé, nor to allow Imperial Britain a monopoly of the market in Malaya and India.

Just as Washington refused to help Britain restrain the weeds of Japanese militarism before 1941, so she insisted upon protecting the frail seedling of Japanese industrialism after 1949. The second course may well have been as virtuous as the first was foolish; but both were short-sighted.

It would be agreeable – but untrue – to report that Pearl Harbour, Yalta and the resurgence since 1950 of Japan's industrial might had cured America's Presidents of the recurring Wilsonian delusion that they could curb all evils, cure all ills and reform all sinners with a few well-chosen words, or a brief visit from the White House.

Eisenhower thought he could do it by ousting Britain and France from Nasser's Suez Canal in 1956 and sending his marines ashore at Beirut in 1958. Kennedy thought he could do it by proclaiming, 'Ich bin ein Berliner,' and sending advisers to South Vietnam. Johnson thought he could do it by continuing the Vietnam war. Nixon thought he could do it by taking himself to Peking.

Carter thought he could do it by bringing Sadat and Begin together at Camp David. Reagan thought he could do it by touring Europe.

Global diplomacy is not a skill one expects to find in haberdashers, generals, lawyers, senators, peanut farmers or actors: it is a professional skill. America's post war Presidents, Secretaries of State and ambassadors have almost all been amateurs from whose dabblings only the Soviet Union and Japan have profited. It is to be hoped that future Presidents will leave foreign affairs to their Secretary of State, who will be a professional and whose ambassadors will be selected from a hierarchy of career diplomats. Foreign affairs are a by-product of foreign minds, which can be understood only by specialists.

*   *   *

And so we come full circle, back to 1941, when we felt threatened by the Japanese but knew nothing about them. Hundreds of books have since been written about them, to read which is to imbibe a veritable thesaurus of adjectives and metaphors, almost all of them true, and none definitive, because they were taken out of the context of total Japaneseness.

It goes without saying that that total concept eludes all Westerners. It even eludes the Japanese when they seek to define it, because theirs is not a language that lends itself to the definition of concepts.

Kenichi Yoshida comments wryly that the Japanese are 'different' because every race is different. What Yoshida omitted to observe was that the Japanese have almost nothing *in common* with the rest of the world.

Having spent two thirds of a lifetime thinking and reading about them, discussing and talking to them, I confess that not since I encountered the inhabitants of the weird world of Greek mythology have I known creatures so alien and complex as the Japanese. Nor, it would seem, has any other Westerner. Consider these descriptions of them from a mere armful of books.

The Japanese are 'short tempered and rash; react with extreme and sudden frenzy when confronted with a frustrating situation; believe in Buddhism's reverence for life but succumb to panic fury and kill wantonly; are an irrational nation; are interesting, neurotic, imponderable and frequently crazy; create illusions and then believe in them; regard all foreigners as unclean vermin; are a tragic people –

and dangerous if crowded; are a dynamic people who move in tremors and convulsions; are childlike; are hard workers and earnest; have a good sense of humour, more broad than subtle; are oddly young; are stubborn and eccentric; accept life as it is and regard the conceptual world as unnatural, impractical and a distortion; smile rather than argue logically; say yes rather than a frank, embarrassing no; are interested only in living, doing, experiencing, enjoying; began their new era of technology mainly by absorbing a vast amount of information which was accumulated and disseminated by computers; got all their computers from America; and all their information from others; can copy anything; can create nothing; side-step confrontations; fight with a concentrated fury; are incapable of abstract thinking; are selfish; ingrates; tenacious; notorious liars; colossally conceited in success; humble enough to learn from others; utterly uninterested in foreigners; iron-willed; punctilious; enigmatic; paradoxical; ambiguous; deceptive; and insane'.

Said one of Britain's most powerful industrialists: 'The Japanese? I don't trust them, I don't like them, I know nothing about them, and I *never* want to find out.' Say the Japanese, 'Our views are different, yes, but not unintelligible.'

According to the Japanese, from life to death, from the family to the state, the individual 'belongs' – and belonging, finds warmth, security, consistency, serenity and harmony.

But they are also, they confess, 'impulsive and irrational', which all too often has led them to a course of conduct that is 'haphazard and contradictory'. Then only failure makes them examine rationally the thing they did.

Even their perspective of past events differs vastly from ours. Thus, as an example of three significant events in their *recent* history, a professor cited to me the vendetta of the 47 Ronin from 1701 to 1703, the attack on Pearl Harbour in 1941, and the Tokyo Olympic Games in 1964.

They admit without shame (indeed almost with pride) that they do not understand any foreign mind; that their behavioural patterns are 'not quite scientific'; and that they prefer to be ambiguous about themselves, even to one another.

Thus they have two forms of seppuku – one to express a feeling of guilt, the other to deny a sense of guilt.

Thus demonstrations can be mounted to prevent something like the visits to Japan of American nuclear submarines – or to gain something — like concessions from America because anti-nuclear submarine demonstrations would have convinced Washington that Japanese loyalty to the Western cause was waning.

Thus even the short-lived collaboration of Japanese 'terrorists' with the PLO could have been ambiguous. It could have been genuine terrorism; it might have been government-inspired at a time when America – whose market and protection Japan needed – was out of favour with the Arabs – whose oil Japan needed. Ambiguity, like pessimism, is an art.

In discourse, say the Japanese, one should *not* hold fast to views sincerely held or one will be taken to be 'stubborn and bigoted'. The fact that they have not contradicted the West's forceful and ever reiterated demands for the liberalization of their non-tariff restrictions does not mean that they accept the rightness of those demands, still less that they will accede to them: it merely means that they are quite unwilling, by arguing them, to appear 'stubborn and bigoted'.

Anyway, whatever they say, they will be misunderstood. Japanese sentences do not depend on individual words, they explain, but on 'a composite whole' whose meaning depends as much on nuances, emphases and facial expressions as on the words themselves. And should a sentence be long, it is only the concluding words that matter!

Moreover, they admit, their mentality is not suited to abstract or long range thinking. And they can't talk to strangers at all. 'I don't know what he is because he didn't give me his business card,' they complain. 'So I don't know what to talk to him about.'

Should a man greet the first of two friends talking together, he will at once leave them unless he also knows the second. To remain would be to embarrass both himself and the third party, neither of whom would know what to talk about to the other. In this respect, Australians astound them. Australians, they have discovered, will talk to anyone about anything whether they know them or not.

They remain in their groups when abroad, they insist, because of this inability to make small talk with strangers. And because of the language barrier. And because it is impolite to assert oneself. Even at the United Nations their delegates decline to hold up their hands until they are sure they have something important to say. But by that time the debate is over, and they have said nothing. 'Foreigners think we are not frank,' they reflect ruefully. 'The truth is that we never say very much, and hate anything explicit.'

'In Japan,' they say, 'the right of an individual to be an individual has yet to come.' But, says Kosaka Masaaki, such 'non-assertiveness is either inappropriate or insufficient for modern society'.

Modern international dealings are governed by contracts, but, 'We Japanese feel uneasy, insecure, with any contractual clause relating to the future because it leaves us no room to adjust to unforeseen changes.' So they have become adept at inserting clauses of their own which enable them to circumvent other clauses. Payment for Australian consignments of iron ore, for example, are only made once the freight is aboard their trading company's ship. If the steel market momentarily collapses, their trading company abstains from sending its ship.

It was this ambivalent attitude to contracts in relation to unforeseen changes (combined with their conviction that no one was ever meant by the gods to deny them what they want) that enabled them to accuse the Russians of 'unpardonable and unlawful' conduct for revoking a six year Neutrality Pact that had ten contractual months to run. It never even occurred to them to reflect that they had seriously considered revoking the same six year pact when it had five years and ten months to run. But life for them is full of such contradictions.

'We avoid violence in our society,' says one.

'But if ever we do resort to it,' reminds another, 'it is with an utter disregard for logic.'

'We are *not* a logical people,' says a philologist. 'Our language is not a language of logic.'

'Only death is logical,' said a student.

'Yes, we still have a high rate of suicide,' a doctor agrees. 'Too many school children kill themselves. And even more old women – because the modern family feels less need of the grandmother; or the wife dislikes the traditional authority of her mother-in-law. More old women kill themselves in Japan than anywhere else in the world. Because they have decided that they no longer belong. Also, now that we have a free medical service, the young often bring their old people to our hospitals and leave them there while they go for their holidays. Some even try to leave them there for good. They think that one can belong in a hospital.'

'We are a meritocracy of seniority,' an industrialist explains, 'not of the competitive labour market. There is only competition for promotion if just one position is available to two men of equal seniority.'

But illogic will always prevail in Japan: Matsushita is notorious for disregarding the ladder of seniority (whereon all may patiently await their turn at the top) and has not hesitated to raise a man five rungs above both his status and those who previously stood above him.

'We have lost our inferiority complex,' says a youthful graduate. 'Since 1964, when we Japanese were first allowed to go overseas as tourists, we have become more cosmopolitan.'

But not less Japanese. They may not believe in Kitabatake Chikafusa's thirteenth century dictum that 'Great Nippon is a Divine Nation. Our Divine ancestors founded it; the Sun Goddess let her descendants reign over it; no other nation has the like of it; and this is why our Nation is called Divine,' but they concur wholeheartedly with Konosuke Matsushita when he says, 'I am beginning to believe that the twenty-first century will be one centred on Asia – in whose achievements Japan will play a very important role.' A race which became nationalistic three centuries earlier than any of its European rivals, and six centuries before the USA, is hardly likely to abandon the habit when world supremacy – political as well as economic – seems imminent.

'At school we now teach about foreign countries,' says a headmaster whose task it is to prepare his pupils for their role in twenty-first century Japan. 'Cultures and environments are changing, and we are becoming more aware of foreign countries and foreign people.

'Education in Japan is better today because pupils are beginning to assume responsibility for themselves, to choose a future for themselves, in some cases even to choose some of their curriculum.

'There is no longer the daily recitation of the Education Rescript. Students don't even care to use all the honorifics of our language as everyone once did. But that is less important (although we must take care that our language does not become debased) than the new relationship between teachers and students, which is today more one of intimacy than respect, as it used to be.

'If a teacher feels that students are behaving improperly, however, he, or she, has a responsibility to explain to the offending student. Here the parents of each student choose to pay half a million yen (£125) a year for fees and a uniform, and that is a lot of money for poor parents, so an explanation of misbehaviour is usually enough. But in the free schools for boys, discipline is maintained by increasingly severe methods.' Little wonder the Japanese are so literate: the Imperial Japanese Army defined their attitude to us as 'severe'.

At school or at work, though, the old precepts prevail – those of the thirteenth century Hogo Shigetoki no less than those of the eighteenth century samurai. 'On every occasion,' Shigetoki adjured, 'try to be charming.' And, 'When you employ knights, labour soldiers, foot soldiers and others, never hire those who are querulous or argumentative.'

But once you *have* hired people, 'Remember that if you speak scathingly to them, you may leave them resentful.' Western experts on labour relations would do well to read the aphorisms of Shigetoki.

'Deliberately take a low posture. Be polite even to persons of no consequence,' he commands. And, 'Never punish a servant when you are angry.' And, 'When you take leave of a person to whom you owe particular respect, follow him for some distance.' At last I know why Matsushita's receptionist bowed low and remained rectangular till my car had turned the corner: as one who had been allowed to talk to Matsushita, I had become worthy of particular respect.

Until the fifties it was common in Britain to see a sign on the top deck of buses prohibiting spitting. Seven hundred years earlier Shigetoki had imposed an even wider ban. 'Spit into a piece of tissue paper,' he ordered – and the Japanese have obeyed him ever since. 'Long distance spitting is vulgar and brings you into contempt,' he warned – and British soccer players, like American tennis stars, have ignored him ever since.

Finally, to what do the Japanese themselves attribute their present success? Not surprisingly (because they have all read the same article in the same quality newspapers) they reply as one, 'First, the government was skilful. Second, we exported efficiently. Third, we converted from light industry to heavy industry. Fourth, life-time employment and enterprise unions. And fifth, the rapid diffusion of information about markets, technology and future plans.'

No mention anywhere of spirit – but that, to the Japanese, is a *sine qua non*. Perhaps it is because they never mention it that the West has convinced itself that it is only by the unfair application of non-tariff barriers that Japan has triumphed. But all five of the Japanese criteria for success are as unexceptional in any industry as are a head, a body, two arms and a pair of legs to any athlete: it requires motivation to transform an athlete into a champion.

A Japanese economist of the sixties defined the element that first motivated (and now almost intimidates) his compatriots. 'For years our people learned to cope with poverty,' he wrote. 'We do not know yet how to cope with plenty.'

211

CHAPTER TWENTY-THREE

>>>>>>>><<<<<<<

'For the Year 2000 There are
Various Scenarios'

IMAGINE, PLEASE, a meeting of eight of Japan's most influential men as they discuss their country's almost embarrassing economic success and the sad situation of the Western world. In fact, it was me they met, and singly not collectively; but artistic licence is a marvellous device, and I shall take full advantage of it.

All these distinguished men are about to assemble in a conference room on the ninth floor of the Head Office of the Mitsubishi Bank in Tokyo, and once they have stopped bowing to one another – which will take some time – and taken their seats, I shall quote each of them quite faithfully.

The words I quote will, of course, be the words they spoke to me; but they will interest you more if they come in the form of a colloquium; and should their conversation flag, an interpreter will prompt them from the list of questions with which I have had the foresight to provide him – not that I delude myself that the ensuing answers will be gems of plain speaking or anything like home truths. 'Foreigners think that we are not frank,' I remember being told. 'The truth is that we never say much and hate anything explicit.'

As each of them enters the Bank, he is greeted by a handsome woman in a kimono who directs him into a large, marble-floored lobby to the right. The lobby is empty, apart from a broad desk against the far wall, and looks as if it was designed by Speer for Hitler in the early days of the Third Reich. Two receptionists, who could be twins with their identical blue jackets and glossy heads, stand behind the remote desk, smiling: then bowing in perfect unison, and in time with the echoing footsteps of the honoured guests approaching them.

Another bow and a pair of blinding smiles as the visitor reaches them. They know his name, of course, (somehow they know the name of everyone who clatters across that floor) and one of them, gesturing prettily, beseeches him to make his way leftward, and then right again, to the elevators. A man materializes, deferential but bleak, probably a minder, to ensure that the visitor does not get lost.

The elevator is by Speer for Hitler after he had changed his title from Chancellor to Fuhrer. It sighs upwards and its doors slide open soundlessly.

No marble now but carpet with a pile so deep it could suck the boots off a navvy; and, in the remote distance, to the left, another pair of twins, bowing, smiling, bowing.

They deliver the visitor to a middle-aged man in a dark grey suit who stands ram-rod straight against a Mitsubishi pillar. Almost palpably he has a black belt in each of the deadly martial arts. Almost certainly a minder. (And also, I suspect, one of my ex-guards from Thailand.) It would be a rash group of assassins who sought to storm their way past him to the sanctum within.

He escorts the visitor some half dozen paces down a broad hall to the right – where a secretary materializes, her hair marcelled, her dress sensible. She bows, smiles coolly, and ushers the visitor into the conference room.

This is a large, low, brownish, rectangular room in the centre of which is a large, low, brownish, rectangular table. The table is surrounded by large, low, brownish, rectangular, plump, leather chairs. Opposite each chair, on the brownish, ceramic tiles that cover the table, is a massive square ash-tray. And propped against each ash-tray is a tiny, virgin box of matches. There are no cigarettes.

Mr Tajitsu waves his various peers to their seats. He looks too frail and old a man, and too tiny, to be the senior statesman of so powerful a banking concern as Mitsubishi. Devoid of vanity, he wears a dark, heavy suit with a thick leather belt to hold up his trousers. When he walks, he toddles, as if he had been wound up and must reach his chair quickly before he winds down. When he sits, he clasps his tiny, slightly arthritic hands. His face is old, round, unlined and still – but alert.

He is of samurai stock, and some of his guests are not, but he will at no time reveal the fact that he is aware of a distinction between himself and the commoners present: that would be a solecism. 'There is dignity in serenity,' a samurai believes; and Mr Tajitsu is serene. 'There is dignity too in clenched teeth and flashing eyes,' a samurai believes; but it is unlikely that his confrères will provoke him to either.

Certainly Kenosuke Matsushita will not, for his is almost the serenity of a mystic. A small man, nearly ninety years old, he stands straight and slim, immaculately groomed and tailored, his shirt crisply white and his dark tie neatly knotted. He moves slowly, but not at all uncertainly (more, it would seem, from a lack of haste than the onset of physical frailty). Mr Matsushita has presence; perhaps because he has worked for a living since he was seven years old.

His father speculated in rice in the late 1890s, and lost all his money. So little Kenosuke left home to work in a bicycle repair shop in Osaka. When tram cars came to the city he was fascinated by them – or rather, by the electricity that propelled them. He joined an electrical firm when he was fifteen years old and 'did wiring jobs'. When he was twenty-three he was promoted to the rank of inspector.

The following year he borrowed a little money and set himself up in business with his wife and brother-in-law. Electricity for domestic purposes had just come to Japan's small urban dwellings – one socket to a house. Matsushita invented and manufactured a two-way socket. Everyone bought one. Then he invented a battery lamp for bicycles. Then a lamp for household use. And next an electric heater. By 1929 he had 300 employees and was a rich man.

The Depression that began in that year hit his sales as pitilessly as anyone's, but he remained optimistic and refused to reduce his staff. Instead, he reduced their working hours by half, while paying them their full wages. Ever since, his employees' loyalty to him has been total.

'The loneliest thing in life,' he nevertheless observed, 'is when your work cuts you off from your neighbours' – and transformed his work force into a family, each of them a neighbour to the other.

In 1931 he began making radio sets. 'The purpose of production,' he exhorted his employees, 'is to serve the needs of society and improve the quality of life.' That creed has been repeated on the anniversary of his firm's foundation ever since.

The Militarists laid their bloody hands on industry in 1936, and when hostilities broke out in 1941 Matsushita was required to convert his hugely successful firm to war work. When defeat followed, he took up the Emperor's cry and proclaimed, 'Industry is the foundation stone of reconstruction.' But MacArthur, accusing him

214

of criminal involvement with the Militarists, purged him. It was not until 1947 that his case was reviewed and he could return to lead his 15,000 employees to even further successes.

In 1952, Phillips of Holland had the good sense to enter a joint venture with him. He followed that up with trading agreements with American firms, and a five year project with the Thais.

In 1961, he retired as Chairman; but was recalled when a world slump hit his company as well as every other. Assembling all his staff and dealers, he said, 'Tell us what you want and we will give it to you.' The company recovered swiftly.

In its more than sixty years of constant innovation and expansion (it now employs 135,000 men and women) Matsushita's Electrical Company has purchased some 49,000 patents and produced everything from electricity plugs to the latest electronic gadget; and Matsushita himself has never hesitated to be so un-Japanese as to promote for reasons of merit rather than seniority, or to demote an appointee who proved unsuccessful.

'Management by wise men is not enough,' he declared. 'Management by great men is not enough. And management by fools is disastrous! I believe in management by consensus.'

His great rival, Masaru Ibuka, the founder of Sony, is almost as old as Matsushita, and just as straight, slim and well turned out, but taller. He too has presence – but more that of a super salesman than a thinker.

He went into business with thirty employees just after the war because he, too, was fascinated by electricity – and would be one of the first to see a future for electronics. He also does not hesitate to be un-Japanese.

'I believe in Western individualism,' he announces without a trace of shame. 'Which is not at all natural to Japan, where there is a belief in groups and harmony.' He is a smiling man, at ease in any company – and, like Matsushita, has the strong, flexible fingers of a professional electrician.

Soichiyo Honda is very different: not young, but looking only middle-aged: not serene, but thrusting, confident, almost frenetic. He could be a television magnate, or a retired bandleader from the forties, or a vaudeville comic: he could not possibly be the founder of a hugely successful automobile company – until one remembers that he started as a manufacturer of motor cycles. It is not at all difficult to imagine Mr Honda roaring round the city (like a Japanese Sir Ralph Richardson) astride a 1000 cc motor cycle. His coral pink suit, among the seven other suits of dark navy blue and grey is vividly incongruous. Also he is visibly impatient for the proceedings to start. As one who had been a mere country mechanic until he started his new career after the war at the age of thirty-nine, he hates to waste time.

Wataru Hiraizuma, on the contrary, is completely relaxed. A wealthy member of the Diet, who was once a Cabinet Minister, a sumptuously tailored cosmopolitan who loves French literature and silk ties, a born conversationalist in a number of languages, he combines an air of flamboyance with the languor of a bon viveur and is in no hurry to confine himself to any single topic. When he is required to, however, he can be both eloquent and controversial.

No less eloquent is Masaya Miyoshi, who resembles nothing so much as a middle-aged but very popular Japanese film star. He has a broad face and forehead, a broad and ready smile, an easy, idiomatic command of English and an astonishing Jekyll and Hyde-like ability to switch from an unassertive Japaneseness to an almost American bonhomie. Not surprisingly, the Keidanren has made him its Executive Director.

Schichihei Yamamoto, whom you will recognize by his long, iron-grey, slightly dishevelled hair, has a thin body that is febrile with unanswered philosophical problems, the strangeness of a bookless room and his longing for a cigarette. He wears a brown suit, a tan polo-necked sweater, brown socks and tan shoes. He looks trapped – like a wild pony in a circus ring.

And finally there is Professor Inohara of the Institute of Socio-Economics at Tokyo's Sophia University, who admits cheerfully that he will talk to anyone so long as there is coffee to drink and a cigarette to smoke. His self-deprecating humour belies the fact that he is not only a distinguished academic but also a widely travelled authority on labour relations in Japan and the West. To his students he must be a refreshing change from their less extrovert professors: to him the majority of his students are a disappointment.

'They give no evidence at all of knowing why they're there,' he complains ruefully. 'All they really care for is the kudos and status of being University students. So it is not surprising that industry is beginning to reject their type. If they *are* employed, they have to be re-trained. And while they're on the campus they treat the teaching staff as if they were dustmen. They are there only to obtain the advantages of a degree, and they are not sincere. There is a minority that works very hard, however and is very honest.'

216

The only thing that offends Professor Inohara more than the thought of his insincere and dishonest students is the picture he carries in his mind's eye of Englishmen sitting in a sunny park doing cross-word puzzles. 'Cross-word puzzles!' he explodes. 'They don't read books, they do cross-word puzzles. *Very* slowly.'

At last, then, all eight are seated – in their correct positions, of course – but, before they start, yet another pretty girl will float silently in and serve each of them a small cup of pale, green tea. She vanishes and they sip it politely.

Except for Mr Hiraizumi, who is completely relaxed in his vast, low-slung leather chair, they all sit bolt upright. Mr Tajitsu glances at the interpreter, who glances nervously down at the list of questions with which I have provided him, and advises (in a suitably modified form) that the first question is: *After the war, your one-time Foreign Minister Shigemitsu wrote a book called* Japan and Her Destiny. *What do you envisage as that destiny?*

'Precisely speaking,' says Tajitsu, 'it's difficult to say anything about ten or twenty years hence, but I'll try. What matters most, in that respect, is the national spirit – and the national spirit seems to be in a state of decay, in as much as our people are getting more and more materialistic. Economic growth seems to have caused a spiritual illness, and to cure it will take longer than it took to become ill.'

Matsushita nods, but (with a slow, stroking gesture, as if soothing an irritable cat) seeks to dispel the worst of Tajitsu's fears. 'Assuming that Japan could become the basis of a world society, she can safely say that she would provide a good basis on which to build,' he suggests. 'After 1945' – and every head nods while he prepares his next soft, measured phrases – 'we knew the depths of misery. We were at the very extreme of pain, poverty and hunger. And that taught us to work. Maybe' – gently – 'other countries still have that lesson to learn.'

Honda, who had been making little *um, umming* noises of agreement throughout, now takes the argument a stage further. 'Before and during the Pacific War,' he observes, 'we lacked the techniques of swift communication, and were ignorant of the outside world and its problems. But today we Japanese know exactly what is happening in the United States and Europe. We understand the frictions that have developed between the West and ourselves – how they began and how they grew – and in the same way' – taking off his glasses – 'I hope that the West will have understood how it was that

217

we Japanese achieved our successes. I fully understand that we are not easy to know; but, I repeat, with today's instant communication techniques there should be plenty of time in which to arrive at mutual understanding and to achieve peace.

'Right after the war, when we were occupied, there was a period of starvation, and people who are now middle-aged learned that to survive you've got to work. But today,' he waves a deprecating arm, revealing a copper bracelet on his wrist, 'there's a degrading of that work-morale in the younger Japanese. And tomorrow, who knows that the European and American working-morale may not rise, so that Japan will need *their* help? And so on, one wave following the other. But not until the waves intersect' – bringing one raised forearm emphatically across the other – 'will we get true understanding and real co-operation.'

Miyoshi flashes his actor's smile and steps smoothly in, aware that everything they say is for the ears of foreigners. 'When communicating with our compatriots,' he mocks kindly, 'the politer one is the better. That is our way. But most Americans and Europeans don't understand this method of communication, so we have to be like Jekyll and Hyde – polite here, and candid there. We have to switch from one mood to the other. But we have lacked this ability in the past: we have lacked this communicating mechanism.

'Also, after our defeat, we could not afford the luxury of ideologies or social planning. We simply had to concentrate on industrial survival. And we did survive; and now we can afford the luxuries of the Western world; but now the Western world accuses us of "laser beam" attacks.' His nose wrinkles with distaste. 'It used just to be "a flood" of Japanese exports the EEC and America talked about. Well, people can survive floods, so that wasn't too bad, did not worry us too much. But laser beams: they're killers; and that has made us think.'

Hiraizumi is not so conciliatory. To him there are many faults on the other side, and he is politician enough to know that his colleagues will leave any discourse thereon to him.

'The Soviet Union, Germany, China and Japan suffered the worst of World War II,' he reminds. 'For one thing, huge losses of population. And it was always the brightest who died. In a war like that one, the bright could not hide, they had to lead. But it's all those millions of bright young men who should be leading the *world* today. Instead . . . look at our Prime Ministers, at all the men of the Soviet Politburo, at China's Chairman and his colleagues, America's President – all of them in their seventies when their positions should be held by men in their late fifties or early sixties.'

Apart from the Professor and the philosopher, all his companions – whose average age is over eighty – gaze expressionlessly at the wall opposite them. Then Mr Matsushita smiles, and murmurs, 'Youth is the state of being young in heart,' and Hiraizumi discreetly switches his line of attack.

'There is an element of hatred in the attitude to Japan of Europe and America,' he insists. 'They simply cannot *stand* the idea of Japan being richer and more stable than they are, and technologically superior to them. But the fact remains, in terms of our respective economies, *we* are now the most resilient.'

Mr Ibuka is swift to point out that the West also has its virtues. 'I believe in Western individualism,' he counters, no less soft-spoken and deliberate than Matsushita, 'but that isn't the norm in Japan. We Japanese believe in harmony and groups and the consensus. But I resist this desire for a consensus. Just after the war, I started my company with about thirty employees; and to avoid the competition of the big organizations I decided to make only what they didn't make.

'Perhaps Mr Matsushita and I are thinkers and individualists because we both know that electronics can, and do, change absolutely anything. And this means that most of mankind will have to be re-educated as to how to use its new environment.

'But Mr Matsushita's company and mine are rivals. Only keen competition produces so great a variety of goods in our industry. Should he and I *harmonize*, the rivalry that produces the consumer's ideal video-recorder, or Walkman, or calculator, is lost.

'Nevertheless, we do now have to re-think the necessary balance between Japan's industries and their foreign rival industries. After World War II our first thought was survival – and only after we had survived did we turn our minds to a degree of economic growth.

'The Japanese people were very loyal to this plan. We all just worked steadily toward our modest target without ever sparing a thought for other countries. But now that we have captured more than ten per cent of the world's total trade, we must start thinking about other countries – about their need for their share of the world's trade.

'All our previous international trade relationships were considered as something from which *we* might derive some benefit: that approach to the rest of the world must now be drastically re-thought.'

Yamamoto leans forward, a cigarette in his right hand. 'The end of World War II erased the effects of the Meiji era,' he says. 'And the advantages of that were that feudalism was abolished painlessly, and that the introduction of Western institutions destroyed the concept of a divine Emperor – thus removing that ambiguity in his role which had been abused, and the confusions about his status which even induced some of his subjects to believe that he was not only the Emperor of Japan but also the King of England.

'Whenever the Emperor speaks of the war, he says that twice in his life-time he has had to defy the constitution. The first occasion was the February mutiny in 1936, which he personally suppressed, and against which he was even prepared personally to lead his Imperial Guards: the second was when he terminated the war.

'So, in one way, he had absolute power; in another, no power at all. That anomaly does not exist today. It can never be misused again.'

'Also,' Professor Inohara reminds, 'we have been very fortunate to have been given both macro and micro opportunities. The wars in Korea and Vietnam brought us booms; and they were followed by the decline of the West.

'The causes of this decline are both economic and motivational. The economic causes spring from the inadequacies of capitalism, which are job specialization and job demarcation, both of which lead to total inflexibility.

'We Japanese, on the other hand, are driven by a kind of voice that says we *must* work. We work for ourselves, admittedly; but, unlike the West, we are very homogeneous – and each goal of each stratum supersedes the goal of the lower stratum. The West is not motivated in this way.

'Also, the Japanese approach to any problem is both logistical and circumstantial. In the present problem of a trade conflict with America and Europe we try to communicate with the West at every level; but the solution to that problem can only come from the West itself. It must produce more, and better.'

'Although this is a very private view,' Matsushita ventures to interpose, 'I also am very concerned about our relationship with the EEC and others. *We* have been able to rehabilitate. *We* can say: "We have done this and we have done that".' He sips at his tea. No one interrupts. 'But as to whether we can continue – whether the resis-

220

tance now coming from the United States and others means that we must do certain different things – change direction – I do not know. Japan is now in a situation where we must all give thought to the problem, and I am grateful that you have prompted me to do so.

'The Keidanren tried to ascertain exactly what the EEC was thinking – and the United States – and found that there was a much worse reaction against Japan's export drive than it had expected. It found that America and Europe were beginning to believe that to continue their free trade policy was dangerous to them – that Japan should find a solution to their problem, exercise self-restraint, seek the formula whereby we and they could enjoy a mutual prosperity.'

At this moment his fingers are tightly, almost angrily, interlocked. He relaxes and raises one hand. 'But their language' – and now his hand begins to chop disapprovingly down on each successive adjective – 'was distressingly high . . . loud . . . and severe.' He pauses again; and again no one interrupts, though all of them resented the tone of the language to which he has referred no less than he. Almost contemptuously, he brings his contribution to a close. 'I believe,' he murmurs indifferently, 'that the government *is* now seeking a way to counter these difficulties.'

'I have just remembered what Toynbee told our Prince on his visit to Japan,' Mr Tajitsu says. 'He said that one of the reasons why Japan enjoys such unique prosperity in Asia is that our management has been governed by, and practised in accordance with, the rules of Bushido.

'In the pre-war years, the Mitsubishi group was guided by the Iwasaki family, whom General MacArthur later proscribed. But those who then took over from the Iwasakis took with them the principles of the old Mitsubishi group. And I remember that when Chou En Lai asked me how we had become so successful again, I replied that when a customer wanted something, a Mitsubishi factory would make it, a Mitsubishi warehouse would stock it, a Mitsubishi ship would transport it – and Mitsubishi itself would always be looking for more customers! This *corporate* approach is one explanation of Japan's present success; and people respect such group success nowadays.'

'Well I don't know about *other* people,' Mr Honda demurs, 'but I do know that *I* don't like to lose. I compete! Not for the sake of the country, or the sake of others, but for myself! I am loyal to myself! I don't even begin to understand those who say, "What I do is for the good of the nation" – and I don't believe them. I have rivals overseas and rivals in Japan; and I try to beat them all – for me, Honda!'

Miyoshi, the diplomat of the Keidanren, hurriedly glosses over this bushido anathema. 'It is our national tradition to worship perfection,' he reminds. 'It is a reverence we inherit from our ancestors, whether they were samurai or commoners. And after the war we combined that perfectionist spirit with the spirit of competition, and spread it over a much wider field of industry than we had ever done before.

'Absolute equality between either individuals or trading nations is, of course, impossible. One cannot change a people's genes or biological structure. But we Japanese are as egalitarian as the biological and genetic facts permit – and you can see the virtues of that egalitarianism in all our factories.'

'Also,' Hiraizumi concurred, 'we do not consume so much as other nations. We are *savers* of money – the highest by far in the world – and the extra power of those savings is being lent by banks to industry, which translates it into the extra power of our exports.

'Our life style is frugal. The Japanese were born poor, and they think poor. They don't, and won't, spend unnecessarily.

'From 1610, when they closed their ports to foreigners, to 1860, when they were forced to open them again, the Japanese allowed no one in and had no desire at all to venture out. In fact, for the last fifteen centuries the only thing we have willingly imported is books.

'Our whole infra-structure of roads, railways, factories and so on is based on plans and instructions taken from imported books. As late as 1850 people had to write in classical Chinese, which was as dead a language as Latin. Only women were allowed to write in living Japanese. Admittedly the Meiji era changed all that, but until 1860 our knowledge of that compulsory classical Chinese was derived and sustained entirely by the import of Chinese books.

'We also have been, and still are, the biggest importers of books in the history of the literate world; and it has made us the most literate race in the world; and one of the main reasons why we are so successful in industry, and the West so unsuccessful, is that the West's labour force is simply not literate enough to be taught the required technology.'

'Speaking not for Japan but for myself,' Mr Honda announces, 'during World War II we had great victories at first, when we were fighting relatively close to home; but, later, long lines of communication and technological gaps in our weaponry caused us to be defeated. But that is history. We both learned lessons – the victors and the vanquished – and we are now all friends.

'But if, many decades ago, we had had the kind of trade troubles we have today, we would long since have triggered off a war. I do not believe that will happen this time. Today – again because of a better communications system – we have learned to cope with one another's problems – to help one another, as we of Honda, for example, are doing with British Leyland; as we've been doing in the United States with our motor cycle plant; and *will* do with our automobile plant – so gradually we all approach the ideal of working together and sharing our profits.'

He scratches his calf, a third of which is visible below the cuff of his coral pink trousers and above his purple socks. 'I even hope to see the day when the Japanese won't care where ideas come from, so long as they are good.'

Yamamoto exhales emphatically. 'Today's Japanese think like they used to before the era of fanatical Emperor worship,' he insists. 'And in those days one clear concept prevailed – that the incompetent shall never be respected.'

'But as to the future,' Miyoshi warns, 'all of us Japanese will have to assume the Jekyll and Hyde mentality of which I have spoken. How we will achieve it, I don't know, because on the one hand we see an ever-expanding willingness to be international (for example, in the study of foreign languages: twenty per cent of our people have now, at some time or other, studied English) and, on the other hand, we see a growing tendency toward Japanization.'

'The stumbling block is America,' Hiraizumi counters. 'From about 1915 until Mao's time, the United States felt that it just *had* to have China, to match Britain's possession of India. It was – and is again – deep in the American subconscious – this need for a United States-Chinese relationship. I feel that this hypothesis deserves examination, explanation.

'The 1945 experience was a good one for both of us. The Americans were magnanimous and generous. Still are – unlike the British, who are mean, having been dreadfully influenced by their long experience of India, by those days when any little school teacher from England could go out to India and become a District Officer ruling the lives of hundreds of thousands of natives.

'But in 1941 the Americans could not understand how the miserable little country of Japan could be the one that was thwarting their ambition to own the heart and mind of China. Hence their obsession with China and the Soviet Union today.

'This deeply Christian republican country just cannot understand its own black and imperialistic desire to possess colonies; yet it is that, as much as its trade deficit with us, and its frustrated desire to invest in our country to the same extent that we have invested in hers, that has lately made her so angry with us.'

'The trouble is,' Miyoshi explains sadly, 'there is a lack of risk-taking policies, of a *systematic* approach, among all Westerners who desire to invest in Japan.'

'Yes,' Tajitsu agrees. 'And it is bad that in Britain, for example, the banks and other financial institutions won't support new industry; but it's not just that. I visited Britain in 1955, to investigate the computerization of banking techniques, because Japanese banks, at that time, were still using the abacus. But Britain's bankers told me not to worry about computerization, that it wasn't necessary! At that time, of course, England was blessed with good traditions and spirit. But I soon realized that that spirit was dying; and I wondered why, and decided that it was because of the Welfare State. The Welfare State is something Japan should also dislike. I myself believe in the spirit of Bushido. But various managers have various ideas, and to discuss them is to discuss philosophy.'

Matsushita, who has been fiddling with a match box, replaces it carefully – and again (as also with those other one-time mechanics, Honda and Ibuka) one is struck by the strength and flexibility of his fingers. 'I'm not very conversant with this sort of situation where foreigners hope to set up their own factories in Japan,' he confesses; 'but if it could happen, if such a plan could be concretely explored, and should any prejudice on our part be revealed, then *government* should act to remove it. On the other hand, Britain already has more than ten per cent unemployment: Japan could not tolerate such a level: Westerners can. *That* is a piece of data Westerners often ignore.

'For two years after the war – while I employed 15,000 people – I managed to survive only by borrowing from my friends (because General MacArthur had proscribed me) and I've never forgotten it. We had to export just to survive, and very fortunately we were able to produce what was most acceptable to our customers abroad. Had our products not been acceptable, we could not have exported.

'Now we used to believe that this attitude of ours would lead to mutual prosperity. This, we thought, was the only way. But even then we would not have denied our oriental belief that things done to excess are worse than things not done at all – that too much done too quickly always creates difficulties. *Has* created difficulties! And we must acknowledge that again today. So we must make it easier for the Japanese people to import foreign products.'

Tajitsu nods and castles the fingers of his tiny hands. 'The problem arises, if we curb our exports, that we ignore the needs of consumers abroad: so really we should concentrate on encouraging imports from other countries – or, of course, the Western consumer could stop buying Japanese goods.'

He ponders this improbable solution before resuming his discourse. 'In the pre-war years, Japan captured the textile industry from Lancashire. Now Korea and Taiwan are taking it over from us. In the same way, in other *new* industries, countries like Great Britain will one day compete with Japan because success in any one trade is always a passing phenomenon.

'For that reason, Britain – which now has oil from the North Sea enabling her to buy foreign goods – will not have that oil forever. Then she will have to find new industries.

'But as to the danger of tariffs, curbs, artificial economic weapons being used against us, the EEC will one day notify Japan of its proposed counter-measures and demands; and the Japanese government, being rather timid, will of course comply. But,' he warns, 'if ever we do reach that kind of situation, the government will have many problems!'

Honda is quick to take the point. 'The trouble with our government is that, after so many years almost of isolation, it is just not equipped for diplomatic action. And anyway our trade expansion happened so suddenly that it has caught all of us unprepared to deal with its international consequences. Changes are already in hand; but it will all take time. It is easier to modify an automobile than a human being.'

'Maybe we *have* become too productive too quickly,' Matsushita concedes, 'and thereby caused others problems. And maybe we will be able to help others with those problems. But whatever the case, we *must* export. For the future we must therefore search for a mutual optimum.'

'Nevertheless,' Miyoshi qualifies on behalf of the Keidanren, 'we have studied the problem, short term and long term, and short term measures are available – like reducing tariffs on 27 various items. Long term measures, as we see the problem, could include mutual investment (but not necessarily as equal partners), technology

225

exchanges, and co-operation in Third World projects which may be either industrial or to do with the infra-structure.

'In Japan, we are shifting from labour-intensive mass production to value-added reprocessing industries using robots, computers and so on. So conditions are not only changing here, but our industrialists are also highly motivated to invest in Europe and America.

'As to the question of those other countries investing in Japan . . . there are many barriers . . . language, property costs, distribution methods and so on . . . but few legal barriers. And those that have not already been reduced or abolished the Keidanren has asked the government to remove. It has also asked the government to simplify the existing import and investment structure. But, I repeat, most Westerners who would like to invest here lack risk-taking policies and a systematic approach.'

There is a silence, and at long last the interpreter looks at his list of questions – most of them already answered. Finally he asks, 'What can the West export to Japan that Japan does not already make better and more cheaply?'

Matsushita holds his hand at shoulder height, as if to acknowledge a greeting. 'The answer is simple,' he says. 'Anything that is better in quality,' folding one finger, 'cheaper in price,' folding a second, 'that the Japanese people need,' folding a third – and drops his hand on to his knee.

'Raw materials, naturally,' says Honda; 'but as far as manufactured goods are concerned, I can't think of many. The government is thinking of facilitating imports, I know, but I do not think that is the solution. I think the solution is for *us* to invest overseas.

'For example, I think our venture with British Leyland is a good thing. But who knows that one day we won't get a good idea back from them? After all, Nissan got their first plans for an automobile from Austin: one day we at Honda may well get the plans for an entirely new kind of automobile from British Leyland. Things change. Everything changes.

'From 1931 to 1945 everything we had in this country went to the military, and by 1945 we were eating grass – literally. Then the Emperor stepped in – and his final words gave me personally great encouragement – and everything changed. And when MacArthur came and purged many of the older aristocratic generation from power, things changed again. People of my class and age (I was then 39) were for the first time able to move into positions of power – and make changes of our own.

'Now take the case of British Leyland. I am told that labour relations there are sometimes difficult. I personally have no knowledge of how unions are organized, or management functions, in the United Kingdom; but I do know that right after World War II, when we were in such a state of devastation, we had many agitators in all our factories. So many that I even thought of closing my own. But reconciliation always comes in time; and in time it came to Japan. Also I was fortunate that, as an engineer myself, I could work with my employees at the bench – and that impressed them, and softened their opposition.'

Professor Inohara is now on familiar ground. 'The lesson is not to take Japan as a model,' he says, 'but as a mirror. We are not really past-orientated (the British are; and the Americans are future-orientated) but present-orientated – and flexible.

'Japanese companies set up in the West have an absolute minimum of regulations for their employees, to allow of flexibility. And in Japan there is a mutual trust – an acceptance of a state of interdependence – between management and labour.

'No Japanese will stop working. To stop means death, and our imperative is to survive, which means to produce, which means to attend, not to be an absentee. One *must* show up – even when retirement is available. But this is not expansionism: it is simply, as I have said before, an expression of our national pessimism. We await the next earthquake or typhoon: we lack the natural resources: we export or we do not survive.'

'And,' says Ibuka, 'we produce things with a high added-value which others – if we bankrupt them – won't be able to buy from us! At the moment we have ten per cent of the world's gross product: so we *could* feed ten per cent of the world's population. Maybe we should feed them. We Japanese look inwards and take it for granted that life has become better; but now we must look outwards, at those for whom it may have become worse.'

'I am not so sure about that kind of supremacy,' Matsushita gently demurs, 'because of Japan's sheer lack of land space. That would make it very difficult for us to become the world's greatest economic nation. To achieve that, we would need to double our land space.'

The others realize that he is not preaching aggression: it has long been a hobby horse of his that the Japanese – having given due consideration to all matters environmental and ecological – should raze half their mountains, turn them into arable land, tip the tailings

227

into the sea and build factories on the areas reclaimed.

'Also,' he points out, 'the basic deprivation that motivated our generations has vanished today. The young know nothing about it; and when the twenty-first century arrives the Japanese will no longer be motivated as we are. Assuming that they have in fact become number one in the world by then, will they be able to retain that position – or will other people take it from them?'

'We must decide now how best we can help other nations redress their problems,' Honda argues. 'I have been saying it for years – I have been trying to persuade a hundred million Japanese that other people's problems are our problems too. But it is difficult. There is no immediate solution.

'You cannot suddenly tell a hundred million people they must stop thinking the way they have always thought, stop working the way they have always worked. But Honda's products are now being made in 31 countries outside of Japan. This is a new trend; and it helps the other countries concerned. Not everyone in Japan has understood that, however.

'I repeat – if only every Japanese corporation would learn the lesson of the benefits that come from overseas co-operation, we would all be much better off. But I cannot, unfortunately, convince them.'

Miyoshi decides to sum up. 'For the year 2000,' he says 'there are various scenarios, each of them dependent on varying intervening factors – such as OPEC springing yet another massive increase in the price of oil, or a war somewhere, or the West imposing massive tariffs or very restrictive quotas on our exports. But I personally anticipate that the status quo will prevail – and that means that by the year 2000 Japan's per capita income will be far higher than that of the United States. Then, as the world's richest nation, Japan will have to become the world's principal donor to less fortunate nations.'

'The new age of electronification is near,' Ibuka promises, 'and the integrated circuit will make it economical. We will be able to use our computer-ware to change the world. Our problem will not be *whether* we can use it, but how to use it. To achieve such a technological revolution will not be difficult; but to bring about a revolution in the way we humans think, about what we consider to be life's needs and fulfilments, that will be very difficult.

'Technology-oriented industry is now our forte. Industries of such a kind, that require a lot of land space, or consume a lot of energy – both of which we lack – will function more efficiently elsewhere. Once our techniques are completed, therefore, we will transfer them to less developed countries. But all of this requires that we rethink our future – and receive the support of our government. Certainly our present prosperity will continue; but I am not certain that we Japanese will know how to handle it.'

The colloquium is finished: the bowing and the departures begin.

CHAPTER TWENTY-FOUR

>>>>>>>><<<<<<<<

'A Shadow has Fallen over the Giant'

THE JAPANESE TACTICS in today's export war are identical with those they employed so successfully in 1941/42 against a bigger army than theirs in Malaya: they attack individual units 'with surprise and with our strength concentrated'.

In 1941/42, their campaign was based on intelligence gathered since 1934. They began gathering their intelligence for today's war in the middle fifties; and stepped up the process in 1964, when overseas tours were first permitted. In 1941/42 their intelligence was collated by Colonel Tsuji's small Unit 82 on Taiwan: today it is collated on the spot, and then disseminated, by a trading company.

In military terms, a trading company is a skilled band of spies and fifth columnists safely ensconsed behind the host nation's lines. It plans the invasion and, when the invasion comes, acts in concert with, or, as an independent commando unit, in obedience to the orders of the general in command – who might be any one of dozens of major industrialists.

Against these sophisticated (and perfectly legitimate) intelligence-cum-commando units the West either despatches individual commercial attachés (with a small staff) to its embassy in the host nation, or a salesman with a briefcase and an expense account.

The 1941/42 analogy can be employed indefinitely and ad nauseum, but it becomes depressing. 'And anyway,' commented a complacent senior executive of a major British industry, 'the Japanese lost the war!'

The implication, of course, is that they will also lose this war; that they may be as apparently invincible today as they were in May 1942, but look what happened to them at Midway in June 1942. It is not altogether reassuring, however, to compare the morale of the West today with the morale of the Allies in early 1942 – when, despite a series of appalling defeats round the world, no American or Briton doubted that the Allies would emerge triumphant.

It is regrettable that Western industrialists, unlike their Japanese counterparts, are adamant in their refusal to have their views on the present economic crisis specifically attributed to them. It is equally regrettable (but, by the nature of their profession, understandable) that the diplomats who have offered their views may, in most cases, not even be identified by nationality. And it is tragic that politicians say nothing on the subject that is remotely relevant. You are asked to accept the quotes that follow as representative and faithfully reported, albeit anonymous.

'The Japanese now make one third of the total world production of motor vehicles,' one of the West's most defiant managers of an automobile industry admitted early in 1982, 'so it's no longer a question of *whether* we can beat them; we can't. Not on their own grounds, anyway; not as manufacturers. But we will soon begin to hold our own in the market place – in the show rooms – because the average European and American is beginning to feel sick to his stomach about what the Japanese are doing to us; and one day soon he's going to refuse to buy another Japanese car.

'Not only that. The Japanese can export a car to Europe at a price $1400 lower than we can from the United Kingdom. But there's $1500 worth of labour in each of our cars. There's no way we can make a $1400 cut at the moment. So the ordinary guy on the *American* factory floor is already beginning to say, "The company can't survive this: I'd better take a wage cut or I'm out of a job."

'That doesn't solve the productivity problem, though. So we're going to automate. Robots. Seven hundred and fifty of them by the end of 1984.

'Now I'm not saying that that'll solve all our problems. We've arrived at the point where, to do that, we'll have to have a social revolution. Heavy industry's got to go on shedding labour; and that means that here in the United Kingdom we've got to reconstruct our society so that it can absorb the redundant three million. But *if* we can cut down our labour force – by wastage and voluntary retirements – and *if* the unions will see that it's essential to accept our technology, and abandon their demarcation disputes, so that skilled men are prepared to do other jobs than their own – even sweep the floor if it needs sweeping – and *if* we can get production up to capacity, and ninety-five per cent of our cars out of the paint shop with "first run capability", perfect, like the Japanese do, instead of

231

sixty-five per cent . . . if we can do all that, we'll survive. Our Western competitors probably won't, but we will, and there'll be enough left of the European market – left by the Japanese that is – for us to stay in business.'

'As we function now, we can't live with the Japanese car industry's exports into Europe any more than other industries have lived with them,' confessed another British expert. 'Japan has creamed the market.'

It was left to an American, John Naisbitt, vice-president of a respected Opinion Research firm, to spell out the unpalatable truth. 'The United States,' he said, 'has lost its place as the world's chief car maker.' By 1989, he predicted, Chrysler and Ford could well be out of business, and the world's thirty automobile firms of today could be reduced to as few as four – of which two would be Japanese.

No one in any industry is unaware of the methods the Japanese have employed. Everyone can reel them off: high productivity, constant automation and heavy investment. Plus their work ethic, minus our labour disputes. Toyota, they tell you, had its last strike more than a dozen years ago.

'But we're too civilized to have a work ethic like theirs,' I was assured. 'And the day I have to come in here, bow to the manager and recite the company prayer, this lot can say good-bye to me.'

It is also pointed out that the materials out of which cars are made (despite the fact that they have to be imported raw, and then reprocessed) are cheaper in Japan than they are in Europe. Nor does Western management deny that its labour force is worse trained, less educated, less versatile, three to six times larger, and less conscientious than Japan's. And only the labour force has yet to be convinced that, in any industry that finds itself competing with the Japanese, the guiding principle must be, '*Fewer* jobs, or *no* jobs'.

Compare that with Matsushita's nostrum, 'A firm will soon lose its vitality if it fails to provide its employees with dreams.' Or his advice to statesmen: 'To inspire its people and instil optimism, it is government's task to promote strong ideals and a prospect of grandeur.'

No one in Western management denies that the Japanese have harnessed productivity to a daily continuity of supplies, which we have not; and that components are delivered from one factory to the assembly line of another as often as three times a day over distances of twenty kilometres or more, which we would not dare to do.

No one in Western management denies that a change-over of dies which takes our skilled workers three to four hours is performed by Japanese skilled workers in five to six minutes.

No one in Japanese management denies that to depend on supplies of components arriving daily at the assembly line, or thrice daily, makes them vulnerable to strikes in the factory manufacturing the components; but all Japanese managers know that such strikes will not happen – because the company's profits would suffer if they did; and when the company's profits suffer so does the worker's twice yearly, very substantial bonus.

When asked the secret of their non-strike record, Toyota reply with a typically Japanese parable. 'Three hundred years ago,' they say, 'if a bird would not sing, one killed it. Realizing that this hardly remedied our songless situation, we switched to a second policy: if the bird would not sing, we made it. But today, if a bird won't sing, we wait a while.'

'What does it mean?' a British marketing expert asked me. I told him that it meant that three hundred years ago, if a man wouldn't do what his master wanted him to do, his master chopped off his head. Later, if a man wouldn't do what his master wanted him to do, his master beat him. But today, if a man won't do what his employer wants him to do, the employer waits for a consensus.

'Seems ludicrous to me,' he commented.

No one in Western management denies that Japan's threat to the survival of his industry increases year by year, whatever sympathetic utterances on the subject may have emanated from Tokyo.

All say, 'We must improve our productivity and, at the same time, cut down on our work force, or we won't survive.'

But none say, 'As well as improving our productivity, and reducing our work force, we must aspire to a work ethic like theirs.' A work ethic like theirs, say the British, is not only unattainable, it is even, in some indefinable way, undesirable. Yet in reality (as has been proved by a number of Japanese-owned, locally-manned factories in the United Kingdom, America and Europe) it involves no greater sacrifice than membership of a house union and the willingness, having changed a die in five minutes instead of four hours, to man another machine rather than stand idle, or even to sweep the floor.

The American attitude is both more robust and more aggressive than Britain's. 'We're trying to get the Japanese to import more manufactured goods,' one of their diplomats explained. 'Our primary products – beef, citrus, coal – are at about the upper limits already – although Japan's oil-saving campaign means that by 1990,

233

provided we have the facilities at the mineheads, and the necessary transportation, coal's gonna be huge. Japan'll take all she can get from us.'

(In fact, Canberra is hoping that Japan will take all the coal she needs from Australia. But that is a comparatively remote problem. If Washington fails to solve the problem of its ever-increasing trade deficit with Japan before 1990, America will be too poor to afford even the inadequate minehead facilities and transportation system she has now.)

'But where we're really hoping and trying now,' the diplomat continues, 'is in the area of manufactured goods – which THEY say puts THEIR factories out of work.

'We argue that, on the contrary, they should adhere to the principle of both free trade *and* comparative advantage. In this latter respect, we argue, they must at last act like a sophisticated industrial nation, not like a mere mercantile power.

'They're way beyond the point where they can go on hollering that they export simply to eat. They're not just eating, they're living and exporting like a major industrial power.

'Anyway, THEY ship sophisticated manufactured stuff to us and Europe, and WE accept it, so why shouldn't they do the same for us?

'Look – we could sell them solar energy equipment, units for houses, things like that, by the million. But no dice: the Japanese are beginning to develop their own solar energy industry, so they're protecting it till it's unassailable.

'Same thing goes for pharmaceuticals and medical equipment. They simply will NOT buy our dialysis machines, hepatitis kits, stuff like that, which we make better and cheaper than anyone in the world.

'Plus there's hundreds of electrical appliances. For over *three years* we've been working to get them to accept OUR United States stamp of approval for electrical goods; but they quibble, say they've got to apply their own safety tests, and then take forever. But that same United States stamp of approval is good enough for *them* when they want to ship their stuff to us.

'And we've got plenty more to offer. About sixteen items that are competitive in price and quality. Things like automotive parts and equipment, avionics, analytical and scientific instruments, industrial controls, building projects, security and safety equipment. But THEY want to get into all those areas too, so they don't open up to us.

'Another example – they need enormous amounts of fertilizer, for their rice etcetera. But all they'll import is the phosphate rock, not our processed fertilizer, which we make cheaper than they'll ever make it.

'Now, don't get the idea that it's our trade deficit that's making me so mad. But 1980's $10 billion trade deficit was bad news – so the Japanese promised it'd go down in 1981. What happened in 1981? It went UP, to $15 billion. So the Japanese promised it'd go down in 1982. And what happened in 1982? It's gone UP, to $20 billion. By 1990 it could be $500 billion. Jesus, no country can tolerate that! No wonder we're screaming.

'Mind you, all their inroads into our economy are in the more glamorous areas of industry – cars, TV, electronics, things like that. But in other areas, like banking, insurance, department stores, their record's not so impressive. Over *all*, our productivity is thirty per cent higher than Japan's. So is Germany's. Japan's productivity is higher only in specific industries. And all of them make *huge* use of robots – which we Americans invented.

'True our auto industry'll never be the same again. Oh, it'll survive; but many of its employees won't. But in the United States we got tie-ups with Isuzu, Toyota and Honda; and Europe has tie-ups with Nissan, Toyota and Honda. Good thing too. We like it. But we'd also like them to have tie-ups with us in Japan. We'd like the Japanese to open up their market for *us* for investment similar to theirs.

'Nominally, there's been no restraint on that since 1972; but in reality there's a barrier they fling up of excessively high prices, the language, distribution methods – you name it, they use it. One prefecture in Japan actually *invited* us to come in, offered us all kinds of incentives; but generally they're completely unreceptive.

'For example, a United States company wanted to put a caustic soda plant at Hokkaido; but they wouldn't allow us a one hundred per cent investment – a one hundred per cent ownership of the plant. Said they wanted a joint venture. It so happened, of course, that the American company had a new process and was afraid the Japanese'd simply go in with them, pinch their idea and start up a plant of their own. That's what they do, you know.

'Despite all of that, though, I believe the amount of trade between our two countries is so incredible that it's vastly important to us both that it goes on. With such an enormous volume of trade, some difficulties must occur from time to time.

'So this thing isn't all black. I mean, they *like* us! They're grateful for what we did for them in 1945 and after! If only they knew how to *give*. But Jesus – they'd better learn quickly!'

'The only industrial rivals Japan now sees on the horizon are those from the Third World,' commented an Australian civil servant. 'Korea, Taiwan, Hong Kong, even India. Apropos of which, it's the Koreans not the Japanese, as you'd expect, who've just won a West Australian contract to build a power station near Bunbury. And it's the Koreans, I'm told, who are Japan's main rivals in the bidding for a contract to replace the P & O's ship, *Atlantic Conveyor*, which the Argentinians sank off the Falkland Islands.

'But by the time any of her new rivals become too competitive, Japan is confident she'll have created new industries and moved on. Japan's always on the move; and unafraid. Don't imagine, though, that America won't fight back – and won't, if necessary, fight dirty. They're getting mighty sick of the Japanese admitting to certain non-tariff barriers on the one hand and saying, tongue in cheek on the other, "You could sell to us if you really wanted to – if you really set yourself to learn our language, study the market and understand the system." '

Mr Yoshiro Inayama, chairman of the Keidanren, replied to some of these complaints in the customary elliptic and inconclusive Japanese manner. 'Only if the Japanese people decide to lower their living standards can Japan reduce its exports. You can't say that Japan doesn't *have* to export. But what we must do is create a situation where material-exporting countries will gladly sell to Japan, and product-importing countries will gladly buy from Japan.

'We have to think about what kind of exports are favoured by importing countries. It's not that foreign countries *won't* buy from Japan – they don't say that – the problem arises when sometimes Japan exports so much that importing countries feel unhappy about it. To solve this problem, we must export goods in an orderly, well thought-out manner.'

The West is unlikely to find any consolation in those few words, and even less likely to hear anything more consoling from any other source in Japan. The bleak reality of the matter, as the Japanese themselves see it, is that, after the war, they deliberately switched from light to heavy industry, from old to new industries, from heavily manned to automated industries and from domestic-oriented sales to foreign-oriented sales; and if the Western world is not now prepared to do the same, it must expect to eat stones, drink gall and sleep on logs forever.

As the West negotiates with Japan today it must bear in mind the lessons of the past. It must remember that Japan's is so different a time scale from ours that it was quite natural to her to wait 40 years before putting into practice General Katsuro Taro's grandiose scheme to conquer Malaya, the Dutch East Indies and the Philippines; that she has been content to wait 40 years to see the first of the three options offered by the Liaison Conference over which Tojo presided in November 1941 come to fruition; that the insults of 1895, 1915, 1920 and 1924 so rankled that she walked out of the League of Nations in 1933 and in 1939 flung herself into the arms of Hitler (than whom no Westerner can ever – with his vulgarity, loudness and assertiveness – have been more repugnant to her); that her Government made conciliatory noises about the China Incident – but did nothing – from 1931 to 1940; that from 1941 to 1945, having been crowded, she became fanatically obdurate; that from 1945 to 1951 she demonstrated her blind acceptance of the doctrine of *force majeure*; and that for the foreseeable future it is in her hands, not ours, that *force majeure* again resides.

Nor should Japan's attitude to treaties and agreements be disregarded. Simply stated, it is that such clauses therein as are beneficial to Japan are regarded as contractually binding, while such clauses as are rendered inexpedient to Japan, by altered circumstances, are instantly to be dropped – or, at best, renegotiated. In such case, as they see it, it is not they who have dishonoured an agreement to which they have appended their signature, but circumstances.

And least of all should their semantic storm-warnings be ignored – especially the fact that Premier Suzuki, Kenosuke Matsushita and Masaya Miyoshi, in almost identical words, have already hoisted them.

'This kind of action against another country is hard to understand,' Suzuki rebuked America's outspoken congressmen.

'The West's voice is distressingly high, loud and severe,' chided Matsushita.

'Criticisms are harsher than we expected,' warned Miyoshi.

It should not be forgotten that they resigned their membership of the League of Nations in 1933, rejected Cordell Hull's note of 1941, and wanted to reject Truman's 1945 note about the implications of 'unconditional surrender' because, in each case, the West had been 'rude' to them. Improbable though it is that the West can now satisfactorily negotiate with them from a posture of weakness, it is certain that such negotiations will fail if conducted in the kind of language that the Japanese deem unacceptable. Even Mrs Thatcher had to moderate her language when she made an official visit to Tokyo.

Furthermore, the West should abandon the American premise that, 'They like us.' Except that they believe us to be in a state of decline, and that some of them still harbour an understandable longing for revenge, they have no feeling for 'us' of any kind. To the Japanese, the West is merely an agglomeration of customers.

Hence the widespread indignation in Japan when Premier Suzuki, on a 1981 visit to Washington, and in a moment of euphoria, referred to the United States-Japan Security Pact as an 'alliance'. An alliance, to them, implies an almost emotional relationship such as they imagined they had mutually enjoyed with Britain between 1902 and 1922: their Security Pact with the United States means merely that America will protect them from Russia, in return for which they will do as they please short of making an alliance with anyone else. When Suzuki came home from Washington, his critics called him 'Baka' – which is what our guards called us, and very rude indeed.

Finally, the West must take cognizance at least of the Japanese vision of the twenty-first century. 'A brief review of the world's history,' said Matsushita thoughtfully in a recent interview, 'reveals that civilization and prosperity originated in the area of Egypt. Later it moved and was inherited by Greece and Rome, leading to the full blossoming of a European civilization. Eventually, though, it made its way to the United States; and although the United States is still the most prosperous of all the nations in the world, I see that a shadow is beginning to fall over the giant. The next region in which such prosperity should prevail is Asia, centred on China and Japan.'

Asia itself is by no means disinclined to believe him. For one thing, everywhere it looks it sees the outward and visible signs of Japan's industrial supremacy – plants, factories, installations, cars, television sets and neon signs; for another, Matsushita's vision conforms with its own – that by the year 2000 the colonies of 1941 will be members of the richest, most highly populated bloc in the world. Even now they do not hesitate to snub and rebuke their one-time masters. Malaysia in 1982 blatantly obstructed every British attempt to win contracts anywhere in her federation of sultanates – and awarded most of them to Japanese companies instead; and the Philippines' Foreign Minister openly berated Britain's Foreign Secretary for staying at the British Embassy during a 1982 conference instead of a government Rest House.

In the world of the twenty-first century, as the Ibukas and

Matsushitas and Hondas of Japan see it, there will be only a small part for the West to play. Should Tojo's envisaged war between Russia and America come to pass, Japan plans to stand aside from it, convinced that there will be nothing left of either once it is over. Should it not come to pass, Asia's thousands of millions, fully 'electronified', importing from and exporting to one another, powered and motivated by Japan, and protected from Russia by China, will be rich beyond all imagining – and the West will buy from them whatever it can afford, and work for them in *their* European and American factories.

At the moment that is no more than a Japanese scenario – as was General Taro's plan to capture South East Asia in 1900. At least, though, they have a scenario: the West has only science fiction. For Europe and America, the alternatives are either a second industrial revolution, based on a new technology which it will refuse to sell to Japan, or conversion to the Japanese spirit of industry, so that an exports war can be waged, as the Battle of Midway was waged, on almost equal terms. Neither, as yet, is even, as Matsushita would put it, a dream.

Let it not be imagined, however, that the Japanese are content merely to dream. Already they have bred a better nourished and healthier generation of five to twenty-year-olds whose IQ, according to Professor Richard Lynn of Ulster's New University, is significantly higher than that of the same generation in America, Britain, France and other industrial countries.

Already, as Professor Edward Feigenbaum of Stanford University, California, warned a London conference on computers in July 1982, they have bred a new and privileged generation of computer programmers dubbed 'knowledge engineers'.

Already they have announced to the world that their government has set aside £200 million, and that Japanese industry will contribute £600 million, to expedite the construction by these knowledge engineers of a fifth generation of computers that will be more intelligent than people – that will be able to see, hear, talk and think. Such a fifth generation, which the Japanese promise will be on the market within fifteen years, will sweep much of the West's high technology into oblivion. It will result, Professor Feigenbaum said, in 'an electronic Pearl Harbour'; and the loss of face that would ensue from a failure to fulfil their promise means that the Japanese are confident of their ability – indeed are obliged – to launch just such an electronic onslaught upon all their rivals before the end of

239

the twentieth century.

Meantime their latest five year economic plan commenced in 1983, and Japanese economists predict that Japan's real Gross National Product will grow at an average rate of 4% per annum for the rest of this century.

In 1981/82, it grew at only 2.7%. For 1982/83 growth was predictably not much more – but than that of any of her rivals. The juggernaut's progress may have been impeded by world recession, but its thrust is as relentless as ever. By the year 2000 Japan (with less than half the population of the United States) expects her share of the world's Gross National Product to rise from 10·1% today to 11·9%, while America's will fall from 22·4% to 19·8%, West Germany's from 6·7% to 5·9%, and Britain's from 3·3% to 2·9%.

'Rapid industrial growth,' a report commissioned by Premier Suzuki warned in 1982, 'causes friction, so sufficient time must be allowed for other countries to adjust. Japan must take account of this.' But a fifth generation of seeing, hearing, talking, thinking computers within fifteen years allows other countries no time to adjust to anything; and one of Japan's greatest weaknesses has always been her inability 'to take account' of the protests of her rivals. More frighteningly still, she has never yet practised the virtue of magnanimity in victory.

It is to be hoped that America's magnanimity to her in 1945 has convinced her that such a virtue exists. It is also to be feared that America's inability to compete with the beneficiary of *her* post-war magnanimity will have convinced the Japanese that it is a virtue that yields no dividends.

'We will be able to use our own computer-ware to change the world,' promised Mr Ibuka of Sony. And added, 'Once our techniques are completed, we will transfer them to less developed countries.'

Among those less developed countries, Mr Matsushita foretold, will be America and all the nations of Western Europe – between whom they will be able to pick and choose.

This they are already doing. Britain hoped desperately that the Nissan Motor Company would set up a plant in the United Kingdom to produce cars and provide jobs. But: 'There is strong opinion within our company,' Nissan's President Takashi Ishihara announced on 2 July 1982, 'that the project is very risky. We cannot push a project for which we cannot obtain consensus.'

'We must decide *now* how best we can help other nations redress their problems,' Mr Honda insisted for the benefit of Western ears. But was his insistence genuine? 'I am pleased to find that you are in general keeping discipline and working diligently,' Colonel Nakamura politely congratulated the Allied prisoners of war who built the railway through Thailand as badly as possible while they died of starvation, disease and brutality. 'At the same time,' he added, 'regret to find seriousness in health matter . . . due mainly to the fact for absence of such firm belief as, "Japanese health follows will" and "Cease only when the enemy annihilated".'

That was as close as he could bring himself to saying that we had lost, we were wrong and we deserved every misfortune then befalling us. In victory again today, Japanese health continues to follow will; but this time *our* seriousness in health matter is the result not of their brutality but of our lack of will. What remains to be seen is whether, this time, Japan will cease only when her one-time enemies, real and prospective, are annihilated. I am not convinced that they will so cease because I am not convinced that they can. I am not even convinced that they should, because they have earned the right to a total victory. I simply hope that they will look into their hearts and decide – by consensus, of course – that they must.

That, though, will depend more on tomorrow's Japanese than today's: upon those like the eleven hundred students who graduated from the Soka University in March 1982 and were exhorted by their Honorary President, Daisaku Ikeda, 'The world you are about to enter is not an easy one. In order to become victors in life, you must be healthy, you must have tenacity and a persevering spirit, and you must have the will-power not to succumb to hardship.'

Sheridan – who knew nothing of the Japanese, because he died in 1816 – wrote in *The Critic:*

> *I open with a clock striking, to beget an awful attention in the audience. It also marks the time, which is four o'clock in the morning, and saves a description of the rising sun, and a great deal about the eastern hemisphere.*

Not as amusing, perhaps, as *Pooh's Hum*, but apposite. The drama of Japan's unique spirit since 1894 demands nothing less than 'an awful attention' from Western audiences. Thus far it has been received with little more than our supercilious indignation.

ACKNOWLEDGEMENTS

T. Akiyama *Soka Gakkai*
N. Anemiya *Japanese Foundation,*
London
K. Asomura *Foreign Office, Tokyo*
Australian War
Memorial *Canberra*

Captain R. M. Baird *R.A.N.*
E. Bean *National Panasonic, London*
Mrs J. M. Burgess *Research –*
Sydney
E. Hamanishi *Japan Foundation,*
Tokyo
R. Harasawa *Mitsubishi Bank,*
Tokyo
Y. Hatano *Japanese Embassy,*
London
J. Hartwell *Australia House, London*
D. J. Healy *Editor, London, Sydney*
Mrs A. Heard *UN Association,*
Cardiff
W. Hiraizumı *Member of Diet,*
Tokyo
S. Honda *Honda*

M. Ibuka *Hon. Chairman, Sony,*
Tokyo

K. Ikemi *Honda, Tokyo*
Prof. H. Inohara *Sophia University,*
Tokyo
International House *Tokyo: Staff*
and Library
Todashi Itoh

J. Kato *Foreign Office, Tokyo*
K. J. Kelly *Research, Sydney*

J. Lehner *Importer, Sydney*

Y. Maeda *Mainichi Newspapers,*
Tokyo
K. Matsushita *Matsushita Electric,*
Osaka
M. Miyoshi *Managing Director,*
Keidanren

Dr T. Otsubo *Nomura Institute,*
London
E. Onishi *Matsushita Electric*
R. Osborn *Chargé d'Affaires,*
Australian Embassy, Tokyo

K. Sakiyama *Publisher*
Mrs N. Saneyoshi *Interpreter*
K. Sugawara *Sony, Tokyo*
P. Sutton *Australia House, London*

W. Tajitsu *Hon. Pres., Mitsubishi*
Bank, Tokyo
S. Tani *Matsushita Electric*
R. Tames *School of Oriental*
Studies, London
Toojoeiwa School *Principal and*
Staff, Tokyo

T. Urabe *Foreign Office, Tokyo*

Y. Watanabe *Dep. Pres., Bank of*
Tokyo
A. T. L. Whitehand *Researcher*

M. Yamada *Japan Foundation,*
Tokyo
S. Yamamoto *Author and Essayist,*
Tokyo
Mrs K. Yoshida *Tokyo*

243

BIBLIOGRAPHY

S. Adler   *The Uncertain Giant*   (1965)
Y. Aida   *Prisoner of The British*   (1966)
Lord Avon   *Facing The Dictators*   (1962)
T. Asada   *The Night of a Thousand Suicides*   (1970)

C. Barnett   *The Collapse of British Power*   (1972)
D. Bergamini   *Japan's Imperial Conspiracy*   (1971)
J. H. Boyle   *China and Japan at War*   (1972)
C. Browne   *The Last Banzai*   (1967)

K. Caffrey   *Out in the Midday Sun*   (1974)
Lord Chatfield   *It Might Happen Again*   (1937-45)
W. S. Churchill   *The Second World War*   (1948-50)
W. Craig   *The Fall of Japan*   (1967)
R. L. Craigie   *Behind the Japanese Mask*   (1946)

O. Dazai   *No Longer Human*   (1954)

D. J. Enright   *The World of Dew*   (1955)

H. Fersp   *The Road to Pearl Harbour*   (1950)
Fuchida & Okumiya   *Midway*   (1957)

F. Gibney   *Five Gentlemen of Japan*   (1953)
R. Grenfell   *Main Fleet to Singapore*   (1951)
J. C. Grew   *Ten Years in Japan*   (1944)
R. Guillam   *The Japanese Challenge*   (1970)

P. Haggie   *Britannia at Bay*   (1981)
P. Hasluck   *The East and The People*   (1952)
R. Hough   *The Hunting of Force Z*   (1963)
C. Hull   *The Memoirs of Cordell Hull*   (1948)

N. Ike   *Japan's Decision for War*   (1967)
T. Ishimaru   *Japan Must Fight Britain*   (1936)

F. C. Jones   *Japan's New Order in East Asia*   (1954)

T. Kase   *Eclipse of the Rising Sun*   (1951)
M. D. Kennedy   *The Estrangement of Great Britain
and Japan*   (1970)

S. W. Kirby *Singapore: The Chain of Disaster* (1971)

D. J. Lu *From The Marco Polo Bridge to Pearl Harbour* (1961)

V. C. Maxon *Control of Japanese Foreign Policy* (1957)
C. H. Moore *The Japanese Mind* (1973)
L. Mosley *Hirohito* (1966)

B. O'Connell *Return of the Tiger* (1960)
A. Offner *American Appeasement* (1969)
S. Ooka *Fires on The Plain* (1957)

Pacific War Research Society *Japan's Longest Day* (1968)
R. Paull *Retreat from Kokoda* (1953)
N. Perrin *Giving up the Gun* (1979)
W. Plomer *Sado* (1931)
W. Price *The Japanese Miracle and Peril* (1971)

A. Rappaport *Henry L. Stimson and Japan* (1963)
Lord Russell of Liverpool *The Knights of Bushido* (1958)

A. L. Sadler *The Life of Shogun Tokuyawa Ieyasu* (1937)
M. Shigemitsu *Japan and Her Destiny* (1958)
S. Shiroyama *War Criminal* (1974)
Sir W. Slim *Defeat Into Victory* (1956)
Soka Gakkai *Cries For Peace* (1978)
C. Steenstrup *Tojo Shigetoki* (1979)
H. Stimson *The Far Eastern Crisis*(1971)
R. Storry *Japan and the Decline of The West in Asia* (1979)

H. Tasaki *Long the Imperial Way* (1951)
M. Tsuji *The Singapore Version* (1960)
Y. Tsumetomo *Hagakure* (1979)

L. van der Post *The Night of the New Moon* (1970)

S. Yokoi *The Last Japanese Soldier* (1972)
K. Yoshida *Japan is a Circle* (1975)
T. Yoshihashi *Conspiracy at Mukden* (1963)